BRUCE A. WARE

Big Truths for Young Hearts

Teaching and Learning the Greatness of God

CROSSWAY

WHEATON, ILLINOIS

Big Truths for Young Hearts

Copyright © 2009 by Bruce A. Ware

Published by Crossway
  1300 Crescent Street
  Wheaton, Illinois 60187

Cover design: Tobias' Outerwear for Books

Cover photos: iStock

First printing, 2009

Printed in the United States of America

Unless otherwise indicated, Scripture quotations are taken from the ESV® Bible (*The Holy Bible: English Standard Version®*). Copyright © 2001 by Crossway. Used by permission. All rights reserved.

Scripture quotations marked NASB are from *The New American Standard Bible®*. Copyright © The Lockman Foundation 1960, 1962, 1963, 1968, 1971, 1972, 1973, 1975, 1977, 1995. Used by permission.

Scripture quotations marked HCSB have been taken from *The Holman Christian Standard Bible®*. Copyright © 1999, 2000, 2003, 2003 by Holman Bible Publishers. Used by permission.

All emphases in Scripture quotations have been added by the author.

ISBN PDF: 978-1-4335-0602-4

ISBN Mobipocket: 978-1-4335-0603-1

Library of Congress Cataloging-in-Publication Data
Ware, Bruce A.
  Big truths for young hearts : teaching and learning the greatness of God / Bruce A. Ware.
    p. cm.
  ISBN 978-1-4335-0601-7 (tpb)
  1. Theology, Doctrinal. 2. Christian education of children. I. Title.
BT75.3.W37   2009
248.8'45—dc22   2008045248

Crossway is a publishing ministry of Good News Publishers.

VP		19	18	17	16	15	14	13	12	11
17	16	15	14	13	12	11	10	9	8	7	6

Big Truths for Young Hearts

Other Crossway Books by Bruce A. Ware:

Father, Son, and Holy Spirit
God's Greater Glory
God's Lesser Glory
Their God Is Too Small

To my two children,
both precious daughters,

BETHANY CHRISTINA and RACHEL ELIZABETH:

*How deeply thankful I am that God gave me the privilege
of being your dad; how richly blessed I am
to have received unfailingly your kindness, love,
and respect; and how overjoyed I am to see you walking
faithfully and happily in the good and wise ways
of our great God.*

Contents

Foreword

By Bethany Strachan and Rachel Ware

This book is very special to us. As Bruce Ware's daughters, we view *Big Truths for Young Hearts* not only as a rich resource for children and adults, but also as a tangible representation of the teaching we were blessed to faithfully receive from our dad throughout our childhood.

For the past two decades we have lived with a father who loves theology and loves to teach theology. We both remember him teaching us all six verses of the hymn "May the Mind of Christ my Savior" by the time we were three years old. During our annual summer road trips to see family on the West Coast, Dad and Mom used the time in the car to lead our family in singing worship songs, memorizing Scripture, and discussing theology. Dad would often begin a conversation with a question: "So, do you think Jesus had to be both God *and* man?" or "How can God be good and still allow bad things to happen in the world?" Not exactly laid-back vacation banter, but we loved those family conversations. We girls would sit in the backseat of our family Toyota and rack our brains trying to think of a biblical answer, knowing all the while that Dad had one. He was passionate about sharing truths with us that would give us confidence in our faith. This passion came through in family discussions at dinner, late-night chats in his study, and the "daddy daughter dates" on which he often took us. Though we did not fully realize it then, those conversations were life-changing and heart-shaping. It was Theology 101 given outside the classroom.

Dad really believes the things that are in this book. His theology shapes the way he lives, as we have seen many times. In confronting theological challenges of his day, Dad has displayed uncompromising commitment to God's word. During hard times, he has trusted God and said along with Job, "The Lord gives, and the Lord takes away. Blessed be the name of the Lord." When praised for his gifts, he has had a humble attitude, consistently focusing attention on the Source of every good gift. He is generous with his time and money, faithful in evangelism, untiring in teaching, and devoted to his family. We tell you all this because we want to honor Dad's integrity. Though of course he is deeply aware of his own sin, he strives to live a life worthy of the gospel of Christ.

Big Truths for Young Hearts is the same Theology 101 we learned growing up. It is a rich collection of truths that come straight from Scripture and answer questions about who God is, his work in the world, and the hope we can have through a relationship with Christ. Many people, whether evangelical or otherwise, have misconceptions about the basic doctrines of God. We need to understand these doctrines in order to understand life correctly. This book takes us straight to the heart of the Bible to help us do that.

We want to include a brief word to parents and children. To parents: it may sound cliché, but we followed our father's teaching in part because he practiced what he preached. Like all children, we needed to look up and see our parents looking up at a great God who has great things in store for those who love him. The practice of faith really does make it powerful. To children: we're so glad that you're learning truths about God! It doesn't always seem fun to have to sit and listen to your parents. But this subject is actually more exciting than anything else you could think of. As you get older, you'll be very glad that you had parents who loved you and who taught you about the most important person you could ever know: God.

Lastly, to our dad: we love you so much and are so proud of you. You are a tender father, a loving husband, and a faithful provider. Thank you for raising your daughters so that we, to this day, feel cherished. Most of all, thank you for believing the gospel, teaching it to us, and faithfully showing us through your own life that God is great.

With love,
Bethany and Rachel

Introduction:
On Raising Children to Know and Love God through Raising Them to Know and Love Theology

The beginnings of this book go back nearly twenty years, to when I was teaching theology at Western Seminary, Portland, Oregon. Bethany was six, Rachel was two, and I recall Jodi and me trying to figure out just how best to get two fun-loving, giggly girls to bed in a way that kept our sanity but didn't distract from the sheer happiness they enjoyed that last hour before sleep came upon them both. One night it occurred to me that since they loved being with us this last part of the day and weren't quite ready for sleep yet, I might consider co-opting the time and using it to do what I loved most and what they needed most (though they wouldn't have known this yet)—teach them great and glorious truths of the Christian faith!

What began in those evenings turned into something better than I had planned or envisioned. Surely God led in this despite my mere "play it by ear" endeavor to make something work. I began in those early years spending ten to fifteen minutes with each of our daughters at their bedside, going through the doctrines of the Christian faith. Of course, I didn't explain to them that I was basically teaching them the same theology sequence I taught at seminary, but that is exactly what I did. We started with the Bible's teaching on divine revelation and looked at some key passages about God's revelation in creation and in our consciences and then his remarkable revelation through his Word, both the living Word, Jesus, and the written Word, the inspired Scriptures. We would read a key text or two and then talk about what it means. I'd work at giving explanations they could understand, and it became apparent to me right away when they got it and when they didn't. Facial expressions and questions from children say much about whether they are grasping the ideas and see both their truth and their beauty. When we finished one area of theology, we'd move on to the next, with no set time and no deadlines, so we just enjoyed reading Scripture and thinking about these areas one by one. As much as I longed to convey truth that would help shape their minds and worldviews, I also prayed deeply that God would be pleased to enable them to see the glory and beauty of these precious truths. Mind and heart are both essential in this process, and I knew I must constantly trust God to do this work in them, a work that only he can bring to pass.

I have Bethany and Rachel to thank for the encouragement to write out more formally the kinds of talks we had at bedtimes as well as other discussions we enjoyed on long vacations in the car and for family devotions. Both girls really loved to talk about these matters. Jodi, my precious wife of thirty years, cultivated in them a love for reading Scripture and worked with them to become consistent in their own daily devotions. So when my girls came to me with the idea of writing up our theology discussions, I realized almost immediately that this was something I needed to do. Through their regular encouragement, it now is such a joy to see this book come to pass. Rachel's original suggested title for the book was *Bedside Theology*, recalling obviously the many bedside discussions we had over several of her growing up years. For good reasons, a different title was chosen. Nevertheless, I will always think of this book primarily as the outgrowth of the many bedside theology talks this dad had the joy of having with his precious and much-loved daughters.

In light of the background and history I've just shared, I wish to dedicate this book to Bethany Christina and Rachel Elizabeth. Jodi would want to join me in saying that we have dearly loved and prized the privilege the Lord gave us in being your mom and dad. You've enriched our lives and taught us much, even as we've sought to pass on to you what means the very most to us. Thank you both for the constant love and encouragement you've shown to us. You have both grown now into beautiful and godly women who adorn so well the gospel of our Lord Jesus Christ. We thank God also for the godly and gifted husband that Owen Strachan is to Bethany and for their first child, and our first grandchild, precious Ella Rose. We never will cease to pray for all of you that God will continue his work in your lives, granting you more of the vision of God we've so loved and cherished and longed for you to know as well. May you continue always to know him more richly, love him more deeply, and serve him more fully.

I'm aware that this book may be used in different contexts than the precise one out of which it has grown. Yes, parents may wish to read these chapters with their children, discussing these rich truths together and looking at passages of Scripture that teach aspects of our faith that we need to understand and embrace. Middle and high school students may find it helpful simply to read the book on their own, working bit by bit through some of the core teachings of Scripture on the great doctrines of the Christian faith. Homeschool and Sunday school settings are also places where this book may meet a need. Since it covers the whole range of Christian doctrine, from the doctrine of the Bible all the way through to the doctrine of last things, some may wish to use this as an introductory curriculum for young people to gain a foundational understanding of the whole of the Christian faith. Perhaps also young converts to the Christian faith, no matter what age they may be, will find here a helpful overview of Christian teaching that will give them a better grasp of the truth and beauty God is and has for them to behold.

However this book is used, I hope and pray that God will be pleased to shine forth something of the greatness of his glory, both in who he is as the eternal triune God and in the wisdom and beauty of his work and his ways. God alone is worthy of all glory, honor, worship, praise, and thanksgiving since he alone possesses every quality and perfection that deserves to be so honored. Since to him alone belongs all adoration and worship, to him alone, then, is here given all glory and thanks. May God be pleased to use the truths of this work for the glory of his name, and may his people grow in understanding God as the supreme treasure of their lives.

1

God's Word and God's Own Life as God

God Has Made Himself Known

Has anyone ever kept a secret from you? Maybe it was a birthday present or a special trip you were going to take or what your mom was planning to fix for dinner. If you've had this happen to you, then you can understand how important it is for others to tell us things that we cannot know unless they make it known. No matter how much you might want to know the secret, until someone tells you, you just cannot know what it is.

It is this way with knowing who God is. The only way that we could be thinking together about the greatness of God in this book is because God has shared with us the secret of who he is. We cannot discover who God is or figure him out on our own. We aren't smart enough to do this, and God is way too big for us even to try. One of the very first things we must learn about God is very humbling, and it is this: unless God had decided to show us who he is, unless he had chosen to make known his own life and ways, we simply could know nothing—yes, nothing!—about him. We are dependent completely on God's kindness and goodness to make himself known to us, and for this we ought to be grateful every day of our lives. After all, there is no one more important and more wonderful to know than God. So how thankful we must be that God did not keep to himself, as it were. Rather, he showed us in rich and wonderful ways just who he is.

The Bible talks about several different ways that God has made himself known to us. One of the ways God has shown us some things about himself is through *the world he has made*. Psalm 19:1–2 says, "The heavens declare the glory of God, and the sky above proclaims his handiwork. Day to day pours out speech, and night to night reveals knowledge." And in Romans 1:19–20 Paul adds, "For what can be known about God is plain to them, because God has shown it to them. For his invisible attributes, namely, his eternal power and divine nature, have been clearly perceived, ever since the creation of the world, in the things that have been made. So they are without excuse." As these passages teach, some of the very qualities of God's own life are shown through the world and the universe that he fashioned.

Think with me about some of the qualities of God that we can see by looking at different parts of the world in which we live. When you look closely at a flower, for example, you can see the knowledge and wisdom and beauty of God. How very, very smart God is! God is the one who figured out how to make living things grow, and they all grow according to a lot of very complicated rules that he put into every living thing. The flower we are thinking about came from a small seed, was planted in the ground and watered, and in time grew to be a beautiful, colorful flower. All of its beauty, and each of its parts, has come to be because God has designed just exactly how it would grow from that seed to the full flower. Indeed, God's knowledge is vast, his wisdom is beyond our ability to understand, and his beauty is shown in all of the beautiful flowers, butterflies, trees, and mountains of our world.

We've thought about something on the small side—a flower—so why don't we also consider something big. Think with me about the stars you can see at night. Maybe you live in the country where there are not many city lights, or maybe you've taken a trip out into the woods or to the top of a mountain. On a clear night, when you see all of those stars, it sort of takes your breath away, doesn't it? And to think that we can see only a very, very small number of the stars that are actually there. Just in our own galaxy (the Milky Way) where the earth and solar system are located, scientists estimate that there are about ten billion stars. And the Milky Way is an average-sized galaxy in a universe that contains hundreds of millions of galaxies. Wow! We cannot understand all of this, but it shows us how great and expansive and powerful God is—he made this universe simply by speaking it into existence. Yes, the heavens surely do tell us of the glory of God. His power and wisdom and beauty and greatness—indeed, his Godness—are all seen through what he has made.

Do you remember the story of Job? Job was a very wealthy and powerful man, but to test Job, God allowed Satan to take nearly everything from Job, even giving him sores and boils on his whole body. Job wondered why this happened to him, and he came very close to blaming God. Toward the end of the book of Job, God confronted Job and humbled this man who nearly accused God of doing what was wrong. God asked of Job, "Where were you when I laid the foundation of the earth? Tell me, if you have understanding. [5] Who determined its measurements—surely you know! Or who stretched the line upon it? [6] On what were its bases sunk, or who laid its cornerstone, [7] when the morning stars sang together and all the sons of God shouted for joy? [8] Or who shut in the sea with doors when it burst out from the womb, [9] when I made clouds its garment and thick darkness its swaddling band, [10] and prescribed limits for it and set bars and doors, [11] and said, 'Thus far shall you come, and no farther, and here shall your proud waves be stayed'?" (Job 38:4–11). Consider the greatness of the universe God made, and how detailed and exact everything is that God has fashioned! We truly do learn much about God's greatness and glory just by noticing the world all around us.

Another way God has made himself known is through *how he has made us*, his human creatures. Many things about our own bodies—how amazing are our eyes and ears and heart and brain and on and on—also tell us about God's wisdom and power, just as with the rest of creation. But in addition to this, God has made us with a deep inner understanding of things that are right and things that are wrong. When we lie to our brother or sister or to our parents, we can tell inside of us that this is wrong to do. When we clean up our room or take out the garbage when our mom or dad ask us to, we know in our heart that this is the right thing to do. Where did this inner understanding of right and wrong come from? In Romans 2:14–15 Paul writes, "For when Gentiles, who do not have the law, by nature do what the law requires, they are a law to themselves, even though they do not have the law. [15] They show that the work of the law is written on their hearts, while their conscience also bears witness, and their conflicting thoughts accuse or even excuse them." His point is this: people who don't even have someone telling them that it's wrong to lie or wrong to steal or wrong to murder still know in their own hearts about these things. God has taken something of his own standards of right and wrong and placed them in every human heart. So, not only is God powerful and wise and great, he also is holy and righteous and good. When we do wrong, we have no excuse, because we know from the inside that we should do what is right. God put this into our lives so we would know about right and wrong and so we would know that we are held responsible for what we do. But this also tells us about God—he always does what is right and good and worthy of praise. God is both great, and he is good.

Questions for Thought

1. Can you think of some parts of creation that show just how great or powerful or wise or beautiful God is? What do they show about God, and how do they do this?

2. Have you ever noticed that little voice of your conscience within you warning you not to do something wrong or encouraging you to do what is right? Can you think of any examples from the past week when you noticed this?

Memory Verse

Psalm 19:1—"The heavens declare the glory of God, and the sky above proclaims his handiwork."

God Talks—the Bible Is God's True and Lasting Word

We've just learned that God has made known to us something of himself both through the world he has made and through the sense of right and wrong that he put into every human life. God's greatness, wisdom, power, and beauty are shown in the created world. And God's holiness, righteousness, goodness, and justice are shown through the senses of right and wrong we all have. So yes, God is both great, and God is good. He acts with power, but he always does what is right.

Notice, though, that both of these ways that God has made himself known to us come through his actions—we know he is great and good because we see these qualities shown in what he has made. But there is another amazing way that God has made himself known to us, and it is this: God talks! One of the first things we learn about God in the opening chapter of the Bible is that God is a talking God. For each of the days of creation, he brings about what he makes by speaking. Have you noticed this? The first one comes in Genesis 1:3, "And God said, 'Let there be light,' and there was light." And the words, "And God said" are repeated in verses 6, 9, 11, 14, 20, 24, and 26, where each of the special acts of creation are brought about when God speaks. We learn from this that

God's word is powerful and active, and it is meant to create what is new and glorious, not only to instruct.

Knowing that God is a talking God helps us understand better one of the most important and precious possessions we have in all of life—our Bible. We can far too easily ignore the Bible or spend too little time reading it and learning from it. But when we realize what it really is, we desire to spend much more time learning just what the Bible says. Why? Because the Bible is where we hear what God says. Yes, it is true. What the Bible says is what God says; as the Bible speaks to us, God speaks to us. One of the most important ways that God has spoken is through the very pages of the Bible itself. Consider with me a few verses that help us see this.

Paul describes the Bible this way in 2 Timothy 3:16–17: "All Scripture is breathed out by God and profitable for teaching, for reproof, for correction, and for training in righteousness, 17 that the man of God may be competent, equipped for every good work." Notice that Paul says "all" of Scripture—not just part of it, but all of it—comes from God. So we should see the Bible as a different kind of book from any other book there is. In the entire Bible, God tells us what he wants us to know. Not just parts of the Bible come from God, but all of it is God's own word to us. Also, notice that the Bible is "breathed out by God." This is a way of saying that it comes from God's own mouth. God speaks and breathes out the very books that form the Bibles that we have. Of course, human writers are responsible for writing these books also (we'll say a bit more about this in a minute), but here Paul's main point is that the Bible should be seen as God's Word.

Look next at what Paul says in 1 Thessalonians 2:13: "And we also thank God constantly for this, that when you received the word of God, which you heard from us, you accepted it not as the word of men but as what it really is, the word of God, which is at work in you believers." This helps us because Paul shows that the word spoken to these Thessalonian believers really was God's Word, even though it was spoken to them by Paul. So the Bible is the word of certain men, to be sure. But because God is working through those men as they speak and write, the Bible is really "the word of God," as Paul says.

But how can the Bible be from men but really from God? How can we be sure that humans who spoke and wrote actually have spoken and written what God wanted them to express, so we can be sure that the Bible really and truly is God's Word? Our answer comes from a very helpful statement by the apostle Peter. In 2 Peter 1:20–21 Peter writes, "no prophecy of Scripture comes from someone's own interpretation. For no prophecy was ever produced by the will of man, but men spoke from God as they were carried along by the Holy Spirit." Here is our answer. The Holy Spirit of God, who lives in the lives of all of those who trust in Christ, did a special work in producing the Bible. As Peter says here, the authors of Scripture, who spoke forth the prophesies of the Bible and all of its teachings, were "carried along by the Holy Spirit" as they wrote. So, what they wrote was not as much from them as it was from the Holy Spirit who moved them to write what they did. In this way the Bible is from human authors but even more from God. God, by his Spirit, worked in these writers so that these "men spoke from God" as they wrote the books that we now have in our Bibles. This doesn't take away from the fact that Moses and Isaiah and Paul and Peter and many others wrote different books of the Bible. But it means that with these books, unlike any other books, God worked by his Spirit to make sure that what they wrote would be exactly what he wanted.

Go back again for a minute to something else that was said in 2 Timothy 3:16–17. Not only does Paul say that all of the Bible is "breathed out by God" and so is God's Word, he also says that the Bible is "profitable for teaching, for reproof, for correction, and for training in righteousness, that the man of God may be competent, equipped for every good work." His point is this: because the Bible is from God, it is also very helpful and useful in causing us to grow as we should. Or think of it like this: because the Bible *is what it is* (it is the Word of God), *it can do what it does* (it is profitable to help us grow and be equipped for every good work). But if the Bible were not really the Word of God, we could not be sure that it would work in these positive ways to help us to grow. What the Bible is (the Word of God) enables it to do what it does (help us to grow).

God is a talking God, and how thankful we should be that he "talked" into the very pages of the Bible all of the teachings that he wanted his people to know. How foolish we are when we forget to read and study this book. But how wise and blessed we are when we go to this book constantly for instruction, guidance, correction, and help with living life as God wants. We should thank God every day that the Bible is his Word, that the Bible has the power to help us grow. And we should commit ourselves to knowing the Bible better all the time, so we can learn all that God has for us and live in ways that honor him and bring blessing to our own lives.

Questions for Thought

1. How important is it to believe that the Bible is fully God's Word while it also is the writings of different human authors? That is, why does it matter that the Bible is from God but was also written by men?

2. Since the Bible really is God's Word, that is, since God really talks to us through what is written in the Bible, what should our attitude be to listening to the Bible when it is read? When reading the Bible for ourselves? When hearing the Bible taught and preached?

Memory Verses

2 Timothy 3:16–17—"All Scripture is breathed out by God and profitable for teaching, for reproof, for correction, and for training in righteousness, that the man of God may be competent, equipped for every good work."

God Is God Apart from Us

God is so amazingly great, so perfectly strong, and so completely different from everyone and everything else that he is able to live fully as God without any help from anyone or anything. God doesn't need air to breathe or food to eat or water to drink. He doesn't need help with the work that he decides to do. Rather, God always has, within his own life, everything he needs for being who he is as God and for doing all that he chooses to do. He doesn't need anything at all in the whole world, even though everything in the world needs God. So, God is God—completely and perfectly—without anything in the world helping God to be God.

It is hard to think of God this way, but it is important to learn that this is who God really is. Everything else, and everyone else, in all of the world has to depend on certain things or on certain people. If we listed all of the things we need—things that we don't have in our own lives but must receive in order to live and to do what we want to do—we would be amazed at how long the list would be. But God has no such list! Nothing in the entire world can add to God or can give to God something that he lacks. He has everything—yes, everything!—that really is good, and he has all of this within his own life as God. There is not one single good quality that is not contained within God's own life as God. Anything you can think of that really is good—all truth, all wisdom, all power, all kindness, all love, all righteousness, and every other good thing—is in the very life of God, and it always has been this way. It is simply impossible for God to lack any good thing, because by his very life and being he is the one who has everything that truly and really is good. So, God is God, fully and completely, apart from us and apart from the world that he has made.

When the apostle Paul was asked to tell some people about who God really is, he talked about this very thing. In Acts 17:24–25 Paul said, "The God who made the world and everything in it, being Lord of heaven and earth, does not live in temples made by man, nor is he served by human hands, as though he needed anything, since he himself gives to all mankind life and breath and everything." The reason that God cannot be given anything is clear—God already has it all! For this very reason, God is the one who gives to all of creation what it needs, while nothing in all of creation can give to God anything that he supposedly lacks. Another verse that helps us see this is James 1:17: "Every good gift and every perfect gift is from above, coming down from the Father of lights with whom there is no variation or shadow due to change." If everything that is good and perfect is from God ("the Father of lights"), then this means that God is the one who possesses everything that is good in the first place. You can't give to another what you don't first have. So, for God to give every good and perfect gift that ever is given to each and every person, he must be the one who already has all of those good things. Yes, God is God apart from us, in that he possesses within his own life the fullness of all that is good and perfect.

The prophet Isaiah also helps us see just how great God is by using some examples or illustrations that show us how big and full and wise he is, compared to us. In Isaiah 40:12, the prophet asks some questions meant to help us see God's greatness: "Who has measured the waters in the hollow of his hand and marked off the heavens with a span, enclosed the dust of the earth in a measure and weighed the mountains in scales and the hills in a balance?" Think of that very first image from the verse—who do you know who can hold the waters of the world in the palm of his hand? Imagine for a moment a hand so big that it can cup the waters of the Atlantic Ocean and the Pacific Ocean and all of the seas of the world in the hollow of this huge hand. What a big hand this would be!

Once when our two girls were very young, our family was on vacation along the Oregon coast. At breakfast, I read this passage from Isaiah 40 to my wife and daughters and then asked my two girls if they wanted to do an experiment down at the beach. Bethany was about seven, and Rachel was about three, and they both agreed to come along, excited to see what it was. When we got to the beach, I asked them to stay along the shoreline as I waded out into the Pacific Ocean just a bit. I asked them to watch the ocean carefully, because I was going to stoop down and scoop up water from the ocean, and I wanted them to watch to see how much the level of the ocean dipped as I scooped up water from it. They agreed, and I proceeded to scoop up water with my hands. "Did it change?" I asked them eagerly. A bit disappointed, they said, "No, Daddy, it didn't." I asked them to look very carefully again as I once more leaned over and scooped up a handful of water. "Did it change?" I asked again. "No, Daddy," they again replied.

I walked up onto the shore, knelt down before my girls, and said to them, "Girls, I want you to learn something very important about the difference between how big we are and how big God is. You see, when I went out into this ocean and scooped up all of the water I could within the hollow of my two hands, you couldn't tell that anything had changed at all. But look again at the size of this vast ocean. Imagine a hand so big that if this hand came down right now and scooped up all of the water it could hold, this ocean bed would be dry. That's how big God is!"

Other images in Isaiah 40:12 indicate that his hand is so big that it is able to measure the full extent of the heavens, and his arm is so strong that he could hold the scales on which the mountain ranges of this world are weighed. Indeed, God is great—so great that nothing could add to his greatness. And the greatness of God—the fact that he possesses within himself everything that is good and wise and perfect—indicates to us just how much we should honor him as God and depend on him for all that we need. We should be humble before this great and mighty God, realizing that while we can give nothing to him that he doesn't already have, he has everything that we need. Our hearts should long to praise this God and to live in dependence upon him. Yes, indeed, God deserves nothing less.

Questions for Thought

1. We saw that God always has within his own life everything that really is good. How does this show why God alone ought to be loved and respected and honored above everything and everyone else?

2. What are some things you need that if you didn't have them you wouldn't be able to live? Why should you thank God for giving you those things?

Memory Verses

Acts 17:24–25—"The God who made the world and everything in it, being Lord of heaven and earth, does not live in temples made by man, nor is he served by human hands, as though he needed anything, since he himself gives to all mankind life and breath and everything."

God Is God with Us

Amazingly, even though God is fully God apart from us and apart from the whole creation that he has made, the Bible also teaches that God is a God who is with us. That is, he not only is a God far-off, vast and mighty, big and full of all good things, but he also is a God who has chosen to come near to us, to live with us, to make himself known to us, and to provide for us all that we truly need. Sometimes we might think to ourselves, "Well, of course God wants to be with us; after all, we are such wonderful people." But to think this way is to miss how amazing and truly wonderful it is that God is a God who is with us.

Two things need to be clear in our thinking. First, we must realize that God didn't need to create this world or to create us. Remember that God possesses within his own life everything that is good and wise and perfect. He didn't need the creation that he made, and he didn't have to create us. Some have thought that God made us because he was lonely, but this just is not true. As Father, Son, and Holy Spirit (we'll talk about this more in the next section), he delights in the fellowship he has as three persons in one. And since God already possesses everything that is good within his own life, creation could never add anything to God that he lacked. So, we are not here to fill some supposed emptiness in God or because God needs us somehow to help him out. Second, we must remember that after God created us, we turned against him, rejecting his goodness and wanting to live our lives our own way (we'll talk more about this later also). Because we have sinned against God, we deserve to be rejected by God, not accepted by him.

So, it really is amazing and wonderful that even though God doesn't need us, and even though we have turned away from God in our sin, God comes to us, makes himself known to us, and desires to give himself fully to us. While God is fully God apart from us, amazingly, God is also a God who has chosen to be with us.

Isaiah 57:15 gives us a beautiful description of God in both of these ways: "For thus says the One who is high and lifted up, who inhabits eternity, whose name is Holy: 'I dwell in the high and holy place, and also with him who is of a contrite and lowly spirit, to revive the spirit of the lowly, and to revive the heart of the contrite.'" Can you see both of these truths about God in this verse? First, God is "high and lifted up," and he lives "in the high and holy place." As such, God is God apart from us. In himself, he lives fully as God apart from this world that he has made. But even though God is so great and full in his own life, he has chosen also to come and "dwell" with those who are "contrite and lowly." Why has he chosen to do this? Has he come because he needs something from us? No, rather God sees that we need something—everything!—from him. God chooses to come to those who are humble before him, "to revive the spirit of the lowly, and to revive the heart of the contrite." In other words, God comes to us not so we can fill up some emptiness in God (there is none), but so he can fill up the huge emptiness in us. Even though God doesn't need us, he loves us, and he wants us to receive from him all of the goodness, blessing, and joy that he has for those who will be humble and dependent before him.

One thing this makes clear is how different God's love for us is from our love for each other. A husband may truly love his wife, and the wife may truly love her husband, and yet in their love for each other, they both have needs that the other person must meet. Their love for each other, then, is a matter of both giving to serve the other and receiving what one needs from the other. But since God has no needs that he himself does not meet within his own life as God, his love for us is completely unselfish.

God's love, as C. S. Lewis put it, is "bottomlessly selfless, by very definition; it has everything to give and nothing to receive" (*The Problem of Pain*). God's love for us is not a *because of* love; God doesn't love us for what he can get from us, as if he needed anything we could give him! Rather, God's love is an *in spite of* love; God loves us even though we cannot benefit him, and even though we have sinned against him. As Paul puts it, "but God shows his love for us in that while we were still sinners, Christ died for us" (Romans 5:8), and John says, "In this is love, not that we have loved God but that he loved us and sent his Son to be the propitiation for our sins" (1 John 4:10).

This last point raises a very important truth that we will look at much more in later chapters. For God to be a God who is with us, he must come to us in our sin. And yet God is pure, holy, and sinless, and so he cannot live joyfully and fully with us as sinners. So, God chose that he would come to be with us in the person of his own Son, who would live a perfect life in all of the ways that we as sinners had failed to do. As one who was perfect and sinless, God's Son, Jesus, could then pay the penalty we deserved to pay for our sin. When Jesus died on the cross, his Father placed upon Jesus our sin, so that Jesus died in our place, paying the penalty of death that we deserved to pay. Only in this way would it be possible for our sin to be taken away or forgiven, so we could be viewed by God no longer as sinful but now as pure and righteous. As Paul states it, "For our sake he [God the Father] made him [Jesus] to be sin who knew no sin, so that in him we might become the righteousness of God" (2 Corinthians 5:21).

What God calls us to do is to admit that we have sinned against him, that we deserve death for our sin, and now to believe and trust that Jesus died in our place, paying the penalty we deserved for our sin. When we turn from our sin and trust in Jesus' death as a full payment for our sin, God promises to forgive us of our sin and to make us clean before him. Paul states, "For the wages of sin is death, but the free gift of God is eternal life in Christ Jesus our Lord" (Romans 6:23). Although we deserve to die because of our sin, God's gift to us through faith is life with him that never ends. How amazing that even though God is holy and sinless, he has come near to us, especially in his own Son, providing a way for us to be saved from our sin and brought into his presence forever. God truly is a God who is with us—with us forever through faith in Christ.

Questions for Thought

1. Why do we sometimes think that God loves us because we deserve to be loved by him? What are some reasons we should realize that we do not deserve to have God's love or kindness shown to us?

2. If God loves us when he doesn't need us and when we don't deserve his love, how should we respond to his great love?

Memory Verse

> Romans 5:8—"God shows his love for us in that while we were still sinners, Christ died for us."

Some Truths about God's Richness That Make Him God

How important is it to know someone well, and to know his or her character? Imagine, for example, asking a perfect stranger to stay in your house and watch your pets while you're on vacation. Would you trust him? Isn't it true that only in coming to know someone are you able to decide whether he can be trusted, whether she is true to her word, whether you can depend on him or her? The very same thing is true in our relationship with God. We need to seek to know him much, much better so that we will be drawn to love and trust him more. Knowing him better should be one of the main things we seek through all of our lives. Here we'll consider three ways in which the character of God is seen in God who lives fully as God, apart from the world. There is a richness to God that is true of him totally apart from whether he made the world or not. God is God *period*. As we've seen, God does not need the world in order to be God, even though the world needs God for everything that it is and does. So, what are some of the ways that God's richness can be seen as he is—the true and living God, apart from the world?

First, God is *eternal*. This means that God's life has no beginning, and it has no ending. Unlike everything else that has ever existed, God does not depend on anything else for his life, since he always lives and can never die. This is a very difficult idea for us to understand, since we do not know of anything like this—and that's because there is nothing in all of creation that is like God. Your own life had a beginning, when you were first conceived, and then nine months later you were born into this world. And your mom and dad both began at some time, as has every dog, cat, lion, elephant, tree, and insect. Everything else has a beginning to its life. But this is not true of God. God has no beginning, since he always lives. And because life is part of what it means for God to be God, his life can never come to an end. A psalm written by Moses offers this way of seeing God as always living, as eternal: "Lord, you have been our dwelling place in all generations. Before the mountains were brought forth, or ever you had formed the earth and the world, from everlasting to everlasting you are God" (Psalm 90:1–2). When Moses speaks of God as living "from everlasting to everlasting," he means that as far back as you can think (even before God created the universe and created time itself) to as far forward as you can think (imagine heaven that continues millions and billions of years from now), God has always lived and will always live. From the everlasting past to the everlasting future, God has always existed as God and always will. So, the true and living God has life in himself. No one has given him life, and no one can take away that life. Because God is God, he always lives.

Because God has life in himself, this also means that God has everything that he needs for his life in himself. After all, since God lives forever, it must be true that God has lived most of his life when there was nothing else. God lived before he created the world, and he was still fully God then. So, for God to have life in himself, it means that he also must have everything that he needs for his own life within himself. We can think of God, then, as being both self-existent (he has life in himself) and self-sufficient (he has everything he needs for his life in himself). This reminds us of what we spoke of earlier, that God has no need for the world, since everything God needs to be God is found in his own life. Because God is eternal, because he has life in himself, it also means that he has every good thing within his own life. Nothing can be added to the richness that God has because God has it all, without beginning and without ending.

Second, God is *holy*. The Bible often speaks of the holiness of God, and it emphasizes this truth about God as of the highest importance.

For example, Isaiah once had a vision of God sitting upon his throne in his temple. Mighty angels flew around him, and they cried out to one another, "Holy, holy, holy is the LORD of hosts; the whole earth is full of his glory!" (Isaiah 6:3). To be holy means to be different from all else—to be unique or separate or set apart. These angels are proclaiming that God is different from all else; there is no one like him. The Song of Moses says the same thing: "Who is like you, O LORD, among the gods? Who is like you, majestic in holiness, awesome in glorious deeds, doing wonders?" (Exodus 15:11). And, of course, the answer to this question is, "No one is like the Lord," and so, God truly is holy. He is one-of-a-kind, unique.

One of the most important things about God's holiness is that he is completely separate from all that is wrong or impure or sinful. He has a life that cannot be stained by anything that is bad. Because God is truth, he cannot tell a lie or believe a lie. Because God is faithful, he cannot go back on his word or break a promise. Because God is righteous, he cannot do what is evil or consider the evil that others do as okay or acceptable. Another way to think of God's holiness is this: because God is holy he cannot be less than who he is as God, and he cannot be other than who he is as God. God is wise and good and righteous and truthful and faithful, and God simply cannot be different than this. He is holy, and so he is separated from anything that is contrary to his own life as God.

Third, God is *unchangeable*. We should be able to understand this from what we've just seen of God's holiness. God is God, and this means that God cannot be less than who he is as God, just as God cannot be other than who he is as God. God has every quality within his own life as God, and because of this, he simply cannot change for the better or for the worse. A beautiful statement of this truth is expressed in Psalm 102:25–27: "Of old you laid the foundation of the earth, and the heavens are the work of your hands. They will perish, but you will remain; they will all wear out like a garment. You will change them like a robe, and they will pass away, but you are the same, and your years have no end." Yes, indeed, God is the same, and his years never come to an end. God is who he ever is, and nothing in the very character of God can change.

Considering that God is eternal and holy and unchangeable should bring to us both praise for God's greatness and trust because of the faithfulness of his character. Knowing God is this way, we truly can count on him. He always lives, and he always has all power and wisdom and goodness that he alone has as a holy God. He can never change in his character, becoming less or other than he is. We know that we can believe his word and trust his wisdom and power to do what is right. Knowing the richness of God, then, leads us to honor him, worship him, trust him, and humble ourselves before him. God alone is God, and God's richness is without measure and without end.

Questions for Thought

1. God is so different from us. What are some of the ways God is not like anything he has made? How does this show God's greatness?

2. God never changes in being the perfect God that he is. How does this truth about God bring comfort, strength, and hope to those who trust in God for what they face in their lives?

Memory Verse

> Exodus 15:11—"Who is like you, O Lord, among the gods? Who is like you, majestic in holiness, awesome in glorious deeds, doing wonders?"

Some Truths about God's Kindness That Make Him God

In learning who God really is, we find that he not only is separate from us in his richness and fullness as the eternal God, but he is also with us as a patient, gracious, forgiving, and loving God. So, not only is God rich in his life as God, he also is gracious and kind in his relationship with his people. Here we look together at three truths about God that show the greatness of his kindness, truths that help us know God better and realize even more why our hope and trust and dependence should be placed in God.

First, God is *wise*. In fact, the Bible teaches that God's wisdom is so vast and perfect that it is right to call him "the only wise God" (Romans 16:27). Even though people may have some bits of wisdom—some more than others, and all of it from God!—only God is perfectly wise.

To understand what it means for God to be wise, we should talk for a minute about the difference between knowledge and wisdom. Knowledge has to do with having certain facts or information stored up in one's brain. A person can know the multiplication table or the order of the presidents of the United States or the names of the planets of our solar system. Knowledge is factual, and one can acquire much knowledge, but not necessarily be wise. What's the difference? Wisdom depends on knowledge, but it goes beyond knowledge. Wisdom takes factual knowledge and puts it to use to figure out how best to solve a problem or how to plan for something that might happen in the future. Wisdom, then, is knowledge applied; it is knowledge put to use for some practical purpose. But there's more. To see this, stop and ask yourself, what is the difference between someone who is wise and someone who is cunning or crafty? A cunning or crafty person probably uses knowledge to accomplish something, but he does this for bad purposes. A thief may be very cunning, but his use of knowledge of how to steal something should not be considered wise, right? So wisdom, then, is a use of knowledge, but it is a use of knowledge to bring about something that is good and right and helpful.

Now ask yourself two questions about God. 1) How much knowledge does God have? Answer: God knows everything that can be known. He knows everything about the past, the present, and the future. He knows things exactly as they are, and he is never wrong about anything. 2) What guides God's use of this perfect knowledge as he makes his plans and carries out his will? Answer: God's own holy and righteous nature guides him. This means that everything he decides, and every use of his knowledge, will bring about what is completely good and right and best.

No wonder the Bible talks about God's wisdom being shown through his creation of the world (Psalm 104:24) and in his salvation of sinners (1 Corinthians 1:18–25). In these two greatest works of God we see how God took his vast knowledge and applied it to bring about what was good and right and beautiful and best. Both creation and the cross of Christ display the wisdom of God like nothing else ever has or ever could.

Second, God is *all-powerful*. Think with me for a minute: what if God were wise, in the ways we've just seen, but suppose he didn't have the power to bring about what his wisdom had planned? What would we think about God then? Well, we might respect God for having such vast knowledge and perfect wisdom, but we would also feel sorry for someone who knew the best things to do but who couldn't do them. But what if God had all power and yet suppose that he wasn't actually wise? What would we think then? It doesn't take long to realize that if this were true, we would be terrified of God and of what he might do. After all, to have all power but to lack wisdom that directs its use is a very scary idea. But here is the truth—the true God, the God of the Bible, is both perfectly wise and almighty in his power! He is able to plan what is best, and nothing can keep God from bringing about what he knows is best to do.

Abraham and Sarah learned about God's great power. They were both very old, and they had not yet had the son that God had promised they would have. As the years went by and Sarah got older and older, she began to doubt that God could make it possible for her to have this baby boy. When God told Abraham that he would work in Sarah's body so that she would give birth to a son named Isaac, Sarah laughed. God heard this, and he responded, "Why did Sarah laugh and say, 'Shall I indeed bear a child, now that I am old?' Is anything too hard for the LORD? At the appointed time I will return to you, about this time next year, and Sarah shall have a son" (Genesis 18:13–14). Interestingly, the name *Isaac* that God said to name this son means, "he laughs." So, even though Sarah laughed, thinking she was too old for God to fulfill this promise, God instructed that her son be named "Isaac," "he laughs." God's power was so great that God got the last laugh. God's power is without limit. As the prophet Jeremiah states, "Ah, Lord GOD! It is you who has made the heavens and the earth by your great power and by your outstretched arm! Nothing is too hard for you" (Jeremiah 32:17). Nothing? No, nothing!

Third, God is *all-good*. How encouraging to know that yes, God is *all*-good. Even though we are very glad that God is completely good, this is another truth about God that is sometimes hard to believe. After all, we do not know anyone who is completely and perfectly good. Because we are sinners, and all the people we know are sinners—even really fine Christian people still sin and do what is wrong sometimes—we find it hard to believe that God is purely and perfectly good. But good he is! Psalm 5:4 declares of God, "For you are not a God who delights in wickedness; evil may not dwell with you." God has no wickedness or evil in him at all. Rather, as Psalm 119:68 says of God, "You are good and do good." God's very life is good, and all of his actions are good. There is no evil in God at all, and all that God is and all that God does is completely good.

Part of what it means for God to be good is that he longs for his own people to be blessed and to experience true and lasting joy. He loves his own people deeply, and the proof of his love for his own people is seen in the grace and mercy shown to them despite their sin. Even though we deserve God's just punishment, God has sent his Son to pay for our sin and bring us into right relationship with himself. Such grace (kindness given to those who deserve punishment instead; see Ephesians 2:8–9) and mercy (kindness given to those who are hopeless and helpless; see Ephesians 2:1–4) are the expressions of God's love and goodness to his own people.

So, God is perfectly wise, all-powerful, and completely good. We have every reason to trust him, then. God plans only what is best (he is perfectly wise), and God cannot be hindered in bringing it about (he is all-powerful), and we know that his plans will work out for our best (he is completely good). Like sitting on a three-legged stool, we need to sit by faith on top of these three supports: God's wisdom, power, and goodness give us every reason to put our trust in God, and in God alone.

Questions for Thought

1. Why is it good (and wonderful) that God is both all-powerful and all-wise? How does our trust in God depend on God being both all-wise and all-powerful?

2. How is your confidence in God and his ways strengthened even more by knowing that God is always good? What are some ways your doubts or fears can be removed by trusting in God's wisdom, power, and goodness?

Memory Verse

Daniel 2:20—"Blessed be the name of God forever and ever, to whom belong wisdom and might."

2

God as Three in One

There Is Only One God

We live in a world in which there are many different religions with different beliefs and practices. Along with this, each religion has its own idea of who god (or the gods) must be. Some believe in many gods (as in Hinduism and Mormonism), and others believe in only one God (as in Islam, Judaism, and Christianity).

What is true today has always been the case. All the way back in the days of Abraham, Moses, and the prophets of Israel, we find that the nations that surrounded Israel believed in many gods. There were many different religions in those days, and most people believed there were many gods. One of the most common ideas among the religions of Israel's neighbors in Old Testament times was that different gods were responsible for different parts of the world. Certain gods were in charge over certain areas, while other gods had control over other areas. Because of this, when you traveled, you would have to be aware of when you passed from the area controlled by one god into an area controlled by a different god—different gods, over different areas, with different laws that applied in each of those areas. It's sort of like when you drive from one state into another state or one country into another country. You have to watch to see if the speed limit or other rules of the road change. Since now you are in a new place, there may be different laws to obey than you had before.

The beginning of the book of Genesis, then, is very important in light of the different religions and gods that were followed by Israel's neighbors. The opening verse of the Bible reads, "In the beginning, God created the heavens and the earth" (Genesis 1:1). And so right off the top, the Bible makes clear three very important truths: 1) there is one and only one God, 2) this one God has made absolutely everything—"the heavens and the earth"—that exists, and 3) because the true and living God has made everything that is, he alone has rightful rulership over everything that exists. The principle is something like this: to make something is to be the rightful owner of it, and to own something means you're the only one who can say how it is to be used. Well, since God made everything, he owns it all. And as Creator and owner of everything, he alone has the right to be in charge over absolutely everything that exists. This is why the Bible calls God both Creator and Lord. He not only created everything that is, but he rules over all that he has made. Because God made the whole world, he owns it; and because he owns it, he rules it as he pleases.

Have you ever heard the story of Elijah when he confronted the prophets of Baal? In 1 Kings 18 we read that Elijah wanted the people of Israel to decide whether they would worship and serve the true God (the God of Israel) or whether they would serve instead the false god Baal. Because many of Israel's neighbors worshipped Baal, the Israelites were tempted to do the same. So Elijah said to them, "'How long will you go limping between two different opinions? If the LORD is God, follow him; but if Baal, then follow him.' And the people did not answer him a word" (v. 21). Because the people of Israel were not sure about following the Lord God of Israel, Elijah challenged the prophets of Baal to make an altar and pray to Baal to come down and burn up the altar with fire from heaven. Well, they built the altar and prayed, but nothing happened. They tried hard to get Baal to burn up the altar, but he didn't seem to hear their prayers, no matter how much they tried.

So Elijah built an altar and even put lots of water on it, making it harder for it to be burned up. Then Elijah prayed with all of his heart, and the true God, the Lord God of Israel, consumed the altar with fire. By this, Elijah had shown all of the people that the God of Israel was the true God and that Baal was not really a god after all.

One very interesting thing about this story is where it took place. Elijah confronted these prophets of Baal at Mt. Carmel, an area that was supposed to be where Baal was in charge. The worshippers of Baal would not have been surprised to see the God of Israel consume the altar with fire if this had happened in Jerusalem. They thought that Jerusalem was the place where the God of Israel was in charge. But on Mt. Carmel, Baal was supposed to be in charge. So when the God of Israel responded to Elijah's prayer and consumed the altar, this showed two things: not only was the God of Israel the true God, but also the true God was in charge everywhere, not just in certain places. Because God is the true God, and because he has made all that is, he also alone is the rightful ruler of all that he has made. The prophets of Baal learned that on that day.

Some other passages in the Bible help us see that Scripture teaches clearly that there is only one God. Deuteronomy 6:4, for example, states, "Hear, O Israel: The LORD our God, the LORD is one." The God of Israel, then, is the only true God, and amazingly, this true God is "our God." Israel should have rejoiced and been humbled, and we also should rejoice that this one and only true God has made us his own people as we trust him and follow in his ways. Or listen to what Solomon prays in his prayer of dedication for the Temple. After reminding the people that they are God's chosen people and should serve him with their whole hearts, he calls for them to live faithfully before God, "that all the peoples of the earth may know that the LORD is God; there is no other" (1 Kings 8:60).

Over and over in Isaiah 41–48 we see something amazing. The true God, the God of Israel, challenges the false gods to prove that they are gods. Any real God, says the God of Israel, will be able to predict what will happen in the future and control history's events, and if he cannot do this, he's not really a god. So for example, God challenges the false gods, "Tell us what is to come hereafter, that we may know that you are gods" (Isaiah 41:23a). A bit later we also read the words, "I am he [God]; there is none who can deliver from my hand; I work, and who can turn it back?" (Isaiah 43:13), and, "I am the LORD, and there is no other, besides me there is no God . . . ⁶there is none besides me; I am the LORD, and there is no other. ⁷I form light and create darkness, I make well-being and create calamity, I am the LORD, who does all these things" (Isaiah 45:5–7). The Bible is clear: there is one and only one God. The God of the Bible, the God of the Israelites, and the God shown through Christ is the only true God. We close with Jesus' own words, showing that he also believed there is only one God. He said, "And this is eternal life, that they know you the only true God, and Jesus Christ whom you have sent" (John 17:3). We praise God that he alone is God, and we rejoice that this God has come to us and has made himself known. May we know him better and learn his ways, so we may walk in his light and trust him always.

Questions for Thought

1. What are some other religious beliefs you've heard about? How do those other religions' understandings of "God" differ from what the Bible teaches about God?

2. What difference does it make to know that there is only one true God?

Memory Verse

> Deuteronomy 4:35—"To you it was shown, that you might know that the LORD is God; there is no other besides him."

One God in Three Persons

Some things in the Christian faith are easy to understand, and others are harder. The topic we have here is one of the harder ones for sure. And yet, understanding how God is both one and three at the same time is important for two main reasons. First, this is who God really is. So, if we are to know God as he is and not think of him in ways that we just make up or guess at, we need to understand what he's told us about himself. And one thing he's told us is that while there is one and only one God, this one God is also three at the same time. Just what this means, we'll work at understanding in a minute. But right here it is important for us to accept this teaching of the Bible as good and right because it tells us who God really is, as he has made himself known to us. Second, seeing God as both one and three is important because through this we can understand better the ways in which the Father, the Son, and the Holy Spirit relate to one another and do their work. Each Person—the Father, the Son, and the Holy Spirit—has very important work to do, and yet as they all do their work, they relate to each other and to us in the process. We can learn much about God, and about how we are to relate to others also, by watching carefully how this one God does his work through being three Persons in relation to one another.

We've seen in the previous section why we should believe there is only one God. The Bible is clear on this point, as the passages we looked at showed. But the Bible also speaks of God as three. The Father is God, the Son is God, and the Holy Spirit is God. Let's begin by looking at a few passages of the Bible that show that God is three while also being one.

One of the most important passages comes from the words that Jesus spoke after his resurrection and before he went back to be with his Father. He said to his disciples, "Go therefore and make disciples of all nations, baptizing them in the name of the Father and of the Son and of the Holy Spirit, [20] teaching them to observe all that I have commanded you. And behold, I am with you always, to the end of the age" (Matthew 28:19–20). When Jesus commanded his disciples to baptize believers in the "name" of the Father, Son, and Holy Spirit, he used the word "name" as a singular noun, not "names" as a plural noun. This is meant to show that there is one God, since there is one and only one nature of God as indicated by his one "name." There aren't many gods with different names, but only one God with one name. But interestingly, this one God's name has three parts: Father, Son, and Holy Spirit. So there is one God, but the Father is God, and the Son is God, and the Holy Spirit is God. There is only one God, but this one God is expressed in three Persons, as the Father, Son, and Holy Spirit. Each is God and shows what God is like.

Another passage that helps is the very last verse of 2 Corinthians. Here Paul gives a final blessing to the people, saying, "The grace of the Lord Jesus Christ and the love of God [the Father] and the fellowship of the Holy Spirit be with you all" (13:14). Of course, Paul knows that there is only one God, and he is here giving a final blessing from this one God. And yet how he offers this blessing is interesting. He uses the language of three in this blessing that he offers from the one God. So, in Paul's mind, "May God be with you" becomes "May the grace of Jesus, the love of God the Father, and the fellowship of the Spirit be with you." One God, yes; three Persons of the one God, also yes.

One last passage we'll consider is Ephesians 2:18: "For through him [Christ] we both have access in one Spirit to the Father." Paul is speaking here about the fact that both Jews and Gentiles who have trusted in Christ are now in right relationship with God. They both have been brought to God through faith in Christ. But the way he speaks of this truth involves all three members of the Trinity. Both Jews and Gentiles who have trusted Christ are able to come to *the Father* because of the work of *Christ* and through *the Spirit* who now lives within them by faith. So Father, Son, and Holy Spirit are all involved in the way a person is able to be joined again with God.

A question often asked is whether there are any examples, any analogies or illustrations, to the Trinity that can help us understand how God is both one and three. Some have suggested that the Trinity is like a triangle—three sides make up one triangle, so you have three in one. This example helps for a bit, but when you think about it more deeply, you can see it isn't quite right. You see, the Bible teaches that there is one God, and the Father is fully God, the Son is fully God, and the Holy Spirit is fully God—not three gods but three Persons, each of whom expresses fully that one God. But a triangle is not this way. Yes, it has three sides, but each of the sides is not fully a triangle, right? So, while a triangle shows one thing made up of three parts, it doesn't show one thing that is fully expressed by each of the three parts.

Some have thought that perhaps the Trinity is like three men, say Peter, James, and John. They all are human, but they are three persons. Will this work to show us the Trinity? Here the problem is the opposite of the problem with the triangle. Each person is fully human, but in this example you not only have three persons, you have also three human beings. After all, Peter is a man, but a different man from James, who is a different man from John. So if we followed this illustration we would end up with three gods as well as three persons who are god.

Yet others have thought that H_2O (water) shows us the Trinity since H_2O can be three things: solid (ice), liquid (running water), and vapor (steam). But the same H_2O molecules cannot be all three at exactly the same time. H_2O is a good illustration of modalism (a false teaching of the Trinity that we'll learn more about later) where God is first the Father, then the Son, and then the Spirit, one at a time. But the Bible teaches that God is Father, Son, and Holy Spirit *all at the same time*. Each Person lives eternally as God.

The closest thing I've imagined to the Trinity is drawing one circle using three colored markers (perhaps red, blue, and green). If you draw the same circle three times, with each color overlapping exactly the previous one, you have one circle. But the red line is not the blue line, and the blue line is not the green line. Yet all three lines enclose only one circle. While this illustration may work in a very small part, the truth is that there simply is nothing in our experience that shows us exactly what the doctrine of the Trinity teaches. Nothing quite works to show what it means for God to be one in his nature as the one true God, yet three in Persons as the Father, Son, and Holy Spirit, each fully God. But we should not be surprised at this. After all, the Bible has told us many times that there is no one like the Lord (Exodus 8:10; 9:14; Deuteronomy 33:26; 34:11; Jeremiah 10:6–7). He is the one and only true and living God, and he also is unlike anything or anyone else.

There truly is no one like the Lord. He is one God, but that one God lives and is expressed through the three Persons of the Father, the Son, and the Holy Spirit. Each Person is fully God, yet each Person is also distinct from the other Persons. We have here a biblical teaching that in the end we must believe even though we cannot understand it fully. And what we can learn from this is that God is greater than anything we can imagine and more beautiful than anything we've seen. The doctrine of the Trinity calls us to wonder and marvel at just how great God is. Three in One and One in Three—this is God, and there is no other!

Questions for Thought

1. Why is it important to know that God is both one (only one God) and three (the Father, Son, and Holy Spirit), and each is fully God?

2. Why should we not be surprised if we cannot completely and fully understand the doctrine of the Trinity?

Memory Verse

> Ephesians 2:18—"For through him [Christ] we both have access in one Spirit to the Father."

The Father Is God

There is one and only one God. But that one God lives and is expressed always as the Father, the Son, and the Holy Spirit. So there is one God but three Persons, each of whom is fully God. And each of the Persons of God is responsible for certain parts of the work that God does in the world.

For example, it is true (and glorious) to say, "God saves us from our sin." This is a wonderful truth we'll think more about in later chapters, and yes, it is God who does this. But if we think more carefully, we realize that "God saves us" only as the Father does his own particular work along with the Son who does his own particular work along with the Holy Spirit who does his own particular work in saving us. The Father is the One who planned our salvation and chose to send his Son into the world to save us from our sin (John 3:16–17). But the Son (not the Father and not the Holy Spirit) is the One who came to become a man and to live a perfect life and then die on the cross (Philippians 2:5–8). The Holy Spirit worked to help Jesus during his life (Luke 4:14–21) and works in our lives so that we are able to put our faith in Christ and be saved (John 3:4–8). So the Father, the Son, and the Holy Spirit each play different roles, and together they accomplish the one work of salvation that the one God brings to us.

Let's think more about the work that the Father does as God. The Bible presents the Father as the One who has planned everything that takes place in all of creation. The Father not only planned to create the world, he also planned all that would happen in the world. For example, the Father planned what the world would be like, and he planned to send his Son to die for sin, and he planned that certain people would truly be saved through faith in Christ, and he planned that one day all of creation would be under the rule of his own Son. Yes, the Father stands behind everything as the careful planner, the wise designer, of all that takes place in our world. Paul makes this point in Ephesians 1:11, where he writes that "In him [Christ] we have obtained an inheritance, having been predestined according to the purpose of him [the Father] who works all things according to the counsel of his [the Father's] will." Yes, the Father is the One who has planned all that takes place, and the Father works to make sure that his purposes and plans happen just as he desires.

This is why we see in the Bible that the final praise and thanks will be given to the Father. He is the One who stands behind everything that the Son and the Holy Spirit do in saving sinners and making all things new. For example, in Ephesians 1 Paul explains a number of reasons why we should give praise to God for the many wonderful gifts he brings to us. But rather than saying, "Praise be to God," speaking of the oneness of God in his gifts to us, he says, "Blessed be the God and Father of our Lord Jesus Christ, who has blessed us in Christ with every spiritual blessing in the heavenly places" (v. 3). Notice that Paul very carefully and specifically gives this praise to God the Father rather than expressing it to "God" more generally. It wouldn't have been wrong for Paul to say, "Blessed be God for all the blessings he has brought to us," but it is more exact and precise to say what he does say. Notice that he indicates that final praise is given to "the God and Father," showing that this praise goes to the Father specifically. But notice also that he says that all of the blessings that the Father brings to us come "in Christ."

So, the Father brings us every blessing we receive, but every blessing we receive comes always and only through what his Son, the Lord Jesus Christ, has accomplished by his work for us. And notice finally that these blessings are "spiritual" blessings, showing that the way we receive these blessings is as the Holy Spirit brings them to our lives. So we learn here that the Father is the wise and gracious Giver of all of the blessings that God gives to us. And these blessings from the Father are blessings that the Son has won for us by his life, death, and resurrection. And these blessings, from the Father, through the Son, are brought to our own lives through the work of the Spirit. Praise be to the Father, and through him for the Son, and through him for the Spirit.

Another passage that helps us see that the Father is the One who rightly receives the final praise and honor for all the work of our salvation is Philippians 2:8–11: "[Christ] humbled himself by becoming obedient to the point of death, even death on a cross. ⁹ Therefore God [the Father] has highly exalted him and bestowed on him the name that is above every name, ¹⁰ so that at the name of Jesus every knee should bow, in heaven and on earth and under the earth, ¹¹ and every tongue confess that Jesus Christ is Lord, to the glory of God the Father." The Father planned not only to send his Son into the world (John 3:16–17; 6:38), but also that after his Son had died on the cross, the Father would raise him, exalt him, and give him the greatest name of all. The day will come when every single person who has ever lived will bow his or her knee before Christ and say with his or her own lips, "Jesus Christ is Lord." But when all human beings do this, they then will also give final praise beyond the Son "to the glory of God the Father" (cf. 1 Corinthians 15:25–28).

Seeing the Father as the One highest in charge and having authority over all is important for many reasons. One way it helps is in how we think of prayer. If you notice as you read the prayers in the New Testament, most of them follow the very pattern that Jesus taught his disciples. Jesus said, "Pray then like this: 'Our Father in heaven, hallowed be your name'" (Matthew 6:9). Why would Jesus instruct us to pray to the Father? Simply because the Father is the One who has the highest authority of all. Even the Son right now, who is over everything created, sits at the "right hand" of the Father (Ephesians 1:20), indicating that the Father is highest of all. So, prayers in the New Testament most often are made to the Father. Consider Paul's prayer at the end of Ephesians 3. He begins this way: "For this reason I bow my knees before the Father, ¹⁵ from whom every family in heaven and on earth is named, ¹⁶ that according to the riches of his glory he may grant you to be strengthened with power through his Spirit in your inner being" (vv. 14–16; see also Ephesians 1:16ff.; 5:20; Philippians 4:19–20).

Prayer, then, should normally be directed to the Father. But we can only come to the Father because of what Christ has done for us through his death and resurrection. When we trust in Christ, then we can come "in Christ" to the Father. So our prayers are to the Father, in the "name" or the authority of the Son. But we also need the Spirit to direct us to pray as we should. So we should normally pray to the Father, in the name of the Son, by the power of the Holy Spirit (see Ephesians 6:18). Ephesians 2:18 gives us this pattern. It speaks of how both Jews and Gentiles who have trusted in Christ are brought into relationship with the Father. Paul says, "For through him [Christ] we both [believing Jews and believing Gentiles] have access in one Spirit to the Father." So, praise be to the Father, who through his Son's death and resurrection and by the work of the Spirit makes the way for us to be brought into right relationship with him. What a privilege to pray to and to praise the One who has highest authority over all.

Questions for Thought

1. Have you noticed how often in the Bible we are called to pray to the Father or give thanks to the Father? Why is this?

2. What are some of the main things that the Father does for which we should give him our praise and thanksgiving?

Memory Verse

Ephesians 1:3—"Blessed be the God and Father of our Lord Jesus Christ, who has blessed us in Christ with every spiritual blessing in the heavenly places."

The Son Is God

When we think of Jesus, we should think of the One who was sent by the Father to come and save us from our sin. He is the eternal Son of the Father who came down from heaven to take on also full human nature. He was, then, fully God and fully man. He had to be both fully

God and fully man in order for him to live a perfect human life, pay the enormous penalty that we deserved to pay for our sin, be raised victorious as our Conqueror, and then reign forever as King of kings and Lord of lords over all. He had to be man in order to live a perfect human life and die in our place. But he had to be God so that the payment he offered would meet the standard that God his Father required. You see, if we paid for our own sin, we would never finish paying. Forever and ever we would still be paying for our sin because our debt is that big. But because Jesus was God as well as man, he was able to pay the full penalty for our sin so we could be saved by faith in him.

So, it matters that Jesus was God, right? If he wasn't God, he couldn't save us from our sin. But it also matters that Jesus lived life fully as a human, right? If he wasn't really and fully human, he couldn't have lived the life we should have lived—a life of perfect obedience to God—and qualify then to die in our place, bearing not his own sin (he didn't have any!) but bearing our sin. What a great Savior Jesus is! And this could only be true because he was both God and man.

In later chapters we'll talk more about the human nature of Jesus and how he lived his life of obedience, dying then for our sin. But here we need to understand the Bible's teaching on the fact that Jesus was fully God. There have been people all through history, as there are some people today, who did not believe that Jesus was fully God. Some think that Jesus was created by the Father, just as we are created. They think that Jesus had God's Spirit living in him, but that he wasn't God himself. But the Bible is clear that Jesus was never created; rather, he created all things that have been created! And while the Spirit did help Jesus live his life as a man, Jesus also lived his life fully as God.

Where does the Bible teach that Jesus is God? First, the very name *God* is sometimes used of Jesus. One of the most important passages is John 1:1, which says, "In the beginning was the Word, and the Word was with God, and the Word was God." "The Word" that John refers to here is the Son of the Father who then became a man. We know this because in John 1:14 John says that "the Word became flesh"—that is, the Word who is the eternal Son became a human being. This, of course, is Jesus. So we now know that back in John 1:1 "the Word" is Jesus before he became also a human being. This verse says of him that he always has been with God his Father and that he also always has been God. So, as Son of the Father he has been with his Father forever, but as God he always has had the very same nature as his Father as God. Because Jesus has the one nature of the one God, Jesus is actually called "God" (see other passages where "God" is used of Jesus: John 20:28; Romans 9:5; Philippians 2:6; Colossians 1:15; Titus 2:13; Hebrews 1:8; 2 Peter 1:1; 1 John 5:20).

Second, Jesus does works that only God can do. For example, right after Jesus is called "God" in John 1, the writer goes on to say that Jesus (before he became also a human) was the One who created everything! John 1:3 says, "All things were made through him [the Word, Jesus], and without him was not any thing made that was made." One interesting thing about this verse is that it teaches that everything made has been made by Jesus. Well, this means that Jesus could not himself be made, right? If Jesus made everything that has been made, then Jesus cannot be made by something else. If you wish, you can see the very same truth taught by Paul in Colossians 1:16 where "all things" made are made by Jesus. If he creates *all things that are made*, this means that Jesus himself cannot be made.

Another thing that only God can do that Jesus does is forgive sin. In Mark 2:1–12, Jesus surprises everyone when he forgives the sin of a man who was brought to him for healing. Some Jewish leaders were shocked. They said, "Why does this man speak like that? He is blaspheming! Who can forgive sins but God alone?" (v. 7). But they didn't realize that Jesus really is God, and so he really can forgive sin. Yes, only God can forgive sin (the Jewish leaders were right), but since Jesus is God, he really can—and did!—forgive sin.

Third, there are certain things true of Jesus' own life that are true only of God. For example, we're told that "Jesus Christ is the same yesterday and today and forever" (Hebrews 13:8). And earlier in Hebrews we are told that Jesus never changes (1:10–12). Well, this is a trait that only God has, the trait of being unchangeable. Everything else changes, but God cannot change in his own life as God. What is true of God alone, though, is true of Christ. So, Jesus is God as shown by his being unchangeable. Jesus also is eternal, which is a trait only true of God. That same passage in Hebrews 1:10–12 speaks not only of Jesus as unchangeable but also as eternal. Other passages teaching this are Isaiah 9:6, Micah 5:2, and Revelation 1:8. Well, if God alone is eternal, and Jesus is eternal, then it follows that Jesus is God.

Fourth, Jesus is worshipped as God. The Bible is clear that only God is to be worshipped (Exodus 20:1–5; 34:14; Deuteronomy 6:13), and the people of God have known this (see, e.g., Acts 10:25–26; 14:11–15; Revelation 19:8–10; 22:8–9). So, how amazing it is to see that Jesus is worshipped and that his Father even wants others to worship Jesus. For example, Hebrews 1:6 says that when the Father brought Jesus into the world, he said, "Let all God's angels worship him." And after Jesus was raised from the dead, you may remember that "doubting Thomas" saw Jesus with the wounds in his hands and side, and he said, "My Lord and my God!" (John 20:28). And in the end of time, when all people honor God, they will worship the Son with his Father, as we see in Revelation 5:8–14. Since only God is to be worshipped, and Jesus is rightly worshipped, Jesus has to be God.

Lastly, Jesus declared that he was God. One of the most amazing statements Jesus ever made is recorded for us in John 8:58, where Jesus said, "Truly, truly, I say to you, before Abraham was, I am." What makes this statement truly astonishing is not merely that he claimed to be older than Abraham, who had lived two thousand years before Jesus! More amazing than that is the fact that Jesus said that he was "I am." By saying this, Jesus was connecting himself to the very God of Israel who in Exodus 3:14 gave as his name, "I AM." So Jesus is God since he claims to be the God of Israel, the true and eternal God.

We have very strong reasons, then, for believing that Jesus was not only a man but that he was fully God. We rightly worship him, and we should long to serve him, for he truly is God. And this won't change when we learn later about Jesus becoming also a man. When he became a man—fully a man—he never stopped being God—fully God. Because Jesus is God as well as man, he was able to pay the full price for our sins that only God could pay. Because Jesus is God as well as man, he deserves our love, obedience, praise, and worship. With Thomas, we should bow before Jesus and declare, "My Lord and my God!"

Questions for Thought

1. The Bible tells us that Jesus has created the world and that Jesus is able to forgive our sins. How do these acts of Jesus show that he is God?

2. Jesus was worshipped by people during his life on earth, and one day all people will worship him (Philippians 2:9–11). Since only God is to be worshipped, what does this tell us about Jesus?

Memory Verses

John 1:1–3—"In the beginning was the Word, and the Word was with God, and the Word was God. He was in the beginning with God. All things were made through him, and without him was not any thing made that was made."

The Holy Spirit Is God

Many things about the Bible's teaching on God are difficult for us to understand. But as we've seen, this shouldn't surprise us since God is so much bigger and greater than we can ever imagine. And one of those challenging areas is this doctrine of the Trinity, where we are called to believe that there is one and only one God, and yet the Father, Son, and Holy Spirit each is fully God, always and forever.

But now, when we begin to talk directly about the Holy Spirit, we face another area that is difficult to see. For on the one hand, the Bible teaches that "God is spirit" (John 4:24), so that God does not have a real body or take up real space, as we do. Now, all of God's life is the life of One who has non-physical or spirit existence. It is for this reason that God can be everywhere (Psalm 139:7–10). God is not limited to being in one place at a time, as we are. He is able to be everywhere at the very same time because he is spirit, and his life as spirit is bigger than the whole universe!

But on the other hand, the Bible also teaches that the third Person in the Trinity is "the Spirit." The Bible's names for the three Persons of God, as we've already seen many times, are Father, Son, and Holy Spirit. You may remember that one of the most important verses in all of the Bible to show that the one God lives his life and is expressed in three Persons is Matthew 28:19, where Jesus says to baptize new believers "in the name of the Father and of the Son and of the Holy Spirit." So we should call this third member of the Trinity by the name "the Holy Spirit."

On the one hand, then, God—the fullness of who God is—is "spirit," and on the other hand, the third Person of God is called "the Spirit." So, while God is spirit, the Holy Spirit is God. So we need to keep in mind that when we talk about God—all of who God is—we are talking about One who is not a physical being and does not take up just a certain amount of space, as we do. Rather, God—all of who God is—is non-physical or "spirit." But we need also to keep in mind that the name the Bible gives us for the third member of the Trinity, who forever lives as God with the Father and the Son, is the name "Holy Spirit." He, too, is God, just as the Father is God and the Son is God. This third Person of the Trinity must also be seen as God.

What teaching does the Bible give to help us understand the Holy Spirit? First, we should see that the Bible teaches that the Holy Spirit is a *real and genuine person*. He is not some force or power like the force of wind or the power of electricity. We know this because the Holy Spirit is treated as a person, and he shows us qualities that are true only if he is a person. For example, the Holy Spirit can be lied to (Acts 5:3) and insulted (Hebrews 10:29), which are things that cannot be done to a mere force or power like wind or electricity. Just try to insult the electricity that is powering your lights or your refrigerator! You can't do it because such forces or powers are not personal. But the Holy Spirit is personal, and so he is treated as a person. Also, the Holy Spirit has personal qualities like having a mind (1 Corinthians 2:10–11—the Holy Spirit knows the thoughts of God), emotions (Ephesians 4:30—the Holy Spirit can be grieved), and a will (1 Corinthians 12:11—the Holy Spirit gives abilities to members of the body of Christ as he so chooses). And maybe most important, the Holy Spirit is called "holy" ninety-four times in the New Testament. He has the character of holiness, which along with having a mind, emotions, and will, is true only of a person.

Furthermore, not only is the Holy Spirit a person, but he is a *divine Person*. That is, the Holy Spirit is God. Here are some of the ways we can see from the Bible that the Holy Spirit should be understood as God. First, there are some places where he is spoken of as God. In Acts 5, for example, Peter rebukes Ananias for lying to the Holy Spirit about the land he has sold. Then Peter says, "You have not lied to men but to God" (Acts 5:4). So when Ananias lied to the Holy Spirit, he was actually lying to God. Another amazing statement that the Holy Spirit is God comes from Paul in 1 Corinthians 3:16: "Do you not know that you are God's temple and that God's Spirit dwells in you?" Here those who belong to God through faith in Christ are called God's temple—the place where God dwells. But just how does God dwell or live with his people? He lives in them as the Spirit of God dwells in them. So, for believers to have the Holy Spirit living within them is to have God dwelling in them. Yes, the Holy Spirit is God.

Second, the Holy Spirit does things that only God can do. For example, the Holy Spirit is involved, along with the Son and the Father, in the creation of the world (Genesis 1:2; Psalm 33:6, where "breath" is the Hebrew word *ruach*, which also can refer to the "Spirit" of God). He also is spoken of often as the One who gives new life to people so they can believe in Christ and be saved (John 3:5–6; Titus 3:5). And the Holy Spirit is the One who worked in the lives of the writers of the books of the Bible so that the Bible would be the Word of God (1 Corinthians 2:13; 2 Peter 1:21). The Holy Spirit is God, then, in order to accomplish these things that only God can do.

Third, the Holy Spirit has certain qualities that are true only of God. For example, the Holy Spirit is referred to as living forever or eternally (Hebrews 9:14), as being everywhere present (Psalm 139:7–10), and as having all knowledge (1 Corinthians 2:10). These qualities—referred to often as eternity, omnipresence, and omniscience—are qualities that only God has. And since the Holy Spirit has them, he must be God.

Fourth, the Holy Spirit is mentioned in some passages along with the Father and the Son as being equal to them. Since the Father is God and the Son is God, for the Holy Spirit to be equal to them must mean that he, too, is God. The most famous passage showing this is one we've seen earlier in this section. Jesus says to baptize new believers "in the name of the Father and of the Son and of the Holy Spirit" (Matthew 28:19). But since they are baptized in the "name" of the Father, Son, and Holy Spirit, it means that they all share the very same name or nature. Just as the Father is God, so also the Son is God, and so also the Holy Spirit is God.

So, we have very strong reasons for believing that the Holy Spirit is both a personal being and that in fact he is a divine Person. All who have trusted in Christ (as we shall see more later in this book) have even more reason humbly to thank and praise God that the Spirit truly is God. For when the Spirit comes to those who believe in Christ, he comes as the very Spirit of God with supernatural power to make us new and make us more and more like Jesus. Praise God that the Spirit who comes to bring God's great power is this Holy Spirit who is fully God. And praise God, who is Father, Son, and Holy Spirit, for his greatness and his grace.

Questions for Thought

1. How do we know that the Holy Spirit is a real person? What qualities does he have that only real persons have?

2. Since the Holy Spirit is God, what is he able to do in the lives of those who have trusted Christ and have received the Holy Spirit into their lives?

Memory Verse

1 Corinthians 3:16—"Do you not know that you are God's temple and that God's Spirit dwells in you?"

How the Father, Son, and Holy Spirit Relate

Have you ever noticed that some of the most beautiful music is made up of different parts being sung together? Rather than each person singing the same notes as the others—that's called unison—instead each singer has a different line of music to sing, but they blend to make a rich and beautiful sound together—that's called harmony. No doubt, there is a beauty to singing in unison, but there is usually a richer and more beautiful sound produced when each singer contributes just the right lines of the music, at just the right times, singing in harmony.

In a very real sense, this is how God does most of his work in the world. The one God does most everything that he does through all three Persons of the Trinity. Each Person does his own distinctive work, each contributing his own part—singing, as it were, his own line of the music— and together they accomplish exactly what is best and perfectly wise and most beautiful. The Father, Son, and Spirit don't usually carry out their work strictly in unison. Rather, they work in harmony with each other as each Person fulfills that part of the overall work that is right and good for him to do. As all three Persons contribute to the overall work, everything is done as it should be and is done with the greater richness that harmony brings over unison.

As we saw earlier, the Father stands atop this work as the One who designs and plans what the work shall be. Because of this, the Father is also the one who is praised most highly in the end. As we saw in Philippians 2, when every knee bows and every tongue confesses that Jesus is Lord, they will do so to the glory of God the Father. So the Father contributes both the goal and plan of the work that should take place, and he also designs just how the Son and Spirit should join him in carrying out this work. After all, the Father has highest authority, and so he chooses the ways in which the Son and Spirit contribute so that the Father's perfect will and work is done just right.

The Son, for his part, is completely committed to doing the will of the Father. As you read the four Gospels (Matthew, Mark, Luke, and John), you will notice how often Jesus mentions that he was on earth to accomplish everything that the Father sent him to do. One of the clearest of these statements comes in John's Gospel. Jesus said, "When you have lifted up the Son of Man, then you will know that I am he, and that I do nothing on my own authority, but speak just as the Father taught me. [29] And he who sent me is with me. He has not left me alone, for I always do the things that are pleasing to him" (8:28–29). Notice the strength of what Jesus says of himself in relation to his Father. Jesus says that he does *nothing* on his own authority, that he speaks *just* as the Father has taught him, and that he *always* does what is pleasing to his Father. We should not understand what Jesus says here as overstatement or exaggeration, because we know that Jesus lived a completely sinless life. To sin even once would have involved his doing or saying something against what his Father had wanted, but Jesus never, never, not even once, did this. So what Jesus says here is completely true. He did *nothing* by his own authority, and he spoke *only* what the Father wanted him to say, and he *always* pleased the Father in everything that he said and did. Amazing!

One more thing this means is this: As the Son of the Father, Jesus lives always under the authority of his Father—in all times past and now and in all times future. During his life on earth he surely did this, as we saw from John 8:28. And as one looks carefully at Jesus' own teachings along with other passages in the Bible, it is clear that Jesus, as the Son of the Father, was always under his Father's authority, and he will always be under his Father's authority. Think, for example, how often we read about God "sending" his Son into the world and of the Son coming to do the "will" of his Father. If the Father sends the Son (John 3:17), and if the Son comes into the world to do the Father's will (John 6:38), then it follows that the Father had authority over the Son before he came into the world to become also a man. And does this relationship continue in the future? Yes, for according to 1 Corinthians 15:25–28, when all things are put under the authority of the Son, the Son will put himself under the Father's authority along with all of creation, in order for God the Father to be shown as supreme. So the Son always stands under his Father and does the will of the Father. And in this, Jesus takes great joy in doing exactly what the Father wants him to do. The Son is not upset about this; he doesn't wish to be the one in charge instead. Rather, as Jesus himself says, "My food is to do the will of him who sent me and to accomplish his work" (John 4:34). Amazing! Jesus loves being under the authority of his Father, and the Father loves to lift up his Son to show how great and glorious his Son truly is.

For his part, the Holy Spirit truly is third among the Persons of the Trinity. As the Son is under the authority of the Father, the Spirit is under the authority of the Father and of the Son. One of the clearest statements of this is found in Jesus' own teaching about the time when the Holy Spirit would come to dwell within those who follow Christ. Jesus says, "I still have many things to say to you, but you cannot bear them now. ¹³ When the Spirit of truth comes, he will guide you into all the truth, for he will not speak on his own authority, but whatever he hears he will speak, and he will declare to you the things that are to come. ¹⁴ He will glorify me, for he will take what is mine and declare it to you" (John 16:12–14). With language very similar to how Jesus spoke of himself in relation to the Father, Jesus now spoke of the Spirit in relation to the Son. Just as the Son did not speak his own words but taught what the Father told him, so the Spirit does not speak what he thinks but speaks what he hears from Jesus. And just as the Son glorified the Father by doing the Father's will, so the Spirit glorifies the Son by taking from the Son what he then passes on to others. The Spirit delights, then, in showing Jesus off, in shining the spotlight on Jesus, and in helping people see just how wonderful Jesus is.

The relation of the Father, Son, and Holy Spirit, then, is one of glorious harmony. Each has his work to contribute, and each does this in recognition of the authority and submission order that is true among these Persons. The Father is highest in authority, the Son is under the Father, and the Spirit is under the Father and the Son. But there is not the slightest hint of discontent in this order. Rather, there is joy and fulfillment both in each being fully God and in each working in the proper lines of authority that exist forever in God. A lesson we can learn from this is that lines of authority and submission are true in our human relationships because they are a reflection of what is true in God (see 1 Corinthians 11:3). The Father, Son, and Spirit are fully equal as God, yet they live gladly within lines of authority. So, too, we humans should live both as equals of each other, yet gladly in God-given lines of authority. May God help us to see the beauty of equality and the beauty of our differences, even differences in the lines of authority that are true in our relationships.

Questions for Thought

1. Since the Son always obeys the Father and we are never told that the Father obeys the Son, does this mean that the Son is not equally God? Or that the Son is less than the Father? Why not?

2. Can you think of some examples in your experience where two people are equal to each other as human beings, yet one is under the authority of the other?

Memory Verses

John 8:28—"When you have lifted up the Son of Man, then you will know that I am he, and that I do nothing on my own authority, but speak just as the Father taught me."

John 16:13–14—"When the Spirit of truth comes, he will guide you into all the truth, for he will not speak on his own authority, but whatever he hears he will speak, and he will declare to you the things that are to come. He will glorify me, for he will take what is mine and declare it to you."

3

Creator and Ruler
of All

Who Made the World? God (the Father, Son, and Holy Spirit) Did

I remember well a song that our children loved to sing when they were very young. The first line asked the question, "Who made the world?" and the second line answered, "God did!" This is true, and we should rejoice in its truth. Yes, God did make the world. As we saw earlier, he made flowers and butterflies and birds and fish and stars and mountains and waterfalls and the oceans and coastlines and *everything* that was made.

And amazingly, God made everything in the whole universe without using any materials that were already there. Anytime we humans "create" something or make something, we have to take things that are already there and use them to make what we want. If, for example, we'd like to make some bookshelves, we have to take boards and nails and perhaps glue and varnish or paint and other materials, cutting and connecting and treating them just right so we end up with the bookshelves that we had in mind. And that is the way it is with anything and everything that we make. But for God—just think how amazing this is—when he decided to create the world and all that is in it, there was nothing yet that existed except for God. He alone is eternal (only God lives forever). So before God created the world, there was nothing else other than God in existence. Rather than taking and using materials already there (for there were none), God merely spoke and brought into existence things that were not already there at all, in any way, shape, or form. As we have seen earlier, God is a talking God, and God merely said, "Let there be . . ." and whatever he spoke came into existence, just as he planned it to be. God created everything out of nothing, and he created by speaking into existence everything that has come to be.

Hebrews 11:3 also teaches exactly this truth: "By faith we understand that the universe was created by the word of God, so that what is seen was not made out of things that are visible." Yes, God by his word brought into being everything that is, and he made all that he made—which is everything that has been made—without using anything already there to make it happen. And Hebrews tells us that we must accept this truth "by faith." Why is that? Simply because we cannot understand how someone could just speak and bring something into being without using any materials to do it. Every time we make something—whether it's your mom making dinner or your sister drawing a picture or your brother building with Legos—we always use things to put together what we make. Only God creates out of nothing. So we must believe this teaching of the Bible simply because God has told us that this is how he made the world. We can't understand it—not really—but we know it is true because God has the power to create in this way and because he has told us that this is how he did it. We believe in God's power, and we trust in God's truthfulness, and so we believe the Bible's teaching. Yes, God created all things out of nothing as he spoke them into being.

When you look at the teaching in the New Testament about God's creation of the world, you find something very interesting. In nearly every passage speaking about God creating the world, it talks specifically about the Son as the One who actually brought the world into being. One of the most interesting of these passages is John 1:3, where it is "the Word" who creates all things. John 1:1–3 reads: "In the beginning was the Word, and the Word was with God, and the Word was God. ² He was in the beginning with God. ³ All things were made through him [that is, through the Word], and without him was not any thing made that was made." Why do you think that the One creating here is called the Word? The reason is this: when you read in Genesis 1 about God creating, he does so as he speaks. That is, as God utters his word, light comes into existence, and stars and planets and everything that is made. So John 1:3 helps us see, then, that the way God creates the world is really as the Father creates through the work of the Son (who is called "the Word" in John 1). The Father, then, stands behind all of the creation as the One who designed just what it would be and planned how it would unfold. But the Father chose to use his Son as his agent to bring the creation into being. It's sort of like your mother deciding to make a pie, but she might ask her daughter to do the pie-making work as she directs. When the pie is done, you might say, "This is mom's pie," but you could also say that the pie was made by her daughter. So, the world is God's world, but God made the world through his Word, who is his Son.

It may help to read a few other passages that point to the Son as the One who actually brings into being everything that is created: "For by him [Christ] all things were created, in heaven and on earth, visible and invisible, whether thrones or dominions or rulers or authorities—all things were created through him and for him" (Colossians 1:16). "Long ago, at many times and in many ways, God spoke to our fathers by the prophets, 2 but in these last days he has spoken to us by his Son, whom he appointed the heir of all things, through whom also he created the world" (Hebrews 1:1–2). "[T]here is one God, the Father, from whom are all things and for whom we exist, and one Lord, Jesus Christ, through whom are all things and through whom we exist" (1 Corinthians 8:6). This last passage is especially helpful because it indicates that the Father is responsible for all of creation since it all comes "from" him. But the Son, Jesus Christ, is the One "through whom" the Father created the world. The Father spoke, and his Word brought the universe into being.

And what about the third member of the Trinity, the Holy Spirit? Scripture indicates that he was also involved in creation. The Spirit of God is mentioned in Genesis 1:2 as "hovering over the face of the waters." And Psalm 33:6 says that creation happens both by "the word of the LORD" (recall John 1:1–3 here) and also by "the breath of his mouth" ("breath" is the same word as for the Spirit). So, somehow the Spirit is also involved in creating. Perhaps his role was in giving life to those parts of creation that were to live. In Genesis 2:7 we see God "breathing" into Adam so he lives, and it may be the work of the Spirit to give original life to those parts of creation. Even though we are not told much in the Bible about this, we know that the Spirit was involved with the Father and the Son in creation.

One final comment might help here. It makes sense to see the Father, Son, and Spirit all involved in creation since all three are also involved in our salvation (or our re-creation, perhaps we could call it). In our salvation the Father designs how we will be saved, the Son comes and accomplishes our salvation on the cross, and the Spirit brings new life to those who then believe in Christ to be saved. All three have vital roles to play in salvation, and it seems all three have similar roles to play in creation.

So, let's go back to the question that began this section: *Who made the world?* The answer *God did* is correct, to be sure. But even better would be this answer: *God the Father, God the Son, and God the Spirit did!* Amen.

Questions for Thought

1. What are some ways we should worship, praise, and thank God as the Creator of all that is?

2. The New Testament books make much of the fact that Jesus is the Creator of the world. What does this tell us about Jesus, and what difference should this make to our relationship with him?

Memory Verse

> Hebrews 11:3—"By faith we understand that the universe was created by the word of God, so that what is seen was not made out of things that are visible."

God Rules the World He Has Made

Let's begin by remembering something we thought about earlier. The fact that God created everything that has been created shows that he alone is God. There is no other god, since only the true God has lived forever and since only the true God has created everything that is. There are not many gods who are responsible for different parts of creation. No, there is one God, and only one God, and he has made everything— absolutely everything!

But since God (and only God) has created all that is, this means that God owns everything. Everything is God's because God made it all. If some other god had made some part of creation, then that part of creation would belong to that god. But there are no other gods, and everything in creation has been made by the one true and living God. Since God created all things, then God (alone) is the rightful owner of all things.

To take it one step further, we can see that since God created all that is, and since he, then, is the rightful owner of all that is, God also is the rightful ruler of all that is. Everything that God made is his, and he alone has rights to rule over it and use it however he wishes. As we have thought about before, to create something is to own it, and to own it is to have the right to rule over it. So, since God has created all that is, he alone is the rightful owner and the rightful ruler of everything—absolutely everything!

How good it is to know some truths about this God who alone has the right to rule the entire world that he has made. If God were this ruler, but if he weren't wise, we would worry that he would direct the world in ways that would not be best. Or if God ruled this world, but if he wasn't good, we would worry that he might use the world for wrong or evil purposes. But how wonderful it is to know that God is both wise and good! His great power has brought the world into existence, and we can be sure that God has wise and good purposes to bring about through the world. God should be praised for his creation of this world since it shows his greatness, and it all works exactly as he knows is best. Revelation 4:11 says this beautifully: "Worthy are you, our Lord and God, to receive glory and honor and power, for you created all things, and by your will they existed and were created." What a great God our God is. He has created everything, and we can be sure that he is ruling over everything he has made so that he will receive all praise and honor in the end.

There are two ways in which God's ruling of this world is spoken of in the Bible. One way is through God's providing for everything that he has made, and the other is through God's guiding and directing everything he made so all things accomplish what God has planned. Let's think about each of these a bit more.

First, God provides for everything he has made. He brings everything into being, but after creating different things, he doesn't leave them alone. Rather, God cares for his creation. He is involved in providing for and protecting every part of the creation so that all of God's purposes are fulfilled. Jesus refers to this when he asks his followers to, "Look at the birds of the air: they neither sow nor reap nor gather into barns, and yet your heavenly Father feeds them. Are you not of more value than they?" (Matthew 6:26). Or again he says, "Consider the lilies of the field, how they grow: they neither toil nor spin, [29] yet I tell you, even Solomon in all his glory was not arrayed like one of these. [30] But if God so clothes the grass of the field, which today is alive and tomorrow is thrown into the oven, will he not much more clothe you, O you of little faith?" (Matthew 6:28–30). Of course, the reason Jesus tells us these specific ways that God, his Father, cares for his creation is so that we will trust God to take care of us, too. As Jesus indicates by his questions, because we are more valuable to God than the birds of the air, and because God has made us to live forever and not be like grass that is here today and gone tomorrow, we can be sure that God will take care of us. If he takes care of the birds and the fields, even more will he take care us, his children. So, God not only creates the world, he also watches over it and cares for it to make sure that all of his purposes with the world are accomplished. And this also means we can trust God to take care of us, watch over us, and provide what he knows is best for us.

The second way God rules the world he has made is by guiding and directing it to accomplish or bring about everything that he has planned for it. A verse we looked at earlier is important to consider again. Paul writes, "In him [Christ] we have obtained an inheritance, having been predestined according to the purpose of him [the Father] who works all things according to the counsel of his [the Father's] will" (Ephesians 1:11). God has a plan for the world he made. He didn't create the world wondering what might happen. He didn't create the world and then leave it alone to run by itself. Rather, God created the world with a very complete plan for how the world would develop and what would be accomplished through it. As Paul has said, God the Father "works all things according to the counsel of his will." We can be sure that all of God's purposes and plans will be brought to pass since the God who made the world also rules the world he has made.

Perhaps one other passage might be helpful to see God's rulership over the world. In Daniel 4 we read that the great king Nebuchadnezzar, King of Babylon, had become very proud of how wealthy and powerful his nation had become. This was wrong of him to do, since he should have known that the only reason Babylon had become great was because God made it great! It wasn't Nebuchadnezzar who did this; God did. So God humbled King Nebuchadnezzar until he learned that the true God was in control of making him and his nation great, and so God alone would be praised. Here, then, are the words of a humbled, corrected Nebuchadnezzar: "I, Nebuchadnezzar, lifted my eyes to heaven, and my reason returned to me, and I blessed the Most High, and praised and honored him who lives forever, for his dominion is an everlasting dominion, and his kingdom endures from generation to generation; [35] all the inhabitants of the earth are accounted as nothing, and he does according to his will among the host of heaven and among the inhabitants of the earth;

and none can stay his hand or say to him, 'What have you done?'" (Daniel 4:34–35). Notice Nebuchadnezzar's statement that God does what he wills to do in "the host of heaven" and throughout "the earth." Stated differently, this means that God does his will in all of creation! Just as "God created the heavens and the earth" (Genesis 1:1), so he rules completely over the heavens and the earth—that is, over all that he has made. And notice that no person can "stay" God's hand. This simply means that no one can keep God's hand from doing what God wants to do.

So, God not only made all things, he has complete control over all that he has made. And we can know, then, that he will direct his creation forward to bring to pass all that he has planned for it. Praise be to God, the Creator and Ruler of all that is!

Questions for Thought

1. Since God created the world, he owns all that he has made, and he alone has the right to rule all that he has made. What heart responses should we give to God in light of this?

2. God rules the world by *providing* for it and by *directing* all that happens in it. What heart responses should we give to God in light of this?

Memory Verse

Revelation 4:11—"Worthy are you, our Lord and God, to receive glory and honor and power, for you created all things, and by your will they existed and were created."

God Provides All Good Things in the World

Many of our family vacations have involved long drives in the car. In order to make good use of the time together while driving, my wife, Jodi, would make copies of portions of Scripture that we would memorize as we drove past yet more cornfields. One summer, our psalm to memorize was Psalm 103, and I can tell you that we all loved reading, memorizing, and discussing this wonderful psalm. It begins like this: "Bless the LORD, O my soul, and all that is within me, bless his holy name! ² Bless the LORD, O my soul, and forget not all his benefits, ³ who forgives all your iniquity, who heals all your diseases, ⁴ who redeems your life from the pit, who crowns you with steadfast love and mercy, ⁵ who satisfies you with good so that your youth is renewed like the eagle's" (Psalm 103:1–5).

Indeed, we should bless the Lord every day of our lives, and one of the most important ways we can do this is to "forget not all his benefits." According to James, there is not a single one of these benefits, not a single good thing we have in our lives, that did not come from our gracious heavenly Father. James writes, "Every good gift and every perfect gift is from above, coming down from the Father of lights with whom there is no variation or shadow due to change" (James 1:17). God our Father is the Giver of every good thing that we enjoy. One of the ways we should rightly honor him as God, then, is to remember all of his benefits and to give him thanks for them.

The Bible indicates that those who have trusted in Christ receive these benefits from the Father in a special way. Every good thing that we as believers in Christ enjoy has been given to us by the Father through the work of the Son. In other words, *all* that the Father gives us, he gives to us through what Christ has done, and never apart from this. Ephesians 1:3 makes this clear: "Blessed be the God and Father of our Lord Jesus Christ, who has blessed us in Christ with every spiritual blessing in the heavenly places." Notice that the Father has given us these gifts (as we've also seen in James 1:17), but the way the Father brings all of these gifts to us is "in Christ" or through what Christ has done for us. After all, how do we receive forgiveness of our sin? Answer: through the death of Christ for our sin. And how do we receive the hope of eternal life? Answer: through the resurrection of Christ, which assures us of our resurrection to eternal life. And how does the Father provide for our needs? Answer: through the never-ending and glorious riches of Christ. Yes, the Father gives us every good thing. And as believers, we honor Christ as the One whose work has made it possible for us to receive all the good things that we enjoy in this life and in the next.

If believers are ever tempted to doubt God's love for them or to wonder if God really and truly wants their best, they should consider the truths that Paul expresses about just how much God is "for us." He writes, "If God is *for us* [believers in Christ], who can be against us? [32] He who did not spare his own Son but gave him up *for us* all, how will he not also with him graciously give us all things?" (Romans 8:31–32). The following is a poor illustration (compared to God and his gifts), but it may help get this idea across. Suppose you had a very wealthy uncle who decided to build your family a new home. Because he was so rich and because he loved you so much, he built a very fine and spacious home, using the best materials. Then he bought furniture for all the rooms and set the whole house up for your family. Well, at the first dinner meal in your new home, you noticed that there weren't any salt and pepper shakers on the table or in the cupboards. Would you think your uncle was not willing to get these for your family? Of course not. So, here's the question we should ask: your uncle, who spared no expense to build and furnish this beautiful home for you, how will he not also, along with this home, give you mere salt and pepper shakers to use at your meals? Do you get the point? If your uncle has done this *big* thing out of his love (built your home), he certainly won't hesitate to do also this very *small* thing (getting salt and pepper shakers). So, too, for God. If God your Father has given you the *greatest* gift possible by offering his own Son for your salvation, then this same God can be trusted to give you everything else that will be good for you to have. We need to remember that the good that God has for each of us is truly good, as he alone knows what is best. This isn't a promise from God that he'll give us a new baseball mitt or laptop computer or dress. But it is a promise that God will give his own children everything that God knows will truly and eternally be good for them. As we read in the Psalms, those who seek the Lord and long to follow in his ways "lack no good thing" (Psalm 34:10; cf. Ps 84:11). What a kind, generous, and giving God this true and living God is.

One of the most important responses to this gracious God who is the Giver of every good and perfect gift is this: we should feel and offer deep and constant thanks to God. Consider Jesus' approval of the one leper (a Samaritan, no less) out of the ten cleansed who alone returned to Jesus and fell on his face, thanking him and glorifying God (Luke 17:15–16). In contrast, Jesus' questions about the other nine could apply to all such acts of ingratitude. Jesus asks, "Were not ten cleansed? Where are the nine? Was no one found to return and give praise to God except this foreigner?" (Luke 17:17–18). Other passages also speak of not giving thanks, and we see what God thinks about that. For example, in Romans 1 Paul describes how God's anger is being expressed against people who once knew him but now have rejected him. Among the charges made against these people is the comment, "For although they knew God, they did not honor him as God or give thanks to him" (Romans 1:21a). And when Paul lists some of the major sins of the people of Israel in Old Testament times, along with mentioning their idolatry and immorality Paul reminds us of their grumbling that brought them God's judgment (1 Corinthians 10:10). Oh, how we should follow the wise and good advice of Psalm 103:2 to "forget not all his benefits."

Indeed, we should thank God for the small gifts and for the great, from our food for breakfast to answered prayer for something that looked impossible. One of the marks of people who know God rightly and who know God well is that they are filled with thanksgiving to God. If we find in our own lives that we are prone to complain or grumble, that we often are unhappy because we didn't get what we wanted, we need to see this for what it is. A grumbling spirit is sinful, because it fails to recognize God's goodness and kindness in providing for us every good thing in life that we enjoy. Instead of grumbling, we should accept both what God gives us and what he chooses not to give us, because in both cases he does what is best for us. Yes, our heavenly Father is the Giver of absolutely every good thing we have in our lives now and will receive in the future. We owe to him our deep and constant thanksgiving and praise. God is good, and all that he gives is good. Praise be to his name!

Questions for Thought

1. As Psalm 103 encourages, what blessings from God's hand can you remember now and thank God for? How can remembering these blessings keep you from grumbling and complaining?

2. What are some ways the Bible helps us understand just how great is God's love and care for his own people?

Memory Verse

James 1:17—"Every good gift and every perfect gift is from above, coming down from the Father of lights with whom there is no variation or shadow due to change."

God Controls All Bad Things in the World

M ost people find it natural and easy to believe that God is in control of all the good that happens in the world. After all, God is good, so it makes sense that when good happens or when good gifts are given, God has been in control. What is harder for many to see is this: God is just as much in control of bad things that happen in the world as he's in control of all of the good that takes place. How can this be? Doesn't this mean that God should be blamed for bad things that happen? What does the Bible really teach about this?

The Bible teaches that God is in control both of all the good things and of all the bad things that happen in life. Even though we tend to think of God having control only over the good, the Bible teaches that he has control over the bad also. Let's look at some of the Bible's teaching, and then we can think about some questions that this brings up.

Before the children of Israel entered the Promised Land, Moses had been instructing them about who God is and what God expects of them. Toward the end of Deuteronomy, Moses taught them a song that they were to learn and sing when they crossed the Jordan River. In this song Moses says this, using God's own words to teach them: "See now that I, even I, am he, and there is no god beside me; I kill and I make alive; I wound and I heal; and there is none that can deliver out of my hand" (Deuteronomy 32:39). Notice that God makes sure that we understand him as the only true and living God. There is no god besides the true God, he declares. So, we should have our ears open to learn just who this real God is and what this real God can do. And what we learn may surprise us. The real God is responsible not only for making alive but also for killing, not only for healing but also for wounding. In fact, God's control over everything good and bad is so strong that no one can stand against God or keep his plan from being accomplished.

A similar statement of how God controls both good and bad things in life comes from Hannah. As you may remember, Hannah was not able to have a child; so she prayed, and God granted her request. She had a son, named Samuel, whom she dedicated to the Lord. After Samuel was born, she spoke a prayer of thanksgiving and praise to God. Within this prayer, we read these words: "The LORD kills and brings to life; he brings down to Sheol and raises up. [7] The LORD makes poor and makes rich; he brings low and he exalts" (1 Samuel 2:6–7). Very much like Moses' song, Hannah states that God is in control not only of positive or good things like giving life, raising up, giving riches, and exalting people—God also is in control of bad things like killing, taking people to the grave (Sheol), making people poor, and bringing people low. In other words, the whole of life, both its good things and its bad, are all in the control of God.

One more passage that makes this same point powerfully is Isaiah 45:5–7, which reads: "I am the LORD, and there is no other, besides me there is no God; [6] . . . there is none besides me; I am the LORD, and there is no other. [7] I form light and create darkness, I make well-being and create calamity, I am the LORD, who does all these things." Again the main point is clear: God, who is the only true God, is in complete control of both every good thing and every bad thing. This passage is very important because it states so clearly, repeating several times, that there is only one true God. From this, the passage then goes on to describe what this true God does to demonstrate or show that he is God. What shows God to be God? Answer: the true God is in complete control of everything in life, all that is good (God forms light and makes well-being) and all that is bad (God creates darkness and calamity).

Some people refuse to accept this teaching from the Bible because they cannot understand how God could control bad things and not be blamed for that bad. So let's consider two things that may help. First, the Bible states that God controls both good and bad; so we ought to accept this as true even though we may not be able to understand fully just how it can be true. We should accept this teaching especially since we have passages where God speaks directly of himself (saying things like "there is no other God besides me") and then states that part of what it means for God to be God is that he controls all good things and all bad things. So, we should not turn away from this teaching just because we find it hard to understand. Since God tells us in his Word that it is true, we must accept it as true. Second, we should not think that if God controls what is bad, then God must be partly bad. This would be a great mistake. Rather, the Bible teaches that while God controls all things good and bad, God himself is good, and he is not bad at all. Here are a couple of verses to set alongside the teaching in Isaiah 45:7. Isaiah 45:7 says that God forms light and creates darkness, but 1 John 1:5 says, "God is light, and *in him is no darkness at all.*" Isaiah 45:7 also says that God makes well-being and creates calamity, but Psalm 5:4 says, "For you are not a God who delights in wickedness; *evil may not dwell with you.*" In the Hebrew Bible, the very same Hebrew word in Isaiah 45:7 (translated "calamity") is used in Psalm 5:4 (translated as "evil"). So, while God controls completely all that is good and all that is bad, we must understand that God is completely good and that he has nothing bad or wrong or evil in him at all.

So we need to avoid two mistakes. First, we should not think that if God controls all good and bad, God must be himself partly good and partly bad. No! While God controls all good and all bad, God in himself is only good and not at all bad. Second, we should not think that if God is only good and not at all bad, he controls only good and has nothing to do with what is bad. Again, no. While God is only and completely good, still he controls everything that is good and everything that is bad. So, both of these truths from the Bible must be accepted together if we are to understand correctly both God and his work in this world.

A word often used when explaining these ideas is the word *sovereignty*. To say that God rules over all things, both the good and the bad, is to say that he is completely sovereign over them. This teaching of the sovereignty of God is one of the hardest areas for all of us to understand. In fact, as with some other areas of our faith, we just have to accept the teaching of the Bible even though we cannot make perfect sense of it. But if God says that he has complete control over light and over darkness, over well-being and over calamity, we have no right to say this cannot be. We must let God speak for himself, since he alone knows everything exactly correctly. What he tells us about himself, then, must be accepted as true. God is sovereign over all things good and all things bad. And God is completely and only good. God said so, and that should settle it.

One last word here: it is only because God has complete control over all bad things that we can be sure that those bad things work to bring about some good purpose that God has planned. If God is not in control of bad things, then we would be led to deep sadness, thinking that a bad thing that is happening will serve no good purpose. But it is not so! Rather, God does control the bad as well as the good. When bad things happen, we can know, then, that God is using them for good purposes. What comfort and peace this should bring to us, since God always does what is best, and God's purposes can never fail.

Questions for Thought

1. Why is it so important to understand that God is completely good and not evil in any respect, ever?

2. Why is it so important to understand that God has complete control over all things good and all things evil?

Memory Verse

> Deuteronomy 32:39—"See now that I, even I, am he, and there is no god beside me; I kill and I make alive; I wound and I heal; and there is none that can deliver out of my hand."

Our Responsibility in the World
God Controls

Do you remember the story of Joseph in the Bible? When we begin reading about Joseph in Genesis 37, we find that he was Jacob's second youngest son in a family of twelve brothers. Jacob loved Joseph more than his other older sons, and Jacob showed his favor of Joseph in ways that made his older brothers jealous and angry. One time the older brothers were far away from home finding pasture for their sheep. Jacob sent Joseph to go and see how his brothers and the flock were doing. As Joseph came close, the brothers saw him and began to talk about killing Joseph. The oldest brother put an end to this and wouldn't let them murder Joseph. But then later when a caravan came along heading for Egypt, they sold Joseph to the traders, and Joseph ended up as a slave in Egypt.

God took care of Joseph, though, and Joseph was very faithful to God even through many difficulties. God gave Joseph the ability to interpret dreams, and one time Joseph was called in to interpret a dream of Pharaoh, the king of Egypt. The king was so pleased that he put Joseph in command over his entire kingdom. The whole region had some good years for their crops, and Joseph stored away much of the extra food during these years. But this was followed by some very poor years when many people were suffering for lack of food, including Jacob and his family. So Jacob sent his sons to Egypt to buy food. When they arrived in Egypt, they actually bought the food they wanted from their brother, Joseph, even though they didn't recognize him. This happened a few times, and finally Joseph decided it was time to let them know who he was.

Let's consider what Joseph said to his brothers when he made himself known to them. Genesis 45:4–8 says, "So Joseph said to his brothers, 'Come near to me, please.' And they came near. And he said, 'I am your brother, Joseph, whom you sold into Egypt. ⁵ And now do not be distressed or angry with yourselves because you sold me here, for God sent me before you to preserve life. ⁶ For the famine has been in the land these two years, and there are yet five years in which there will be neither plowing nor harvest. ⁷ And God sent me before you to preserve for you a remnant on earth, and to keep alive for you many survivors. ⁸ So it was not you who sent me here, but God. He has made me a father to Pharaoh, and lord of all his house and ruler over all the land of Egypt.'"

Notice a few things about what Joseph says here. First, he makes clear that his brothers sold him into Egypt. Anyone reading the story of Joseph would have to agree—the jealous brothers did in fact do this very bad thing. Second, Joseph indicates that even though the brothers sold him into Egypt, God was also involved. When he tells his brothers not to be angry with themselves for selling him, he then says, "for God sent me" (45:5) there in order to save up food that they would need to live. He repeats the fact that God sent him (in 45:7), indicating that the real reason Joseph was in Egypt was God's doing, not the brothers'. Third, the fact that God, not the brothers, had highest responsibility for getting Joseph to Egypt is made completely clear by 45:8, for here we hear Joseph telling them, "it was not you who sent me here, but God." Amazing as it seems, the main reason Joseph was in Egypt was because of God's doing, even though the brothers did exactly what they wanted in selling him into Egypt.

A very natural question now comes to the surface: if the main reason Joseph was in Egypt was because of God's doing, not the brothers', shouldn't we blame God for what happened to Joseph, and wouldn't the brothers be off the hook (innocent of wrongdoing)? A bit later in Genesis, after Jacob has died, Joseph again speaks to his brothers about their selling him into Egypt, saying, "As for you, you meant evil against me, but

God meant it for good, to bring it about that many people should be kept alive, as they are today" (Genesis 50:20). So, God had the highest responsibility in getting Joseph to Egypt, and the brothers actually accomplished what God wanted done. Even so, the brothers were to blame for what they did, but God should be praised. They meant it for evil, and so they were guilty of wrongdoing. But God meant it for good; so he is worthy of praise and honor.

What this story illustrates is very important. It shows us that even though wicked people carry out things to harm others and to bring about what is wrong, yet God works in and through those very wicked actions. And the fact that God works in and through them makes us sure that his good purposes are brought about even though wicked deeds are done. Because of this, the wicked people who have done these bad things are rightly guilty of doing what was wrong. But God, who works through what they have done, is worthy of praise since he brings about the good that he has planned through them. Both men and God can be involved in the very same actions, men doing these actions for evil, and God doing these actions for good. When men do evil actions, even though God works through them to bring about good, they are still guilty of doing wrong. And since God always works through evil actions to bring about good, God is never to blame and always deserves our praise.

Another very important story in the Bible helps us see these truths. Consider for a minute the question, who put Jesus on the cross to die? If you think about this question for a bit, it becomes clear that you have to give two different answers. On the one hand, you have to say that wicked men put Jesus to death. After all, the Jewish leaders were very jealous of Jesus and asked for him to be put to death. Pilate knew Jesus was innocent, but he handed Jesus over to be crucified anyway. The Roman soldiers made fun of Jesus and beat him before nailing him to the cross, even though he had done no wrong. All of these wicked people were involved in putting Jesus on the cross. But on the other hand, we also must say that God the Father put Jesus on the cross to die. After all, we're told that "God so loved the world, that he gave his only Son, that whoever believes in him should not perish but have eternal life" (John 3:16). And we read elsewhere that "it was the will of the LORD to crush him [Jesus]," putting Jesus to death (Isaiah 53:10). So yes, the Father sent his Son into the world in order for the Son to die as our Savior. So the question, who put Jesus on the cross to die? has to be answered two ways: 1) wicked men put him there, and 2) God his Father put him there. And just as in the Joseph story, those wicked men were guilty of doing what was wrong, even though God had highest responsibility for the fact that Jesus was put to death. And God the Father deserves our praise, honor, and thanksgiving for doing the greatest and most loving thing ever done, offering his Son for the forgiveness of our sin.

The true and living God rules over everything that's good and everything that's bad. But he does so in such a way that he always brings about the good that he has planned, while wicked people are rightly held responsible for the wrong they've done. God is sovereign (he's in control), and we are responsible (we are accountable for the actions we do). The Bible helps us see that these two things must be kept together. Although we cannot understand this fully, faithfulness to God and to his word means that we believe both of these teachings of the Bible are true.

Questions for Thought

1. Many people think that when we do something we choose to do, God can't be in control of what we've done. What is wrong with this idea?

2. Can you think of some other examples in the Bible where God is in control of what people do, and yet those people are responsible for what they've done? (Want some help? Look at Isaiah 10:5–15 or Habakkuk 1:5 and following.)

Memory Verse

> Genesis 50:20—"As for you [Joseph's brothers], you meant evil against me, but God meant it for good, to bring it about that many people should be kept alive, as they are today."

Pain and Suffering in the World God Controls

None of us likes to think about pain or suffering. We all hope we will live lives filled with joy and happiness, not ones weighed down by pain. But many people, including many Christian people, have experienced suffering, sometimes lasting for long periods of time. Even though we'd like to avoid it, we should realize that some suffering will probably be a part of most of our lives, and great suffering will come to some. So when we are young, we should develop biblical thinking about suffering so we can be prepared for whatever God may take us through in our lives. Let me suggest here five principles that can help us think correctly about suffering from a biblical and Christian point of view.

First, *suffering is not, in itself, something good that lasts forever*. We know this because the original creation that God made was good and only good (Genesis 1:31), and in heaven that is coming, all evil, suffering, and pain will be done away with completely. Revelation 21:3–4 states, "And I heard a loud voice from the throne saying, 'Behold, the dwelling place of God is with man. He will dwell with them, and they will be his people, and God himself will be with them as their God. 4 He will wipe away every tear from their eyes, and death shall be no more, neither shall there be mourning, nor crying, nor pain anymore, for the former things have passed away'" (cf. Revelation 22:1–5). It is clear, then, that pain and suffering are not part of God's own life, nor are they part of the original creation or the new re-creation yet to come. Suffering, then, is not in itself something good that lasts.

Second, *suffering is often planned and used by God to bring about good*. Even though suffering is not in itself good, God plans for it and uses it to bring about good. Consider some of the ways God plans for and uses suffering, as the Bible indicates. 1) Suffering can sometimes be the tool of God's judgment on those who are opposed to him, even bringing them to death if they continue in their sin (e.g., Numbers 16:31–35, 41–50; Isaiah 10:5–19). 2) Similarly, God designs some suffering as his tool to call disobedient children back to himself (e.g., Proverbs 3:12; Hebrews 12:10). As C. S. Lewis has said, pain is God's "megaphone" calling his children back to himself (*The Problem of Pain*, p. 81). 3) Suffering can be planned by God so that believers grow in trusting him (e.g., Romans 5:3–5; James 1:2–4). When we understand the good that God plans from suffering, we are able to rejoice in our affliction. God's ways are always best, even when his ways involve his children going through trials and suffering. 4) Suffering can show our human weakness so that the greater strength and glory of God will be seen (e.g., 2 Corinthians 4:8–12; 12:8–10). Often we realize how much we need God, how dependent we really are on God, only when we go through very difficult times. When trials help us see our need for God, they serve a very good purpose. 5) Suffering can be given by God so that believers will be better able to help others who, in similar ways, experience suffering in their lives (e.g., 2 Corinthians 1:3–7). Isn't it true that if someone has gone through the same problem you are facing, they can help in a very special way. So God sometimes gives us suffering so that we can help others who face the same trials. 6) Suffering is a part of being a follower of Jesus, being willing to suffer for his sake in faithfulness to him (e.g., John 15:18–20; Philippians 3:10; 2 Timothy 3:12). As Jesus taught, we should accept persecution as Christians with joy because God will bless us for being faithful to his name (Matthew 5:10–12).

Third, *God has promised his children that everything in their lives, even suffering, will be used for their good.* As Romans 8:28 says, "And we know that for those who love God all things work together for good, for those who are called according to his purpose." All through the Bible we see that God plans and uses suffering in the lives of his children to bring about some good in the end. Consider the lives of Job or Joseph or David or Daniel or Jesus or Paul or Peter or so many more. God *does* plan for his good purposes to come about through suffering he directs at his children. Because of this, Christians can have much hope and peace throughout their suffering, knowing that God's good and wise purposes are being done. Yes, God will work all things together for their good.

This explains why Scripture commands believers to give God thanks *in* their suffering (1 Thessalonians 5:18) and to give God thanks *for* their suffering (Ephesians 5:20). Since God has promised that "all things work together for good" (Romans 8:28), and since God has promised that "those who seek the LORD lack no good thing" (Psalm 34:10; cf. Psalm 84:11), then we have good reason to give God thanks both *in* and *for* all that occurs. God will not fail. He rules over the suffering of our lives, and he plans for our good through everything that happens. What hope and confidence and peace and joy and strength we can have even in the midst of suffering because our great and wise God plans for our good even through suffering.

Fourth, *God is more concerned with our character than with our comfort, with our holiness rather than our happiness.* Consider two passages that help us see this. James says, "Count it all joy, my brothers, when you meet trials of various kinds, for you know that the testing of your faith produces steadfastness. And let steadfastness have its full effect, that you may be perfect and complete, lacking in nothing" (James 1:2–4). And in a similar way Paul tells believers to "rejoice in our sufferings, knowing that suffering produces endurance, and endurance produces character, and character produces hope, and hope does not put us to shame, because God's love has been poured into our hearts through the Holy Spirit who has been given to us" (Romans 5:3–5). Only because God plans for our good through suffering can we live with hope even though we experience pain. Knowing that God uses suffering to help us grow gives us the faith to accept our suffering. Suffering should be seen, then, as part of the good purposes of God in our lives to bring about our good.

Fifth and last, *we should pray for God to remove our suffering while we also pray for God to help us accept our suffering.* In 2 Corinthians 12:7–10, the apostle Paul did just this. He prayed three times for suffering in his life to be removed. Praying *three* times indicates that he was serious about wanting God to remove the suffering, but it showed something else also. When he stopped praying, it was because he accepted God's answer of "no." So, while it is right for us to pray for God to take away pain and suffering that comes into our lives, we should also realize that God may have good purposes to bring about through the suffering. It may be God's will for the pain to continue until all of the good that God has planned is brought to pass. In the end we must trust God to know and to do what is best for us. So, praying for suffering to be removed has to be joined with praying for God's help to accept our suffering. Knowing in the depths of our hearts that God is completely good, God is perfectly wise, and whatever God plans for us is best makes all the difference. When we don't know why suffering happens, we can know that God knows, and God always plans and does what is best. Seeing God at work in our suffering, may each of us be able to say, "It is well, it is well, with my soul."

Questions for Thought

1. How is God's love shown when he uses pain or suffering in the life of someone who has turned away from him?

2. How can we see pain and suffering both as something that is bad and something that is good?

Memory Verse

Romans 8:28—"And we know that for those who love God all things work together for good, for those who are called according to his purpose."

4

Our Human Nature and Our Sin

Men and Women, Boys and Girls— God's Masterpieces

If you were asked to pick out the most glorious part of God's creation, what would it be? That is, what part of creation shows more of God's wonderful qualities than anything else? Some might say that forests with their stately trees and delicate flowers show more of God than anything else. Others might point to rugged shorelines and the vast oceans of our world as showing more of God than other parts of creation. For others, what might come to mind are towering mountain ranges that make us feel really small as we stand before them.

The Bible has an answer to our question, an answer that might surprise you. What shows more of God than any other part of creation? Answer: you and me. That is, human beings are really the greatest part of God's creation, the part that shows more of God than anything else. This same question must have been in the psalmist's mind when he penned these words: "When I look at your heavens, the work of your fingers, the moon and the stars, which you have set in place, ⁴ what is man that you are mindful of him, and the son of man that you care for him? ⁵ Yet you have made him a little lower than the heavenly beings and crowned him with glory and honor. ⁶ You have given him dominion over the works of your hands; you have put all things under his feet, ⁷ all sheep and oxen, and also the beasts of the field, ⁸ the birds of the heavens, and the fish of the sea, whatever passes along the paths of the seas. ⁹ O LORD, our Lord, how majestic is your name in all the earth!" (Psalm 8:3–9). Did you see his train of thought? When we look at the heavens, the moon and stars that God has put in place, it would surely seem that this is where we see the greatest display of God's life and character. But it is not so! No, greater than the stars, the moon, the mountain ranges, the oceans, or anything else is "man"—human beings who have been made to display more of what God is like than anything else does in all of creation.

We can see the special place that God gave to us human beings as we consider the creation account in Genesis 1–2. Here are some of the reasons for thinking that God meant for us to see that his creation of the man and the woman was the high point of his creation. Men and women, boys and girls are really his masterpieces!

First, the creation of the man and the woman came at the very end of the creation week. On the first part of the sixth day, God made the animals of the earth, and then on the second part of the sixth day, as the final act of God's creation, he made man. It's much like when you see a well-done fireworks display. They save the best rockets and most beautiful showers of color and light for the very end of the program, the grand finale. In a similar manner, God saved the very best of his creative work for the very end, God's grand finale, as he made man to show forth more of himself than any other part of the creation he had made.

Second, there are things said about the creation of man that weren't said earlier about any other part of creation. For example, Genesis 1:26 begins this way: "Then God said, 'Let us make man in our image, after our likeness . . .'" Here it is as if God is speaking to himself, perhaps a dialogue among the Persons of the Trinity in light of the "Let us." This indicates a special place given to the creation of man that hadn't been true earlier. Also, and more important, is how God says we are made—"in our image, after our likeness." We human beings are the only part of creation mentioned in the Bible as being made in the image of God. This is such an important part of what it means for us to be human that we'll talk more about this in the next section.

Third, as God creates man in his image, he gives to man the right and responsibility to rule over all the animals of the earth. In fact, in Genesis 1:26–28 man is told twice that he has this important job to carry out. In Genesis 1:26 God says, "And let them [the man and the woman] have dominion over the fish of the sea and over the birds of the heavens and over the livestock and over all the earth and over every creeping thing that creeps on the earth." And again in Genesis 1:28, after creating man as male and female, God said to them, "Be fruitful and multiply and fill the earth and subdue it and have dominion over the fish of the sea and over the birds of the heavens and over every living thing that moves on the earth." God's giving the man and woman dominion over the rest of earth's creation indicates that God views mankind as having a special place in authority over creation.

Fourth, the only part of the creation story from Genesis 1 that is drawn out and talked about further is the creation of man. You might think of Genesis 1:26–28 as the snapshot version of the creation of man, but then Genesis 2:4–25 is like the movie version, with much more detail and explanation. Obviously, God cares much about his human creation because most of the rest of the Bible is really about God's relationship with humans. After our sin and the punishment it brought, God designed the most amazing way to bring his rebellious humans back to himself. God values who we are, created in his image, more than he values any other part of creation. This can be seen since the Bible describes God's plan and work on behalf of sinful humans, made in his image.

Now that we've seen that God made men and women, boys and girls, as his masterpieces in all of creation, let's consider a couple of principles that come from this.

First, when we learn things like this—that God values us more than any other part of creation—we must be very careful how we receive this truth. A wrong way to receive this truth would be to say in our hearts, "Since I'm so important to God, I should receive the credit for being so great. I have a right to be proud for how special I am." The problem with this thinking is that it misses something very important—the only reason that human beings are so special is because God made us this way. We had absolutely nothing to do with it. We can't take credit for anything about our lives since everything we are and have is from God, out of his kindness and goodness in sharing with us. So, we need to be humble, not proud, in light of God's goodness to make us in his image.

Second, we should see human life as very dear and precious, never to be taken lightly. God values human life so much that in Genesis 9:6 he requires capital punishment (putting someone to death) for the crime of murder. To murder someone is so horrible in God's eyes because we have wrongly killed one who is in God's own image. We should respect others and treat them as valuable persons since God has made them as well as us in his own image. And while we should care about animals, plants, and the rest of the earth that God made, humans are of much greater value in God's eyes than any other part of creation. God created things this way, and we should see them the way God does.

Questions for Thought

1. The fact that we human beings are God's masterpieces should never lead us to attitudes of pride or arrogance. Why is this?

2. Since all human beings are created in the image of God, what should be our attitudes about all other people, regardless of the color of their skin or the country they are from?

Memory Verses

Psalm 8:3–5—"When I look at your heavens, the work of your fingers, the moon and the stars, which you have set in place, what is man that you are mindful of him, and the son of man that you care for him? Yet you have made him a little lower than the heavenly beings and crowned him with glory and honor."

What It Means to Be Made in God's Image

It is an amazing and remarkable truth that we human beings have been made in the image of God. But what does this mean? In what way or ways are we made so that we "image" or reflect who God is? Some might say that we are images of God sort of like when you look in a mirror. Your reflection in the mirror is an image of who you are. But then we remember that God is spirit, and so it cannot be that we look like God. Might it have something to do with being like God in our inner lives or characters, as when we are called to be holy because God is holy? This is getting much closer, but there is more, and what a joy it will be to see what this is! Let's first take a look at a few passages that talk about being in God's image, and then we'll think more about what this means.

The single most important passage is Genesis 1:26–28: "Then God said, 'Let us make man in our image, after our likeness. And let them have dominion over the fish of the sea and over the birds of the heavens and over the livestock and over all the earth and over every creeping thing that creeps on the earth.' 27 So God created man in his own image, in the image of God he created him; male and female he created them. 28 And God blessed them. And God said to them, 'Be fruitful and multiply and fill the earth and subdue it and have dominion over the fish of the sea and over the birds of the heavens and over every living thing that moves on the earth.'" Notice that although "image" is used more often in this passage, the word "likeness" is used alongside of "image." To be images of God must have something to do, then, with being *like* God. Also notice that both men and women are created completely in God's image (1:27). We should never think of men as having more importance than women or women more than men. Because God made both the man and the woman in his image, they are of equal value and importance to God. Finally, notice that the man and woman are told twice that they should "have dominion" over the rest of creation. Since this is stated so strongly in this passage where we are told about being made in God's image, perhaps part of what it means to be the image of God has to do with our calling to rule or have dominion.

Another important passage to consider is where Jesus is spoken of as being in the image of God. Paul writes, "He [Christ] is the image of the invisible God, the firstborn of all creation. [16] For by him all things were created, in heaven and on earth, visible and invisible, whether thrones or dominions or rulers or authorities—all things were created through him and for him. [17] And he is before all things, and in him all things hold together" (Colossians 1:15–17). Notice that Jesus is the image of "the invisible God." This is to make sure we understand that Jesus was God's image as his human nature (visible) was joined to his divine nature (invisible, on its own). And the way Jesus is the image of God here is as he has dominion over creation. When Paul says that Jesus is the "firstborn" of creation, he does not mean that Jesus was the first created being. This cannot be. Jesus as God was not ever created. Also, verse 16 says that everything created was made by Jesus; so Jesus himself could not be one of those created things. By "firstborn," then, Paul means that Christ has the highest place in all of creation, as the firstborn has in a family (see Psalm 89:27 for "firstborn" used this way). Jesus is over all creation. This is shown most clearly by the fact that Jesus made all of creation (1:16) and he holds together all of creation (1:17). So, Jesus helped us understand what it means to be the image of God as he lived his life and showed his dominion over creation.

One last passage we should think about is in James 3: "no human being can tame the tongue. It is a restless evil, full of deadly poison. [9] With it we bless our Lord and Father, and with it we curse people who are made in the likeness of God" (vv. 8–9). This passage helps us with a question some have had—are we still in the image of God after sin came into the world? And the answer James gives us here is, yes, we are. We should treat all people with respect, all men and women, all boys and girls, since each one has been made in the image and likeness of God. This is true even though all of us have sinned and need to be forgiven and made new by Christ.

Well, let's consider now a few of the main ideas that help us understand the amazing truth that we human beings are made by God in his image.

First, since God is spirit (God has no body), the main way that we are made like God is through the qualities that he has put within us. We have minds and emotions and the ability to choose—all things that God has. But also God made us to be like him in the qualities of our inner lives or our characters. We are to be holy as God is holy, loving as God is loving, forgiving as God is forgiving, truthful as God is truthful, faithful as God is faithful, and so on and so on. Of course, before sin came into the world, Adam and Eve had these kinds of qualities in their lives as God had created them. But sin did great damage to those qualities. Because we are sinners, we often don't live in holy ways or love others as we should or forgive when we've been wronged or speak the truth instead of lying and so on. Because we are made in the image of God, we should be this way, but we are not.

We need, then, to be remade into the image of God once again. And here we see in the New Testament the wonderful news that through what Christ has done for us, by trusting in him for the forgiveness of our sin and the hope of eternal life, we can begin the process of being remade into the image of God as we are made like Christ (see Colossians 3:8–11). Christ is the perfect image of God (Colossians 1:15). All of the qualities of God's character—his holiness, love, mercy, truth, faithfulness, and more—are also true of Christ (see John 1:14). As we are made to be like Christ in our inner lives, we are being remade into the image of God. We become the image of Christ, who is the perfect image of God.

Second, the image of God is not only about the qualities of our inner lives, it is also about our responsibilities—what we are called to do. Adam and his wife were called to do what God commanded them to do, to rule over the rest of the earth. Though they disobeyed God, their calling to obey was part of their being in God's image, acting as God would have them act. Likewise, Jesus was called to obey his Father, to do always and only what the Father had said. Jesus, the perfect image of God, obeyed his Father perfectly, showing us what it means to be the image of God. We also are called to obey God and to follow in his ways. We are to act as God wants us to act. And this is part of what it means to be made in God's image. You see, being in the image of God is not only about who we are, having qualities that are like God's qualities. It also has to do with acting in the ways God would act, living in a way that represents him. Jesus was the perfect image of God in both ways. His character was like God's character, and he always did the will of his Father, living as God would have him live. Since we fail in both ways, God is at work remaking his own people to be like Christ in their character and in their conduct. Only by God's grace can this happen. And as it does, God's people enter into more of the joy of what it means to be re-created in the image of Christ, the perfect image of God.

Questions for Thought

1. What are some ways that God wants us to "image" or reflect before others what he is like?

2. Jesus was the perfect image of God (Colossians 1:15). How does Jesus' obedience to his Father help us understand better what it means to live as the image of God?

Memory Verses

> Genesis 1:26–27—"Then God said, 'Let us make man in our image, after our likeness. And let them have dominion over the fish of the sea and over the birds of the heavens and over the livestock and over all the earth and over every creeping thing that creeps on the earth.' So God created man in his own image, in the image of God he created him; male and female he created them."

Other Features of Being Human

Understanding what it means to be made in the image of God is very important for a correct view of our human nature. But there are some other features or characteristics of our being human that are also important for us to understand. Let's consider four additional aspects of our human nature.

First, there is one way in which we stand in the very same position before God along with the rest of creation. We are creatures, and God is the Creator. As such, we must admit our complete dependence on God for our very life and everything we need in life. All of creation is totally dependent on God. Yet we human beings are in the wonderful position of knowing this; so we can honor God, trust in God, and thank God for his kindness to us every day. As God's creatures, we also owe to God our complete loyalty and allegiance. That is, the only right way for us to live is to bow before God as our Lord and King and give to him our loving devotion and willing service. As Creator, God has complete rights over us, and as his creatures, we should render complete obedience and love to him. Anything less would be a crime against the great majesty of God and would be deserving of everlasting judgment. As humans, then, we are totally dependent upon the God to whom we owe our highest respect, love, and obedience.

Second, God has made us human beings with a certain ability not found in any of the animals or other living things on the earth. He has given us the ability to know the difference between right and wrong and to choose to act in ways that are either right or wrong. The dogs or cats that some of us have in our homes have small amounts of some other qualities that we humans have. Dogs certainly do have emotions, as we also have. Probably the reason that people have said that a dog is man's best friend is because dogs always seem happy to see their masters. But while your dog has emotions and your cat may use its brain to figure out how to catch a moth, what they don't have is what is called a moral nature. A moral nature is simply the part of our inner lives by which we can tell the difference between right and wrong. If a mother of two sons has left two cookies on a plate with a sign saying that each boy may have one cookie, the brothers know it would be wrong if one boy ate both cookies, leaving nothing for the other. If a friend of yours repays the dollar he owes you, you know that what he did was good and right. Our moral natures are gifts to us as human beings (see Romans 2:14–15).

God has given us a moral nature—this ability to understand right from wrong—for a very simple reason. God wants us to hear his word and obey it, doing what we know is right, while resisting temptation to go against God and do what is wrong. God expects us to know that obeying him is right and that disobeying him is wrong. That's why he's given us a moral nature, so we can tell the difference. Of course, because of sin, our ability to tell right from wrong is horribly mixed-up. Often in our sin we consider what truly is right to be wrong, and what God knows is wrong to be right. Thankfully, even as sinners our moral natures are not completely turned around. People around the world, for the most part, still know that it is wrong to steal or murder or lie or commit adultery. But many of those same people may not worship God or seek to honor him as they should. Our moral nature has to be corrected and changed, along with every other part of us as sinners. So, even though they often don't work correctly, our moral natures give us the ability to know right from wrong and to act according to this understanding. And because we do know right from wrong and act accordingly, God will one day judge our actions and the motives of our hearts (Romans 2:5–11).

Third, because all that God created was good (Genesis 1:31), this means that our bodies as well as our inner lives (sometimes called our souls) were created good. Some people throughout history have thought that the body is bad while the soul is good. But we must remember that God is the One who "invented" the human body. He designed it and fashioned it to be part of his greatest masterpiece, a human being. And God was so kind in how he made our bodies. For example, he could have given us hunger so we would feel the need to eat, but he could have kept from us the taste buds on our tongues that make our food so enjoyable and delicious. He could have given us eyesight, but he didn't have to give us the ability to see the range of colors that we so enjoy. God also made us sexual beings, and he intends sex in marriage—but only in marriage—to be a good and joyous experience. How good God is to make our bodies to be able to experience such pleasures. Even though our bodies are damaged by sin, as is every part of us, still the human body is one of the good gifts that God has given to us as human beings. We must remember always, though, that the human body is to be used in just the ways God has directed, since he is Lord also of our bodies.

Fourth and last, God made human beings male and female, and it is important for us to consider what this means. Of course, part of the reason for doing this was so the human race would continue. Remember that God commanded Adam and his wife to "be fruitful and multiply and fill the earth" (Genesis 1:28), which takes both a man and a woman to carry out. But there is more here that we should consider. Notice that God created the woman after the man (Genesis 2:7, 21–23) in order for the woman to be a helper to the man (Genesis 2:18). This means that while the man and the woman are completely equal in value before God (Genesis 1:27), the woman is under the man's leadership and authority since she was created after him, to be of help to him. Paul refers to these ideas in 1 Timothy 2:12–15 and again in 1 Corinthians 11:6–10, in both passages explaining that differences in the roles that men and women may have in the church and in the home are based upon how God created the man and then the woman. Wives should submit to their husbands, and husbands are to love and lead their wives in a Christlike way, because God created them to live and relate in these ways.

To be faithful to the Bible's teaching, then, means accepting two very important ideas: 1) men and women are completely equal in their common human natures, both being made in the image of God, but 2) God gives men and women different roles in the home and in the church. The woman should accept the God-given authority of the man in these settings, and the man should use his authority in God-honoring ways. We are equal and yet different at the same time, and in this we reflect something of how the Persons of the Trinity relate. The Father, Son, and Spirit are equally God, yet they have different roles to play marked by lines of authority and submission in their relationships. So God created men and women in his image fully equal in their human nature, but different in certain roles in which they also have differences in authority and submission. This is part of the beauty of male-female relationships as God has designed them. What a privilege to reflect God's own ways of relating in our human relationships.

Questions for Thought

1. We looked at some important ways of what it means to be human beings. Pick one of these, and talk about what this means to your life personally or at home or with others.

2. Men and women are both made in the image of God, yet God made them different also. What does it mean for a husband and his wife, for example, to see themselves as equal yet different?

Memory Verse

Genesis 1:31—"And God saw everything that he had made, and behold, it was very good. And there was evening and there was morning, the sixth day."

How Sin Came into Our World and What Sin Is

One of the saddest chapters of the Bible comes right after one of its happiest and most beautiful parts. In Genesis 1 we read about God's creation of the world with all of its amazing stars, planets, plants, animals, and the man and woman made in God's image. The closing statement of Genesis 1 makes our hearts sing with joy: "And God saw everything that he had made, and behold, it was very good" (v. 31). And then Genesis 2 continues the joyous story as we see more clearly the creation of the man and the woman. The man was made first and was put to work cultivating the garden and naming the animals. But God said that it was not good for Adam to be alone. So he put him to sleep, took a rib from his side, and fashioned this rib into a woman. God brought her to Adam, who realized how kind God was to give him this companion from his very side to be a helper to him in his work. What joy we feel for Adam and his newly created wife.

Sadly, in Genesis 3 we begin the movement from the good and beautiful creation of God to the damage and harm that will be introduced through sin. We should read the early verses of Genesis 3 and then consider what we can learn about sin from this passage. "Now the serpent was more crafty than any other beast of the field that the LORD God had made. He said to the woman, 'Did God actually say, "You shall not eat of any tree in the garden"?' ² And the woman said to the serpent, 'We may eat of the fruit of the trees in the garden, ³ but God said, "You shall not eat of the fruit of the tree that is in the midst of the garden, neither shall you touch it, lest you die."' ⁴ But the serpent said to the woman, 'You will not surely die. ⁵ For God knows that when you eat of it your eyes will be opened, and you will be like God, knowing good and evil.' ⁶ So when the woman saw that the tree was good for food, and that it was a delight to the eyes, and that the tree was to be desired to make one wise, she took of its fruit and ate, and she also gave some to her husband who was with her, and he ate. ⁷ Then the eyes of both were opened, and they knew that they were naked. And they sewed fig leaves together and made themselves loincloths" (vv. 1–7).

What can we learn here about what sin is and how the tempter can draw us into sin? Notice that the serpent tricked the woman into thinking wrongly both about God and about the tree. Before the serpent had come into the garden and tricked the woman, she had thought of God as good, as One who was concerned about her and wanted her best. She thought of the tree of the knowledge of good and evil as harmful. She knew the warning that God had told the man (Genesis 2:16–17)—if he ate from this tree, he would die. But the serpent led her to begin thinking completely differently, as the tempter always does when he comes to us. The serpent led the woman to question whether God really was good after all, whether God really wanted her best. And he led her to wonder if the forbidden tree might actually be good for her, giving her good things God was keeping from her. By the question the serpent asked, he seemed to suggest that God was stingy in not letting them eat from every tree in the garden. Of course, this was completely false. God had said that they could eat from every tree in the garden except this one tree. That is hardly stingy! But the serpent made it sound as if God were keeping back something good from the woman.

Then the serpent told the woman something that was opposite from what God had earlier said. The serpent said that if the woman ate from the tree, she wouldn't die but instead would enjoy its fruit, be made wise from it, and become like God himself! What a different understanding of the tree from what God had told the man. As we know from the story, the woman believed the serpent and took fruit from the tree and ate. She then gave some to Adam who had been there with her, and he also ate. They both had believed the lies that the serpent told them, and this led them into their sin.

There are a couple of things we can learn about sin from this account. First, sin always works by tricking us, or deceiving us, into doubting things that are true and believing things that are false. The woman believed, wrongly, that God did not really care about her and didn't want her to have what's best. This is just the opposite of the truth that she used to know. But the serpent's trick worked, and she began to think of God as being against her, not for her. And she believed the tree was actually good for her, not harmful. She saw the tree now as able to give her things she wanted, things that she now thought God was keeping her from enjoying. But it was all a lie! God was correct all along! God had always been for her, he had always wanted her best, and so he had warned Adam (who then told his wife) not to eat of the tree or else they would die. And the tree always was harmful, and when they ate, they discovered this right away as sin and death came into the world. Sin always uses the tricks of deception to lead us to believe things that are false and to doubt things that are true. As Romans 3:23 indicates ("all have sinned and fall short of the glory of God"), sin moves us to "fall short" of honoring God and gladly following in his ways. Instead we are led, foolishly, to believe temptation's lie. If we are to resist temptation and keep from sinning, we must know and accept the truth that God tells us, and we must, by God's power, resist and refuse to believe the evil one's lies.

Second, sin is lived out through turning from God and his ways in order to do what we think is best. Even though God had told them not to eat of the tree or they would die, they decided not to believe God but to go the direction they thought would be best. What fools they were for doing this, and what fools we are when we do the same. Sin always involves, then, a desire in our hearts to live our own way, not God's way. Sin always involves thinking we know what is best, not God. Sin always leads us to turn from God and his ways because we think that our ways will end up better for us than God's ways. But this is never true. God's ways are always best for us, and we must resist every temptation to doubt this.

Third, sin always results in harm, ruin, and death. Even though the woman was tricked into thinking that the tree would be good for her, this was a lie. Instead, eating the tree did exactly what God said it would do—it brought her death. In one sense, she died at the very moment that she ate the fruit of this tree. Right away her relationships with Adam and more importantly with God were broken. And sin brought death to her body as she began, at that moment, the dying process. God was right, and the serpent was wrong. Obedience to God always brings blessing, and sin always harms and kills. To understand this will help us resist temptation, knowing that sin always hurts us and is never, ever good for us. But thankfully, God's ways always lead to life and will never, ever disappoint us in the end. May God give us understanding of these truths and a deep desire to believe what he says and to live for him.

Questions for Thought

1. We saw that sin always works by tricking and deceiving us. How can you see temptation to sin doing this in your own life?

2. We also saw that sin always brings about ruin or harm. Why is it that when we are tempted to sin, it doesn't feel like what we are tempted to do will bring us ruin or harm?

Memory Verses

Genesis 2:16–17—"And the LORD God commanded the man, saying, 'You may surely eat of every tree of the garden, but of the tree of the knowledge of good and evil you shall not eat, for in the day that you eat of it you shall surely die.'"

How Sin Has Spread to All People

Here's a very important question for all of us: do we sin because we are already sinners, or do we become sinners when we first sin? Many of us might lean toward saying that we become sinners when we first sin. After all, how can you be a sinner if you haven't sinned? It seems to make the most sense to say that you become a sinner at the time that you actually commit some act of sin. But is this what the Bible teaches? Is it possible that the other answer is the correct one?

One of the most important passages in all of the Bible on this question is Romans 5:12–19. In this section of Romans, Paul explains that Adam's sin in the garden brought to the entire human race that comes from him both sinful natures and God's judgment of condemnation. Because Adam was the first man, and all the rest of us, throughout all of history, have come from Adam, then God saw all of the rest of us connected to Adam and his sin. So, when Adam sinned, all of us who come from Adam would receive sin in our own inner lives (our natures). We are born into this world, then, with sinful natures that trace back to the sin of Adam. And when Adam sinned, all of us who come from Adam also received God's judgment of death, the punishment for sin that God gave to Adam and all who come from Adam. Adam's sin, then, is our sin. Adam's sinful nature results in our having sinful natures. And Adam's guilt and condemnation carry over to our being guilty and deserving death.

A couple of the key verses from Romans 5 will help us see this. Romans 5:12 says, ". . . sin came into the world through one man, and death through sin, and so death spread to all men because all sinned." Paul explains here that Adam's one sin has brought two things to all of us who come from Adam. First, Adam's one sin has brought sin "into the world." That is, all people in the world have sin because of Adam's sin. Second, Adam's sin has brought us "death through sin." That is, Adam's sin has brought us guilt before God so that we deserve the sentence of death. Romans 5:18–19 also helps us see both of these ways that Adam's sin has come to us. Paul writes, "Therefore, as one trespass led to condemnation for all men, so one act of righteousness leads to justification and life for all men. [19] For as by the one man's disobedience the many were made sinners, so by the one man's obedience the many will be made righteous." Verse 19 shows that Adam's one sin has brought to all of us sinful natures (we were "made sinners"). Verse 18 shows that Adam's one sin has brought to all of us God's judgment (Adam's sin "led to condemnation" for us all).

Let me ask our question again: do we sin because we are already sinners, or do we become sinners when we first sin? From what we've seen in Romans 5, the answer now is clear: we sin in our own lives because we were already sinners in Adam. We are born into this world with sinful natures. That is, we are born with inner lives that are directed toward ourselves and what we want and not directed toward God and his ways. Because we have inner lives bent away from God in sin, when we are old enough to know right from wrong, we act in sinful ways. So the correct answer is that we sin because we already are sinners. We come from Adam into this world as newborn sinners, and later when we know better, we act out that sin.

If you still wonder how we can be sinners before we have sinned, consider this illustration. Would you say that a tree bears apples because it already is an apple tree, or does the tree become an apple tree when it produces its first apple? Well, it is pretty clear. I hope we all would agree that the reason the tree bears apples is because it already has been and is an apple tree. In fact, an apple tree (or orange tree or pear tree) can grow as a small tree for many years before it ever produces its first piece of fruit. In those early years it is still an apple tree (or orange tree or pear tree) even though it isn't old enough to bear any fruit. And when it does bear fruit, then we would just say that the tree is producing fruit according to its nature. That is, it produces apples because it is, by nature, an apple tree.

So too we, by nature, have the sin of Adam from the very moment that we are conceived in our mother's womb. As David prayed, "Behold, I was brought forth in iniquity, and in sin did my mother conceive me" (Psalm 51:5). We are, then, sinners by nature who show ourselves to be sinners by choice. For when we are old enough, just like the apple tree that eventually bears apples, so we sinners bear our "fruit" in the form of sin. As Jesus said, "each tree is known by its own fruit" (Luke 6:44). Sinners by nature who show ourselves to be sinners by choice and sinners by action—this is our inheritance in Adam.

Some might think that if we are sinners because of what Adam did, this must mean that we are not responsible for our own sin. After all, since it is not my own sin that makes me a sinner (and that is correct), then I cannot rightly be blamed either for being a sinner or for committing the sinful acts that I do. It's Adam's fault, after all, not mine, so I'm off the hook, this thinking would say.

There are a couple of problems with this line of thought. For one thing, the Bible declares that since Adam was the first human at the head or start of the human race, what he did affected all of us who come after him. We may not like this, but this is how God sees it, and God always sees things correctly, exactly as they are. Plus, we have some examples from our own lives when something like this is also true. Suppose you and a friend are hitting baseballs out in the street (not the best idea!), and on one of your hits, the ball flies right through the front window of your neighbor's home. Your neighbor might come over and insist that your dad pay to have the window fixed. But if your dad said, "Well, I didn't break your window, so I'm not responsible to pay for it," your neighbor could rightly respond, "Because your son broke the window, you as his father are responsible to pay." And the neighbor would be right. As God sees it—and remember God always knows things exactly right and is always completely just—we are responsible along with Adam for Adam's sin.

Another reason we are responsible for the sin of our own lives is this: our sinful thoughts, attitudes, words, and actions are the ones we want to do. When we act sinfully, we act in ways that we desire and intend. So God is right to hold us responsible for our sin. We live in a day when many people want to put the blame on others for what they do. But God knows better. We are responsible for all of the sin we carry out with the sin natures that came from Adam, because when we sin, we do what we want and carry out what we intend. Sin is a very serious matter. We need to accept the fact that as sinners by nature and as sinners by choice, we are deeply guilty before God. We cannot pass the buck. We cannot shift the blame. Before God, we are guilty for our sin, and we cannot pass off our guilt to anyone else. Sometime soon you may want to look in a mirror and remind yourself of this: *in Adam and apart from God's grace, I am a sinner, I am guilty, and I deserve to be condemned.* Until we face these facts we will never understand the glory of the gospel.

Questions for Thought

1. Do we sin because we are already sinners, or do we become sinners when we first sin? What is the correct answer from the Bible, and why?

2. Why did Adam's one sin bring sin to all the rest of us? How does this help us understand why we all (yes, all!) need a Savior?

Memory Verse

> Romans 5:12—"Therefore, just as sin came into the world through one man, and death through sin, and so death spread to all men because all sinned."

The Punishment for Our Sin

It is very important for us to understand correctly what the Bible teaches about the punishment that we deserve as sinners. Why does this matter? There are two main reasons.

First, we need to know just how terrible our punishment should be in order for us to see just how terrible our sin and guilt is before our holy God. We understand how bad our sin has been when we see how bad the punishment is that we now deserve. Otherwise, if we think our punishment before God will be a small thing, then we will also naturally think that our sin was a small thing. For example, if you saw someone being punished with a light slap on his wrist, you would think that whatever he did, it couldn't be very bad. Light punishment and light sin go together. But weighty punishment and weighty sin also go together. So the first reason for understanding correctly the greatness and terror of the punishment we deserve is so that we will see the greatness and the evil of our sin for what it is.

Second, we need to know just how terrible our punishment should be so we can marvel and wonder at our Savior, Jesus, who took our punishment upon himself when he died on the cross. If our punishment is a small thing, then when we learn that Jesus took our punishment upon himself, we think little of this. But when we see our punishment as the great and weighty and horrible thing that it is, then it becomes a wonder and a marvel to us that Jesus took that punishment upon himself for us. For example, if you owed someone five cents, and a friend came along and paid the five cents for you, you would be grateful, but you would not consider it a big deal. After all, it was only five cents. But if you owed someone five thousand dollars or five million dollars, and a friend came along and paid that debt for you, you would be absolutely amazed, and rightly so. Just as weighty punishment and weighty sin go together, in a similar way weighty punishment and weighty salvation go together. If we hope to see Jesus as the Savior correctly and marvel at the greatness of his saving work, we must understand the greatness of the punishment for sin that we deserve, a punishment he has taken in our place on the cross.

The very first warning of sin's punishment comes right away in Genesis 2. You may remember that God told Adam that in the day he ate from the tree of the knowledge of good and evil, he would surely die (vv. 16–17). What becomes clearer as you keep reading the Bible is just what this punishment for sin really involves. The death spoken of here means more than dying physically or having your body die. Death for sin involves most importantly a separation from God and all that God is. If you remember from the earlier chapters of this book, we talked about how God has in his own life every good quality that there is. He alone has all that is good and true and beautiful and wise and joyful. To be separated from God, then, is to be separated from everything that is good, everything that is beautiful, everything joyful, and on and on. As the apostle Paul says, those who must pay for their own sin "will suffer the punishment of eternal destruction, away from the presence of the Lord and from the glory of his might, [10] when he comes on that day to be glorified in his saints, and to be marveled at among all who have believed, because our testimony to you was believed" (2 Thessalonians 1:9–10). The death that our sin brings, then, is in reality the removal from us of every possible enjoyment and good thing that we want badly to have. To be "away from the presence of the Lord" is to be removed from the source of every good thing, from God himself. All good is in God, and in our sin we are separated from God. We have no part, then, in anything that is good forever and ever, for we have no part in God.

But death means even more than this. This separation from God does not only involve our not having good things that we wished we had. It means also that what we do have is painful and miserable and horrible beyond our ability to imagine it correctly. The Bible states clearly that the punishment for our sin involves great misery that can never be ended. Jesus describes some aspects of this punishment in the story he tells about the rich man and Lazarus. After both the rich man and the poor man, Lazarus, died, the two men went to very different places. Lazarus went to be with Abraham and enjoyed being in a place of peace and joy. But the rich man went instead to a place of torment. As Jesus tells the story, "in Hades, being in torment, he [the rich man] lifted up his eyes and saw Abraham far off and Lazarus at his side. 24 And he called out, 'Father Abraham, have mercy on me, and send Lazarus to dip the end of his finger in water and cool my tongue, for I am in anguish in this flame.' 25 But Abraham said, 'Child, remember that you in your lifetime received your good things, and Lazarus in like manner bad things; but now he is comforted here, and you are in anguish. 26 And besides all this, between us and you a great chasm has been fixed, in order that those who would pass from here to you may not be able, and none may cross from there to us'" (Luke 16:23–26).

We see in this story something of how terrible the punishment is that the rich man experiences. His anguish is great, and he longs for some relief. But no relief will be given; indeed, no relief can be given. A great gulf separates the rich man from Abraham and Lazarus, so that no one may cross over to bring him even a drop of water. And worse, the presence of that gulf means that there is never any hope of the rich man crossing over into the land where Lazarus has received so much joy. Deep anguish, absence of relief, relentless torment that is never-ending and always horrible—this describes some of the punishment that awaits each of us as sinners, apart from God's grace in Christ.

Jesus taught much more about this subject, as you may know. He talked about our punishment in hell with phrases like "eternal" or "unquenchable" fire (Matthew 25:41; Mark 9:43), where there is "weeping and gnashing of teeth" (Matthew 13:42), and where the "worm does not die and the fire is not quenched" (Mark 9:48).

As we bring this section to a close, remember one important truth: God is just. He does not punish anyone any worse than he or she deserves. So, when we see in the Bible how great the punishment for our sin is, we realize in new ways just how great our sin is before God. And when we see the greatness of our punishment for sin, we also see better the greatness of Christ's sacrifice to bear our punishment in our place. Let us think deeply about the greatness of our punishment, then, to see more clearly the greatness of our sin, and then (yes!), the greatness of our Savior and Christ's payment of the full punishment for that sin. What horrible sinners we are before God. Just look at the punishment we deserve to pay. But what a great Savior is Jesus. Look even more closely at his grace and mercy as he took upon himself the full punishment for our sin through his death on the cross. Great punishment, great sin; great punishment, great Savior—let's see these as God sees them, to the humbling of our needy souls and to the glory of his matchless name.

Questions for Thought

1. Since God is just, he must punish our sin. What is that punishment like, if we were to receive the punishment for our own sin?

2. We understand how bad our sin has been when we see how bad the punishment is that we now deserve. How does this help us appreciate the greatness of Christ and of his death that pays the penalty for our sin?

Memory Verse

Romans 6:23—"For the wages of sin is death, but the free gift of God is eternal life in Christ Jesus our Lord."

5

Who Jesus Is

A Person Who Was Alive Long Before He Was Born

Have you ever known someone who was alive long before he was born, like thousands and millions of years before he was born? Crazy idea, you might say, and you're right, for the most part! All of us begin our lives when we are first conceived and then nine months later are born into the world. But Jesus is an exception to this rule. Jesus, as the eternal Son of the Father, as the second Person of the Trinity, lived eternally (forever in the past) before he was conceived by the Holy Spirit in the womb of his mother, the Virgin Mary. Jesus, then, is the only human being ever to live long (really long!) before he was born.

Why does this matter? Well, it matters for one very simple reason. In order for our Savior Jesus to be both God and man, he must be God before he becomes also man. Since God has no beginning and no ending (God is eternal or lives forever in the past and in the future), then Jesus as the eternal Son of God also had no beginning and will have no ending. But the human life of Jesus did have a beginning, since all human life must begin at some point. So then, Jesus as God had no beginning. But Jesus as man had a beginning when he was conceived by the Holy Spirit in Mary. Jesus as God lived long (eternally long) before Jesus as the God-man was born into this world.

One of the strongest passages showing that Jesus knew that he had existed as God long before he was born in Bethlehem is his claim in John 8:58. Because this verse also proves the deity of Christ, it is one we have already considered earlier. Listen to the discussion between Jesus and the Jewish teachers. Jesus said, "'Your father Abraham rejoiced that he would see my day. He saw it and was glad.' [57] So the Jews said to him, 'You are not yet fifty years old, and have you seen Abraham?' [58] Jesus said to them, 'Truly, truly, I say to you, before Abraham was, I am'" (John 8:56–58). These Jewish teachers just didn't know what to make of Jesus. He was always making claims and statements that they found hard to understand, and often they didn't like what they heard. So when Jesus said to them that Abraham had seen the day of Jesus, they couldn't understand how this could be. After all, Abraham lived about two thousand years before the time that this discussion took place between Jesus and the Jewish teachers. And as they had observed, Jesus was well under fifty years old. How could Abraham have seen Jesus?

Jesus' answer to them was really a shock! He said to them, "Truly, truly, I say to you, before Abraham was, I am" (John 8:58). The opening words, "Truly, truly, I say to you," is Jesus' way of saying, "What I'm telling you is the absolute truth." But what he tells them seems impossible: "Before Abraham was, I am." That is, "Before Abraham lived, I was already alive." So, Jesus was claiming to be over two thousand years old, yet he was in the body of a man who was under fifty years old. How can this be? Well, the key to the answer is in his words, "I am." Here Jesus was not claiming merely to be older than Abraham, which would seem ridiculous for a man not yet fifty. What Jesus was really claiming was to be the "I am" of Exodus 3, Yahweh, the God of Israel. As we saw earlier, when Moses asked God for his name so he could tell the people of Israel in Egypt who had spoken to him, God said to tell them, "I AM" had sent him (Exodus 3:14). So, Jesus claims to be the "I AM" of the Old Testament, Yahweh, the God of Israel. As God, then, Jesus lived eternally before he was conceived and was born as the God-man, Jesus.

To confirm that Jesus was correct to call himself "I am" or Yahweh, some other passages show that Jesus was in fact Yahweh of the Old Testament. In Isaiah 40:3 we read, "A voice cries: 'In the wilderness prepare the way of the LORD; make straight in the desert a highway for our God.'" The English word "LORD" is the way most of our English versions translate the name of God, Yahweh (literally, "I am"). So Isaiah tells of the day when a voice will call out to prepare the way for Yahweh. This was fulfilled, of course, when John the Baptist preached and prepared the way for the coming of Christ (Matthew 3:3). So Yahweh of Isaiah 40:3 is a reference to Christ.

Another amazing passage that turns out to be about Christ is Isaiah 6. This passage describes the vision that Isaiah had of the holy God who sat on his throne high and lifted up. In verse 3 the angelic hosts call out, "Holy, holy, holy is the LORD of hosts; the whole earth is full of his glory!" You can see that the same word "LORD" is used here, indicating that they see and are worshipping Yahweh. What an amazing thing it is to find out that the vision of this "LORD" of Isaiah 6:3 is actually a vision of the eternal Son who is Jesus, for in John 12 the apostle John makes reference to this vision of Isaiah in Isaiah 6 and then says, "Isaiah said these things because he saw his glory and spoke of him" (v. 41). The point, then, is this: Isaiah had actually seen the glory of Christ and had spoken of him. Jesus is none other than Yahweh of the Old Testament.

We'll consider just two other passages that show that Jesus as God lived eternally before he was born also as a man at Bethlehem. Isaiah 7:14 says, "Behold, the virgin shall conceive and bear a son, and shall call his name Immanuel." Matthew quotes this passage and makes sure that we understand the meaning of the term "Immanuel." As Matthew 1:23 says, this name of Jesus means "God with us." So, Jesus born of the Virgin Mary is God born as man. Isaiah 9:6 also indicates that Jesus born at Bethlehem was God before he became also a man. It reads, "For to us a child is born, to us a son is given; and the government shall be upon his shoulder, and his name shall be called Wonderful Counselor, Mighty God, Everlasting Father, Prince of Peace." The most important term here to show that Jesus was God before he was born also a man is the term "Mighty God." This term is used often in the book of Isaiah for the God of Israel. For example, you can see the same term used in the very next chapter, in Isaiah 10:21. What an amazing statement this is as one thinks carefully about what it says. To us a child will be born, a son will be given, and his name will be . . . Mighty God! A child born who is God! A son given who is God! Yes indeed, Jesus born at Bethlehem was eternally God before he became also a man. Eternal God and a human son—both are true of our Lord Jesus Christ.

Questions for Thought

1. Why does it matter that Jesus existed eternally as God before he came and took on also his human nature? How does this help us see that Jesus is fully God as well as fully man?

2. What did Jesus mean when he said, "Before Abraham was, I am"? How does this help us understand better who Jesus truly is?

Memory Verse

Isaiah 9:6— "For to us a child is born, to us a son is given; and the government shall be upon his shoulder, and his name shall be called Wonderful Counselor, Mighty God, Everlasting Father, Prince of Peace."

The Incarnation—God and Man Together

In thinking about the Incarnation—the joining together of the eternal Son of God with a full human nature—we are in the middle of one of the greatest wonders of all! Just how this can be is for us, in this life anyway, a great mystery. But even more wondrous is the fact that God brought this about for our salvation. The greatest miracle ever done in all of history is the joining together of God and man. And this was not done for show or to prove some point. It was done because this was the only way that our loving and holy God would be able to save us from our sin. Oh, the wonder of the Incarnation. Oh, the wonder of the cross.

The term *incarnation* is from Latin, not Hebrew (the language of the Old Testament) or Greek (the language of the New Testament). In Latin, the term *caro* or *carnis* refers to "flesh" or "meat." We use this Latin word in our English word *carnivore*, a meat-eating animal or plant. So, by *incarnation* Christians have referred to the point in human history when the eternal Son of God was joined with human flesh or a human nature. Full God becoming also fully a man is the wonder of the Incarnation.

Putting together John 1:1 and John 1:14 will help us see what the Bible teaches about the Incarnation. These verses read, "In the beginning was the Word, and the Word was with God, and the Word was God. . . . ¹⁴ And the Word became flesh and dwelt among us, and we have seen his glory, glory as of the only Son from the Father, full of grace and truth." John's use of the opening phrase, "In the beginning," is meant to bring something very specific to our minds. John clearly is thinking about the opening of the book of Genesis, which starts with these very same words: "In the beginning, God created the heavens and the earth" (Genesis 1:1).

The meaning of this phrase "in the beginning" in both Genesis 1:1 and in John 1:1 is this: "Before the beginning of the world . . ." So, we might understand Genesis 1:1 to mean this: "Before the beginning of the world there was God, who as the eternal God created the heavens and the earth." The term "beginning" is not a reference to the beginning of

God, for God has no beginning, just as he has no ending. Rather, the point is just the opposite. Before the beginning of the world, God already had been living his life fully and forever. But now, at this beginning of time, at this beginning of the world, this eternal God created the heavens and the earth.

The meaning in John 1:1 is much the same, but now it has to do with the eternal life of the Word. We might understand John 1:1 to mean this: "Before the beginning of the world there was the Word, who always has existed with God, and who always has existed as God." So, John's point is to help us see two things about this "Word." First, he wants us to see that the Word has always been *with* God. This does not mean that the Word is not God himself, but it calls for us to understand the one God as being more than one Person. But second, he wants us to see that the Word has always been God. Because of this, the Word is eternal and has no beginning. The two truths of John 1:1 then are these: 1) As the Word who is the eternal Son of the Father, this Word has always existed *with* God his Father. 2) The Word is in nature the eternal God, and this Word has always existed *as* God. These are very high and lofty truths, but they are important for us to try to understand since understanding them is the only way to understand who Jesus really is.

Let me summarize what we've seen in John 1:1, 14. John 1:1 can be said to mean this: "Before the beginning of the world there was the Word, who always existed as the eternal Son with God his Father, and who always existed with the nature of God as God." Now when we add the thought of John 1:14, we marvel. John 1:14, flowing from John 1:1, might be understood to be saying this: "This very Word—who is the eternal Son living always with God his Father and who eternally is God in his own nature—yes, this very Word has come to earth and has become also fully a man. As the God-man, he lived in our very midst so that we could see him up-close and observe what he was like. In seeing him over many years, we saw the glory that he had, an only Son's glory that was the same as the glory of his Father, one that is full of grace and that is full of truth." How amazing it is that God should become also a man! There is no one like Jesus!

One other passage we should consider here is the opening of the book of Hebrews: "Long ago, at many times and in many ways, God spoke to our fathers by the prophets, [2] but in these last days he has spoken to us by his Son, whom he appointed the heir of all things, through whom also he created the world. [3] He is the radiance of the glory of God and the exact imprint of his nature, and he upholds the universe by the word of his power" (Hebrews 1:1–3a). As with John 1:1, 14, here the Son comes showing forth the glory of his Father through the physical, visible form of a man that he had also become. The phrase that grips us here is this one: "He [the God-man] is the radiance of the glory of God and the exact imprint of his nature." Clearly the writer to the Hebrews wants us to see this Son as the greatest revelation of God, since now God is speaking to us through his own Son. One might not expect this revelation to be so spectacular. But it is. This Son shows forth the radiance of God's very glory, and this Son is the exact imprint of God's own nature. How amazing, indeed, that full God with the full glory of God should unite with full man in order to make the glory of God known to other men.

We will continue thinking about some further aspects of the Incarnation in the next section. Perhaps it is best to close now by taking a moment to pause and marvel at our Savior, Jesus, who as true God came to earth to become also truly a man. I've asked myself often if there is any analogy that helps us see this. Would this be like you, fully a human being, joining yourself also to the nature of a worm or a slug or a fish? Yes, but . . . . no. No matter how lowly the creature was that you joined with, it still would be one creature being joined to another creature. We simply cannot imagine or understand what God the Son has done in obedience to his Father when he, the eternal and infinite God, Creator of all that is, came and took on also the nature of small, finite, creaturely manhood. God and man, Creator and creature, Infinite and finite, All-powerful and weak— how amazing is the Incarnation, and how amazing is our Savior.

Questions for Thought

1. We ended thinking that Jesus becoming also a man is far greater than if you or I became also a slug or a worm or a fish. Why is this so? And how does this help you honor and worship Christ for coming to earth to become also one of us?

2. Since the eternal Son became also a human being, he can understand the weaknesses and difficulties that we experience in life. Why should this help you trust Christ and pray to him when you go through hard times?

Memory Verse

John 1:14—"And the Word became flesh and dwelt among us, and we have seen his glory, glory as of the only Son from the Father, full of grace and truth."

How Jesus Emptied Himself in Becoming Also a Man

When the eternal Son becomes also a man, does this mean that he has to give up being God? Does he have to give up some qualities that are his as God? If not, how can he truly be a man? How can he be fully God and fully man and live his life as one of us, experiencing life as all humans do? How can this be? In dealing with these questions in this section, we will consider a key passage of Scripture. It is one of the richest and most beautiful passages in all of the Bible that teaches about the Incarnation, the joining together of the eternal Son of God with a full human nature. We will consider what it says and then try to illustrate its truth in order to understand better what it means that our Savior, Jesus, the eternal God, has become also a man for our salvation.

Philippians 2:5–11 reads: "Have this mind among yourselves, which is yours in Christ Jesus, ⁶ who, though he was in the form of God, did not count equality with God a thing to be grasped, ⁷ but made himself nothing, taking the form of a servant, being born in the likeness of men. ⁸ And being found in human form, he humbled himself by becoming obedient to the point of death, even death on a cross. ⁹ Therefore God has highly exalted him and bestowed on him the name that is above every name, ¹⁰ so that at the name of Jesus every knee should bow, in heaven and on earth and under the earth, ¹¹ and every tongue confess that Jesus Christ is Lord, to the glory of God the Father."

The main point of verses 6–8 is that Jesus, who existed eternally as God, chose to humble himself and become also a man in order to serve us by his obedient death on the cross. But there is one part of these verses that has been puzzling for Christians over the ages to understand. At the end of verse 6 and the beginning of verse 7, we read that Jesus, although he was God, "did not count equality with God a thing to be grasped, but made himself nothing, taking the form of a servant." What does it mean that Jesus didn't count equality with God something to be grasped but made himself nothing? Does this mean that Jesus stopped being God as he made himself nothing in becoming a mere servant? Some have taken this passage this way, and they are very wrong to do so. Paul is not saying that Jesus stopped being God; the passage does not teach this. In addition, if Jesus was not fully God, he could not be our Savior (just as he also could not be our Savior if he were not fully man). No, Jesus remained fully God when he became also fully a man. So what does Paul mean in this passage?

One of the keys to understanding this passage is found in the Greek word that begins verse 7. Literally, the word here that is translated "made himself nothing" could also be translated simply as "poured out." It is a form of a very common Greek word that is used in everyday life for pouring water from a pitcher or pouring wine into a glass. Both the NASB and the HCSB translations use the phrase "emptied himself" to render this word.

Here is the idea of what Paul is saying: The Son, who was fully God, rather than refusing to leave the glories of his place with the Father, poured himself or emptied himself out, taking the form of a servant. Notice that the passage does not say that the Son poured qualities out of himself. Again, some have thought very wrongly about this. They've thought that Christ gave up qualities of his deity, like his omnipresence (being able to be present everywhere) or his omniscience (being able to know everything). If so, then Jesus was not fully God. But most important here, this is not what the passage says. It says that Christ "poured himself out," not that he poured out qualities from himself. Do you see the difference? Our Savior poured out himself entirely when he became a man. All of who he was, including all of his deity, was poured out when he took on also full humanity.

Another key to understanding this passage is found in the next word; it is a participle that explains how the pouring out was done. Look at it carefully. Jesus, fully God, poured himself out by "taking the form of a servant." The participle "taking" explains how the pouring out or the emptying took place. He poured himself out (all of who he was as God) *by taking* the form of a servant; he emptied himself (all of who he was as God) *by taking* on human nature. This is odd, is it not?—a pouring out by taking, an emptying by adding, a diminishing by increasing. What is this?

Allow me to give you an illustration of what subtraction by addition might look like and how it might take place. Imagine for a moment that someone, say, an older brother of yours, was shopping for a new car. He went to a BMW car dealership and asked to test-drive a beautiful, shiny, brand-new sports car. The dealer handed him the keys, and off he drove. Now, you need to know that for the past several days it had rained buckets in your area, and your brother decided to drive this shiny new car on the dirt roads out in the country. Well, as you can imagine, the roads were muddy as could be, and your brother drove this car wildly, turning and sliding every which way in the mud before he brought it back to the showroom floor. When he drove it in, absolutely covered in mud, the car dealer exclaimed, "What have you done to my car!" But to this, your brother calmly said, "Oh, you needn't worry. I've not taken anything away from your car, I've only added to it." And, of course, your brother was right. Every quality of that car was still there. It still had its beautiful coat of paint and its luster; nothing had been removed from what was there before. Rather, something had been added to it—a thick coat of mud! But notice what this mud did. It covered over that beautiful shine so that, even though it was still there, you couldn't see it. You might even say that the mud worked to hide the glory and brilliance of the car even though those qualities were still there, just hidden.

In a similar way, the fullness of the Son with every quality of his deity was poured out. Nothing from his deity was lost, but rather his full life was poured out as he took on the form of a servant. As that human nature enveloped, as it were, his divine nature, something of the glory and splendor of who he is as God was covered over—not lost or given up, mind you, but covered over. Since he chose now to live fully as a man, this required that certain aspects of his deity would have to stay hidden. To be a man, for example, he would have to accept the limitations of being at one place at one time, of learning new things as he grew from infancy into manhood, of experiencing hunger, thirst, tiredness, and weakness as all human beings do, and so on. Given this, are we required to say that Jesus gave up these qualities of his deity? No, and again I say, no! Rather we say that Christ willingly gave up the *rightful use* of some of the abilities of his divine nature in order to experience fully his life now as a man. So, while he was in nature fully God, yet in order to live in nature fully as a man, he gave up the *expression* or *exercise* of some of his divine abilities. He did not give up those divine abilities themselves. In this way, Christ emptied himself by adding; there was a subtraction of the use of certain aspects of his deity by taking on the full experience of his humanity. And why? All for the purpose of humbling himself to become our servant, a full human being who would obey his Father to the point of death, even death on the cross. What a humbling he underwent. What a Savior he is!

Questions for Thought

1. What is the main idea of Philippians 2:5–8? How can we learn from Jesus' example in living our own lives?

2. Can you think of any other examples of subtraction by addition, of making something appear to be less by adding something else to it?

Memory Verses

Philippians 2:6–7—" . . . though he [Jesus] was in the form of God, [he] did not count equality with God a thing to be grasped, but made himself nothing, taking the form of a servant, being born in the likeness of men."

Jesus Lived in the Power of the Spirit

The Gospel accounts of Jesus' life and ministry make clear that he had the Spirit upon him throughout his life. In fact, as we'll see more in just a bit, the fact that Jesus would be Spirit-anointed was foretold by the Old Testament prophets. The coming Messiah, they said, would have the Spirit upon him. But at this point some questions might be coming to your mind. For example, if Jesus really was fully God, as we've seen the Bible teaches and is true, then why would he also have the Spirit upon him? After all, what could the Spirit of God add to the divine nature that Jesus already had? Doesn't it seem like giving Jesus the Spirit wouldn't really do any good, since he already had all of the same power in his own divine nature? So why does the Bible seem to make such a big deal about Jesus, the Messiah, having the Spirit upon him? What is the purpose of Jesus' Spirit-anointing?

Before we get at the heart of these questions, let's notice just a few passages that speak of the Spirit at work in the life and ministry of Jesus. Without any question, one of the most important Old Testament passages comes from Isaiah 61, a passage Jesus quotes about himself as he begins his ministry. Isaiah had written, "The Spirit of the Lord GOD is upon me, because the LORD has anointed me to bring good news to the poor; he has sent me to bind up the brokenhearted, to proclaim liberty to the captives, and the opening of the prison to those who are bound; [2] to proclaim the year of the LORD's favor, and the day of vengeance of our God; to comfort all who mourn; [3] to grant to those who mourn in Zion— to give them a beautiful headdress instead of ashes, the oil of gladness instead of mourning, the garment of praise instead of a faint spirit; that they may be called oaks of righteousness, the planting of the LORD, that he may be glorified" (vv. 1–3; cf. Isaiah 11:1–9; 42:1–9). What a glorious passage! Here Isaiah speaks of a coming day when the long-awaited Messiah of Israel would come to bring good news of restoration for the people of God. To do this, the Spirit of God would be upon the Messiah. Through the power of the Spirit at work in his life, the Messiah (Jesus) would preach what he was sent to preach, namely, good news to the poor, to the brokenhearted, and to those in prison. Notice that the ability or power for the Messiah to carry out this calling came from the Spirit who had come upon him.

Jesus referred to this very passage when he was asked to read in the synagogue on the Sabbath. Luke records the following account: "And the scroll of the prophet Isaiah was given to him [Jesus]. He unrolled the scroll and found the place where it was written, [18] 'The Spirit of the Lord is upon me, because he has anointed me to proclaim good news to the poor. He has sent me to proclaim liberty to the captives and recovering of sight to the blind, to set at liberty those who are oppressed, [19] to proclaim the year of the Lord's favor.' [20] And he rolled up the scroll and gave it back to the attendant and sat down. And the eyes of all in the synagogue were fixed on him. [21] And he began to say to them, 'Today this Scripture has been fulfilled in your hearing'" (4:17–21). This account is amazing on many levels, but for our purposes we should notice this: Jesus identified himself as the One who fulfilled the promise of this Old Testament prophecy. Jesus was Spirit-anointed, as Isaiah had said the Messiah would be. The Old Testament had made it clear that the coming Savior would be filled with the Spirit, and Jesus let people know that he was that Spirit-anointed Messiah.

What did the Spirit empower Jesus to do? Well, we've just seen that Isaiah 61:1–3 predicted that the Spirit would give him power to proclaim what God sent him to say. When you think of how much of Jesus' ministry involved teaching and preaching, you realize how much the Spirit was at work empowering Jesus to speak forth exactly what he should. Matthew 12:22–29 is another passage that gives us a window into how Jesus lived his life. Jewish teachers had witnessed a miracle Jesus had done, and they were afraid that some might conclude that Jesus was the Messiah from God. So they offered an explanation for the miracle: "It is only by Beelzebul, the prince of demons, that this man casts out demons" (v. 24). Jesus knew that they had charged him with performing the miracle by the power of Satan. So he responded, "But if it is by the Spirit of God that I cast out demons, then the kingdom of God has come upon you" (v. 28). This would have been a perfect time for Jesus to say, "I cast out this demon by my own divine power since I'm God," if that had been the case. But he didn't. Rather he said that he cast out this demon by the power of the Spirit, and because of this, they should know that the kingdom of God had come. After all, passages like Isaiah 11, 42, and 61 had indicated that the coming King would have the Spirit upon him. So they should know that if this man (Jesus) performed these miracles by the power of the Spirit, then he must be the King, and the kingdom must have come.

One final verse we'll consider provides a summary of Jesus' entire life, ministry, and miracles in one sentence! Once again we'll see the central place that the Spirit plays. In his sermon to Cornelius, Peter declares, "God anointed Jesus of Nazareth with the Holy Spirit and with power. He went about doing good and healing all who were oppressed by the devil, for God was with him" (Acts 10:38). Notice that Peter did not refer to Jesus' own divine nature to explain the power Jesus used in his life and for his miracles. He did not say that Jesus "went about doing good and healing all who were oppressed by the devil" through his own divine power. Even though he *was* the eternal Son of God and *did have* the power of his own divine nature, this is not what Peter talked about. Rather, Peter said that Jesus lived faithfully and performed miracles because God (his Father) had anointed him "with the Holy Spirit and with power," that God was "with him" throughout his life. In brief, as Peter looked at the whole life of Christ, including his obedient living and miraculous power, he explained this by saying that God anointed Jesus "with the Holy Spirit and with

115

power." Jesus lived his life, obeyed the Father, and performed the works he did in the power of the Spirit.

We end with a very important question: why did Jesus have the Spirit of God upon him since he was fully God and could have done all he did by the power of his own divine nature? Answer: even though Jesus was fully God, he did not live his life through his divine power as God, because he came to live a real human life, completely as a man. He came to live as one of us, to experience the limitations and struggles of our life, to undergo the temptations we encounter. But to do this, he could not live truly as a man while also using power that he alone would have as God. To live by his power as God, he would not and could not live as one of us. So instead, as a man, he relied on the Spirit of God to grant him all that he needed to live life faithfully and to carry out everything that the Father sent him to do. As a man, empowered by the Spirit, he fulfilled his calling. And before he left he told his disciples the most amazing thing. He said that the Spirit who had been on him would also be on them (John 14:16–17; 15:26–27; 16:5–15). They, too, would have the same Spirit empowerment Jesus had used. In this way, Jesus lived a truly human life and really is an example for how his followers should live. As he lived by the Spirit, they are called to live by the Spirit. We are rightly called to "follow in his steps" (1 Peter 2:21). As we trust in Christ and receive his Spirit, then, may we look to Jesus and live more and more like him.

Questions for Thought

1. As a man, empowered by the Spirit, Jesus fulfilled his God-given calling and mission. How does this help us in understanding correctly Jesus' own life and ministry?

2. Jesus gave his followers the very same Spirit who had empowered him. How should this affect our understanding of how Christians are to live faithful and obedient lives?

Memory Verse

Acts 10:38—"God anointed Jesus of Nazareth with the Holy Spirit and with power. He went about doing good and healing all who were oppressed by the devil, for God was with him."

Jesus Resisted Temptation, Living a Sinless Life

A question that many have wondered about throughout the ages is this: throughout all of his life, could Jesus ever have sinned? Of course, all Bible-believing Christians believe that Jesus in fact did not sin. But that's not the question. True enough, he did not sin, but was it possible for him to have sinned? Could Jesus have sinned?

Part of what makes this question so difficult, and so important, is that the Bible teaches very clearly that Jesus was really and truly tempted. Hebrews 4:15 goes so far as to say that "in every respect" Jesus has been "tempted as we are, yet without sin." And the verse also indicates that this fact should be a source of comfort and strength, since by his temptation Jesus is able "to sympathize with our weaknesses." So, Jesus was really and truly tempted, even tempted in every respect that we are, but the question is this: how could Jesus really and truly have been tempted if he was not able to sin? Is it possible to believe that Jesus was really tempted, on the one hand, and also believe that he could not have sinned, on the other?

Well, let's start with some of the Bible's teaching that Jesus did not sin. Scripture here is completely clear: "For our sake he [God the Father] made him [Christ] to be sin who knew no sin, so that in him we might become the righteousness of God" (2 Corinthians 5:21). "For we do not have a high priest who is unable to sympathize with our weaknesses, but one who in every respect has been tempted as we are, yet without sin" (Hebrews 4:15). "He [Christ] committed no sin, neither was deceit found in his mouth. 23 When he was reviled, he did not revile in return; when he suffered, he did not threaten, but continued entrusting himself to him who judges justly" (1 Peter 2:22–23, with a quotation here from Isaiah 53:9). "You know that he appeared to take away sins, and in him there is no sin" (1 John 3:5).

Without any question, the Scriptures teach that Christ did not sin. In order for him to be the spotless, substitute Lamb of God to take away the sin of the world, he had to be sinless. And sinless he was. But our question remains: was it possible for him to sin, even though he didn't ever sin? Some have thought so simply because it is difficult to see how he was truly tempted if he wasn't able to sin. But others have held the view that Christ, as fully God, could not have sinned. After all, just suppose for a minute that he did sin. How could he commit an immoral act without that sin staining his own divine nature? And since God cannot sin, how could Jesus, as God, ever sin?

I side with those who believe it is best to think that Christ could not have sinned. The holiness of the divine nature is at the heart of who God is as God. His holiness cannot be marred. God cannot be involved in sin. For God to be who he is as God, it is impossible for his perfect and spotless nature to have sin stain it. But to say that Christ could have sinned seems to work against the idea that God cannot change in his holy and moral nature. If Christ were to sin, it would seem that his divine nature as well as his human nature would be involved. Sin is a moral (actually, an immoral) act. So how could it be possible for Christ to sin and God not be involved in sin? Is there a way, then, to understand the real temptations of Christ while also holding that Christ could not have sinned?

Yes, I think there is. And in this we'll see some lessons for how those who follow Jesus, too, are to fight against temptation. What I suggest here is this: we should understand two different questions as needing to be given two different answers rather than the same answer for both. The two questions are these: 1) why it is that something *could not* happen, and 2) why it is that something *did not* happen? It may appear that these are two ways of asking the same question, requiring the same answer. But this is not true. Allow me to offer an illustration of the difference between these two ideas, and then we'll see how it helps with our question of Jesus' temptations.

Imagine a swimmer who wants to try to break the world record for the longest continuous swim (which, I've read, is over seventy miles). As this swimmer trains, besides his daily swims of five to ten miles, he includes weekly swims that are longer. On some of the longer swims of thirty and forty miles, he notices that his muscles can begin to tighten and cramp a bit, and he becomes worried that in trying to break the world record, his muscles may cramp so much that he could drown. So he talks with some friends, and they decide to have a boat follow along behind the swimmer twenty or thirty feet back, close enough to pick him up if there is a serious problem, but far enough away not to get in the way of the swimmer. The day comes, and the swimmer dives in and begins. As he swims, all the while the boat follows along a little ways back, ready to pick up the swimmer if needed. But no help is needed; with much hard work and resolve, the swimmer keeps going, and in due time he breaks the world record.

Now consider two questions: 1) In this event just described, why is it that the swimmer *could not have drowned*? Answer: the boat was there all the time, ready to pick him up if needed. But 2) why is it the swimmer *did not drown*? Answer: he kept swimming! Notice that the answer to the second question has nothing at all to do with the boat. In fact, if you gave the answer of "the boat" to question 2, the swimmer would be quite puzzled. It simply is not true that the swimmer did not drown because the boat was there. The boat, quite literally, had absolutely nothing to do with why the swimmer did not drown. Why he *could not drown* and why he *did not drown* require two very different answers.

Think again about the temptations of Christ in light of the following two questions: 1) Why is it that Christ *could not have sinned*? Answer: because as God he could not sin. God cannot sin, and Christ could not do something that would stain his divine nature. 2) Why is it that Christ *did not sin*? Answer: because as a man, empowered with the Spirit and filled with God's word, he used everything that was given him by the Father to remain obedient. So Jesus did not sin, not because he made use of his own divine nature, but rather because he utilized all of the resources given to him as a man. He loved and meditated on God's word (Psalm 1, for example, should be seen as first and foremost about Christ). He prayed to his Father over and over throughout his life. He trusted in the wisdom and rightness of his Father's will and word. And very significantly, he relied on the power of the Spirit to strengthen him to do all that he was called upon to do. Although he was God, he did not fight against temptation by the power of his divine nature. Rather, he trusted in the word of his Father and relied upon the power of the Spirit who indwelt him.

When we see this, we realize that Jesus lived his life purposely in a way that we should follow. As Jesus relied on the word of God, prayer, and the Spirit within him, so God has given all of these same resources to believers. Those of us who have trusted in Christ and have the Spirit of God living within us should see in Jesus the greatest example of how we should live. Yes, we should rejoice that we are able to resist temptation and obey as Jesus did, with the same Spirit and word that Jesus had. What grace, what power, and what an example to follow.

Questions for Thought

1. Since Jesus never sinned, he also never gave in to temptation. That means that he always felt the full weight of every temptation he experienced. How does this help us in trusting Jesus when we are tempted?

2. What are some ways that you feel most often or most strongly tempted? What resources does God provide to help you resist those temptations? How can you make better use of those?

Memory Verse

Hebrews 4:15—"For we do not have a high priest who is unable to sympathize with our weaknesses, but one who in every respect has been tempted as we are, yet without sin."

What Christians of the Early Church Came to Believe about Christ

This section will be different than most of the rest of the book, but it is a very important section to include. Here we shall take a brief look at what the earliest church councils (of the fourth and fifth centuries) decided on the question, who is Jesus? We stand in a very long tradition of committed Christians who have thought hard and long about difficult questions of our faith. We benefit from their insight, and we should be thankful for the help they've given us today in remaining true to Scripture's own teaching. So, what have Christians through the ages believed about Christ?

In the third and fourth centuries of the Christian church, one position being considered by many was being taught by an early Christian named Sabellius. He proposed that there is only one God, and the Father is that eternal God. But the Father decided to come to earth in the "mode" of the Son, being born as Jesus Christ of Nazareth. After the resurrection and ascension of Christ, then the Father decided to come to earth in the "mode" of the Holy Spirit. At Pentecost (Acts 2), the Father, now as the Spirit, came and dwelt in the lives of the early Christians. This view, called modalism, believes that the Father is fully God, the Son is fully God, and the Holy Spirit is fully God, but only one at a time. God is first the Father, and then he is the Son, and then he is the Spirit, one at a time, rather than being Father, Son, and Spirit all at the same time, eternally. No church council was needed to convince Christian people that this view simply could not work. All one need do is consider the baptism of Jesus or Jesus' prayer in the Garden of Gethsemane to realize that the Bible requires that the Father, Son, and Holy Spirit must be present *at the same time*. Modalism, then, was rejected by the church.

An even more dangerous view was presented by a bishop whose name was Arius. He developed the idea that although Jesus is way above us, he still is a creature who is not himself the eternal God. Sometimes called subordinationism, Arius taught that the Son was the first created being and was great in power. But only the Father was uncreated and eternal. So even though the Son was great, as a creature he was "subordinate" or lesser in his nature than the Father.

The first council of the whole church, the Council of Nicea, met in A.D. 325 to decide the question of whether Christ was a high but created being or if he was the uncreated and eternal God. The hero of the Council of Nicea was a bishop by the name of Athanasius. Athanasius was a very gifted, godly theologian who defended the deity of Christ against Arius's view that Christ was merely a highly exalted created being. No, argued Athanasius; the New Testament record is so clear and strong for Christ's deity that we must affirm that Christ is of the very *same nature* as the Father. The Greek word that Athanasius used here is *homoousios* (from *homo*, "same," and *ousios*, "nature"), indicating that Christ possessed the identically same nature as the nature possessed by the Father. Some at Nicea proposed that perhaps if we said that Christ was *homoiousios* (from *homoi*, "similar," and *ousios*, "nature") or of a *similar nature* with the Father, this would be enough. But Athanasius rejected this idea. The Nicene Creed that was written and is still recited in many of our churches today followed Athanasius, insisting that Christ was "one nature" or the identically "same nature" (i.e., *homoousios*) with the Father.

The second council was held at Constantinople in A.D. 381. A bishop from Laodicea by the name of Apollinarius had agreed with the Council of Nicea that Christ was fully God. But Apollinarius denied that Christ was also fully man. Apollinarius could not see how Christ could be both fully God and fully man, and so he began to teach that in Christ, the full divine nature had come to rest within a human body but was not joined to a full human nature. So Christ looked like a man from the outside, but on the inside he was fully, but only, God. Christ only "seemed" to be a man, and so this view has sometimes been called docetism, from the Greek word, *dokeo*, "to appear" or "to seem."

The council of Constantinople met and rejected the Apollinarian view, arguing that if Christ had not taken on our full human nature, he could not have offered himself as one of us and died in our place, for our sin. In short, if Christ was not fully human, Christ could not be our Savior. So the full deity of Christ *and* the full humanity of Christ were defended in the first two councils of the church.

The third council was held at Ephesus in A.D. 431. Another teaching had arisen in the church, rightly affirming that Christ was fully God and fully man, but it proved to be a problem in the way it did this. The main teaching came from a bishop in Constantinople named Nestorius. He believed and upheld the decisions made at Nicea and Constantinople that Christ was fully God and fully man, but he thought that if this is true, then Christ must be two persons. Nestorius could not understand how Christ could have the full nature of God and the full nature of man without also being two persons, one divine and one human. The Council of Ephesus rejected this view, though, especially because of the teaching of Cyril of Alexandria. Cyril proposed that the Person of the eternal Son came and joined himself to a human nature, but he did not join himself to a human person. If Jesus was two persons, he would not truly be an individual who lived, ministered, and died on the cross. Rather, Christ is one person with two natures, insisted the Council of Ephesus. Christ, then, is fully God (Nicea) and fully man (Constantinople), two natures in one person (Ephesus).

The fourth council was held at Chalcedon in A.D. 451. Here the final issue at the center of the church's understanding of the person of Christ was settled. The remaining question concerned how the two natures in Jesus were related. Eutyches had proposed that the divine and human natures in Jesus had co-mingled, so that a divine-human blend of natures had resulted. Jesus had both a divinized humanity and a humanized deity in his natures. This is a bit like pouring grape juice from one pitcher and apple juice from another pitcher into a common pitcher. You'd end up with neither grape juice or apple juice, but with some new mixture possibly called grapple juice. The Council of Chalcedon rejected the Eutychian view, proposing instead that the two natures of Jesus be understood as joined together but with "no confusion, no change, no division, no separation." That is, each nature was fully present without "confusion" (our grapple juice is an example of such "confusion"), but also without separation, so that the human and divine natures would be together forever in the Person of Jesus Christ.

So all four councils contributed very importantly to the church's understanding of Christ. Jesus Christ was fully God (Nicea) and fully man (Constantinople), with a divine nature and a human nature that are conjoined but not confused (Chalcedon) in one Person (Ephesus). We are greatly indebted to God's sovereign leading in the church to guide her to the truth.

Questions for Thought

1. Can you give the names or dates of the first four councils of the church and what they declared to be true about Christ?

2. Why is it important for the church to reject false teachings as well as to defend the true teachings of the Bible about God and Christ?

Memory Verse

2 Corinthians 10:5—"We destroy arguments and every lofty opinion raised against the knowledge of God, and take every thought captive to obey Christ."

6

The Work That
Jesus Has Done

Jesus' Death Shows God's Justice and His Mercy toward Our Sin

Did Jesus really have to die in order to save us from our sin? Could God have done the same thing some other way? Many Christians have asked these kinds of questions over the years, and if they are clear about Scripture's teaching, they know the answers. Yes, Jesus did have to die; and no, there was no other way. When Jesus cried out to his Father, weeping in agony, "My Father, if it be possible, let this cup pass from me" (Matthew 26:39), can you imagine the Father turning down his Son's earnest request if there really were another way? The only reason we can possibly understand that "it was the will of the LORD to crush him [Christ]" (Isaiah 53:10) is that through the shed blood of his only Son, and only in this way, could forgiveness of our sin be won and our full salvation accomplished.

Why is this so? What stands behind the cross of Christ that explains just why Christ had to come and die? Here we'll consider three key ideas that try to explain why the cross of Christ was needed. Each of these must be a part of explaining the cross, but only as we put these together do we have a full explanation for the cross of Christ. We're familiar with these ideas, but seeing them together here is important both for understanding the need for the cross and for understanding the gospel.

The first foundational idea needed to explain why the cross was necessary is the sin we have committed as human beings. The Bible teaches that all people have sinned in all of human history (Romans 3:23; 5:12) except for one person—Jesus Christ. Not only are we all sinners, but the punishment or "wages" for our sin is death (Romans 6:23; Ephesians 2:1). That is, if we get what we deserve, no matter who we are or how much good we think we've done, we will get the sentence of eternal death and judgment. Please understand: there are no exceptions to this truth. Every human being in the line of Adam is a sinner who has earned what he has coming to him, namely, the eternal judgment of hell's fire. Also, not only are we all sinners who deserve God's judgment, but none of us can do anything to change our situation. There is no amount of good deeds, no amount of work, no pleading or praying or churchgoing or community service that could ever remove the stain and guilt of our sin before God (Romans 3:20; Galatians 2:16–17, 21). In short, we are sinners, we deserve eternal death, and we can't do anything about it.

The second foundational idea needed to explain why the cross was necessary only makes the bad news of the first point worse. This second idea is that God's justice demands a full payment for our sin. Because God is just and righteous, he always upholds the standards that he knows as God are holy and good and right. Because he is God, he cannot ignore these standards or set them aside, for if he did this, he would not be God. And be clear on this: God is not mocked! Never think for a minute that we can live in disobedience to God and not be required to pay the penalty (Galatians 6:7–8). So God can't ignore our sin, he can't sweep our sin under the carpet, he can't pretend that it hasn't happened or that we don't deserve eternal condemnation. In short, God is just, we are sinners, and as a result God must and will bring judgment on our sin.

Now, were it not for the third foundational idea coming next, we would have no escape at all. We should realize the hopeless condition we are in as sinners before a just and holy God. There truly is no good news in what we've seen thus far, but only bad and bleak news for us sinners. Furthermore, we should not expect that the next (glorious!) point must necessarily be coming. That is, we don't deserve what's about to come; it is not an entitlement (that is, something we have a right to receive). And God didn't have to do what we're about to say. Let's put it this way—God could have drawn a line after points 1 and 2 and said, "That's it. You all deserve eternal judgment, and as a holy and just God, that is exactly what I will give you." Yes, he could have done this . . . But God, being rich in mercy, has chosen not to condemn us all.

So the third and very important foundational idea needed to explain why the cross was necessary is this: God is full of grace and mercy, abounding in love to sinners who deserve eternal condemnation. Why God loves us is completely beyond our ability to understand. We have turned away from him, mocked him, resisted him, scorned him, and in a million other ways have slighted God. So, clearly God's love is not based on how loveable we are; just the opposite, we are wretched sinners and despicable in his sight. And then we hear the words of Paul, and it takes our breath away: "but God shows his love for us in that while we were still sinners, Christ died for us" (Romans 5:8). John's insight also helps:

"In this is love, not that we have loved God but that he loved us and sent his Son to be the propitiation for our sins" (1 John 4:10). For reasons we will probably only come to understand in eternity, God has shown the riches of his love for sinners who deserve the fullness of his wrath. Amazing love, how can it be?

Now we're at a very important point in understanding why the cross was necessary for God to save us from our sin. For you see, God faces here what might be called the problem of mercy (I'll let you think about how opposite this is from the so-called problem of evil). The problem of mercy is this: how can a holy, just, and righteous God show mercy and kindness to sinners who deserve the judgment that he, as God, is obligated to execute? Remember, he cannot ignore sinners' sin. He cannot pretend they're not guilty. As God, he must exercise justice, and to fail to do so would be to fail to be God!

So, here is the genius of the cross. God made a plan by which our sin and its full guilt would be charged against God's own Son. As his Son, the God-man, bore our sin and its guilt in himself, the judgment that we deserved was directed at him, not at us. On the cross, then, Jesus bore our sin and paid the punishment for our guilt, and this did two things at once. Jesus' payment for our sin 1) satisfied the full demands of *God's justice* against our sin, while 2) it provided everything *God's mercy* and love sought to accomplish in bringing forgiveness to sinners. In Christ on the cross, the fullness of God's just wrath against our sin and the richness of God's mercy and love toward sinners meet and are satisfied. As Paul says, God the Father gave his Son, Christ Jesus, "as a propitiation by his blood, to be received by faith. This was to show God's righteousness, because in his divine forbearance he had passed over former sins. It was to show his righteousness at the present time, so that he might be just and the justifier of the one who has faith in Jesus" (Romans 3:25–26). Here is the splendor of the cross. Here is the basis for the gospel. And here is the message one must know in order to believe, in order to be saved. Praise be to God for his indescribable gift!

Questions for Thought

1. Why could God not have simply ignored our sins? Why could he not simply have pretended that they didn't exist?

2. How is God's love for us shown in Christ's death on the cross? What happens on the cross that shows how great God's love and kindness is toward sinners?

Memory Verse

2 Corinthians 5:21—"For our sake he [God the Father] made him [Christ] to be sin who knew no sin, so that in him we might become the righteousness of God."

Jesus Paid the Full Penalty for Sin

One of the hardest things in life for any of us to face is when we have a very large debt to pay, and we don't have the ability to pay it off. You may or may not have felt this yet, but it is a very discouraging feeling and one that stays with you all the time. Debt—owing something to someone else—is a part of life we'd rather not have to deal with. But for most people, debt can't really be avoided. If the debt is small, we're okay. But if the debt is big—especially when it's really big—we might wish we could crawl into a hole in the ground and never come out.

There is one debt that each one of us has about which most people know nothing. And it is by far the biggest and most important debt possible. We owe a debt to God our Creator, the Giver of every good and perfect gift, to honor him, love him, obey him, and serve him with all of our hearts. You see, we can't decide if we would like to love, obey, and serve God. Since God is our Creator, he has complete rights of rulership over us. It is not optional whether we honor God as God. We are *required* to do so. And since we as a race of human beings have turned away from God in rebellion against him and his Law, we now have brought upon ourselves a different debt, a deadly debt, that is so big, so great, so overwhelming and impossible to pay off that we could never, ever pay it fully even if we had forever to try.

How amazing, then, is God's grace in Christ! In his love for us, God the Father planned a way for our debt to be paid by his Son. When Jesus came and was hung on the cross, the Father put upon him our sin, and Christ paid fully the debt we owed to the Father. By trusting what Christ has done for us and nothing else, we can be saved. What glorious news this is about the greatest payment ever made for the greatest debt ever owed.

The Bible talks about the death of Christ in a number of different ways. Each of them tells us some wonderful truth, helping us see the fullness of the cross and all that it means. But some of these are especially important if we are to understand rightly what happened on the cross. Consider with me what seem to many to be the two most important ways the Bible talks about what happened when Christ died on the cross.

First, Jesus died *in our place*, taking *our sin* upon himself, and *paying the penalty we deserved to pay for our sin*. This is the cross as penal substitution. The word *substitution* refers to the fact that Christ *took our place* and died *instead of us* having to die. And the word *penal* refers to the fact that as Christ died as a substitute sacrifice in our place, he *paid the penalty* that we deserved to pay. When you put the two words together, you see that the term *penal substitution* means that Christ paid the penalty of our sin (penal) as he died in our place on the cross (substitution). As Paul says in Galatians 3:13, Christ became a "curse for us" as he died on the cross, accepting the curse of the Law, which is death, that we had brought upon ourselves by our sin. Second Corinthians 5:21 says that the Father made the sinless Christ "to be sin" for us, taking our sin and its guilt upon himself, dying our death, so that we might be saved.

One of the richest and most moving passages in the Bible expressing penal substitution is Isaiah 53:4–6, which reads: "Surely he has borne our griefs and carried our sorrows; yet we esteemed him stricken, smitten by God, and afflicted. ⁵ But he was wounded for our transgressions; he was crushed for our iniquities; upon him was the chastisement that brought us peace, and with his stripes we are healed. ⁶ All we like sheep have gone astray; we have turned—every one—to his own way; and the LORD has laid on him the iniquity of us all." Notice that verse 4 states first what really is happening on the cross—he is bearing *our* griefs and carrying *our* sorrows. Then the verse shifts to what it looks like is happening as Christ hangs on the cross—it looks like he is being stricken, smitten, afflicted by God for his own sin; it looks like he is getting what he's due. Then verse 5 tells us that in truth he isn't getting what he's due, he's getting what we're due. He is being wounded for *our* transgressions; he is being crushed for *our* iniquities. Yes, the truth of the cross is this: the Father placed on Christ "the iniquity of us all" (v. 6) so that he might pay the penalty for our sin, providing a way—the only way—that sinners could be forgiven as they put their full trust in him.

Second, another beautiful part of the cross is that Christ satisfied the demands of God's just judgment against our sin through his death on the cross. The word often used here is *propitiation*, a word that refers to the Father's being satisfied since Christ, by his death, paid the penalty for our sin *fully*. The idea of being satisfied is similar to how we use it today. For example, on vacation your family might check into a hotel room, and the clerk might ask, "Are you satisfied with the room?" What he means, of course is, "Does the room meet your expectations, and is it what you require?" When God looked at the payment for sin that his Son made on the cross, paying for the sin of the world that the Father had put upon him (John 1:29; 2 Corinthians 5:21), God saw that Christ's payment was so complete and full that he was able to declare, "I am satisfied with my Son's payment for sin." That is, "My Son's payment so perfectly and completely fulfills my just demands that no other, and no further, payment is required." As Paul says in Romans 3:25, the Father put Christ on the cross "as a propitiation [satisfaction of God's just wrath against our sin] by his blood, to be received by faith." God saw Christ's shed blood on the cross as fully satisfying his demands against our sin. We are forgiven and saved from the judgment that we deserve as we receive the gift of salvation by faith.

I'm reminded of some songs we often sing in church that might be good to meditate on as we conclude this section. The third verse of Horatio Spafford's great hymn "It Is Well with My Soul" reads: "My sin, oh, the bliss of this glorious thought! / My sin, not in part, but the whole, / Is nailed to the cross, and I bear it no more, / Praise the Lord, praise the Lord, O my soul." What bliss, indeed. The whole of our sin has been paid by Christ as he was nailed to the cross, so that by faith we are set free and forgiven. This is the greatest news possible!

Another verse that captures the idea of propitiation so well is the second verse of "Before the Throne," written by Charitie Lees Bancroft, with music provided in recent years by Vikki Cook. It reads, "When Satan tempts me to despair / And tells me of the guilt within / Upward I look and see Him there / Who made an end of all my sin. / Because the sinless Savior died / My sinful soul is counted free. / For God, the Just, is satisfied / To look on Him and pardon me."

Penal substitution that propitiates the wrath of God against sinners— big words, yes. But more important, big truths about a big Savior with big grace from a big God for big sinners. Amen.

Questions for Thought

1. What does the word *propitiation* mean, and why is this an important biblical truth to understand and believe?

2. Although many people have many big problems in their lives, there is one problem every one of us has that is far bigger than anything else. What is the biggest problem that every single person has? What has God done to provide the solution to this problem?

Memory Verse

> Isaiah 53:5—"But he was wounded for our transgressions; he was crushed for our iniquities; upon him was the chastisement that brought us peace, and with his stripes we are healed."

Jesus' Victory over Satan by His Payment for Sin

We live in a day of superheroes! It seems like one blockbuster movie after another comes out with yet another superhero tale to tell. Amazing displays of power, with more hi-tech equipment than one could dream about in several lifetimes, keep moviegoers spellbound as they gaze intently on the superhero fighting his way to victory once again. As much fun as all of this is, it's fiction, make-believe, even if done with a lot of realistic special effects.

But there is a real story about a real villain and a real Superhero that would embarrass Hollywood if the true dimensions of this conflict could be known for what they are. Satan is the greatest villain, the worst enemy, the most powerful opponent who has ever existed or will ever exist. Some of the ways he is described in the New Testament boggle the mind. He is "the prince of the power of the air, the spirit that is now at work in the sons of disobedience" (Ephesians 2:2). He's "the god of this world" who blinds the minds of all who are perishing (2 Corinthians 4:3–4). He "snares" unbelievers until they are "captured by him to do his will" (2 Timothy 2:26). And to top it off, we're told that "the whole world lies in the power of the evil one" (1 John 5:19).

The good news, though, is that Someone greater, wiser, stronger, and better in every way has come into this world and has defeated the great Satan. Satan is living on borrowed time, we could say, since all of the statements just given about Satan's work today describe this defeated foe. But defeated he is. Christ has accomplished what we never could do by bringing Satan down. When God is done with him, he will throw Satan into the lake of fire to suffer forever (Revelation 20:10).

The three strongest passages in the New Testament expressing the truth that Christ has conquered Satan and all of the powers of darkness are Colossians 2:15, Hebrews 2:14–15, and 1 John 3:8. These passages teach that Christ has "disarmed the rulers and authorities and put them to open shame, by triumphing over them" (Colossians 2:15); that Christ took on our human flesh, that "through death he might destroy the one who has the power of death, that is, the devil" (Hebrews 2:14–15); and that "the reason the Son of God appeared was to destroy the works of the devil" (1 John 3:8). These passages, along with many others, make it clear that Christ, by his death and resurrection, won the victory over the very one who had the power of death. Christ's victorious work, in turn, brings this same victory over Satan to Christ's followers and, in a broader sense, to the whole world that the Son is making new.

But how did Christ win the victory over Satan? Is there any connection between what we looked at in the last section—the death of Christ as a payment for our sin that satisfied God's just wrath against us who believe—and this victory that Christ has won over Satan? Yes, there is. We'll see here that the victory of Christ over Satan happens only as Christ pays the penalty of our sin. Satan's claim on us is based on the sin we've committed that holds us in bondage. So, pay off the sin and the basis for Satan's holding us is removed. Although this connection can be shown in all three passages mentioned above, we'll consider just one to illustrate how the Bible sees Christ's payment for our sin as the basis also of Christ's victory over Satan.

Consider Colossians 2:13–15: "And you, who were dead in your trespasses and the uncircumcision of your flesh, God made alive together with him, having forgiven us all our trespasses, ¹⁴ by canceling the record of debt that stood against us with its legal demands. This he set aside, nailing it to the cross. [15] He disarmed the rulers and authorities and put them to open shame, by triumphing over them in him."

As you can see from this passage, Christ's payment for the penalty of sin is explained first (vv. 13–14) before speaking about Christ's victory over Satan (v. 15). In Colossians 2:13–14 we are told that in Christ we have been forgiven of all our trespasses. Through the death of Christ on the cross, God the Father canceled "the record of debt that stood against us" and "set [it] aside, nailing it to the cross." So, because Christ has paid our debt for us, we no longer are required to pay it. The legal requirement that we had before our holy God to pay off our debt is now removed since that debt was paid fully in Christ. This is sometimes called *expiation*—the liability we owed before a holy God to pay the penalty for breaking his Law is now removed (or "forgiven," 2:13, or "canceled" and "set aside," 2:14). How could this be? Answer: Christ took upon himself our record of debt and nailed it to the cross.

Notice that the teaching of Colossians 2:13–14 is the basis, then, for speaking next of Christ's victory over Satan in 2:15. The way that Christ "disarmed" Satan and the forces of darkness was through his removal of our sin and its debt. So, the ideas in these verses are put in this order on purpose. The only way in which Satan could be defeated is as sin, which gave him the basis for his hold over sinners, was itself paid for and forgiven. Christ's forgiveness through penal substitution, then, is the means by which Christ conquered Satan's power.

Perhaps an illustration will help. In countries that are governed by just laws, a prisoner is only rightly put in jail because he has been found guilty of some crime for which the penalty is time behind bars. Notice, then, that his *guilt* forms the basis for his *bondage*. Only because he has been proven guilty of breaking the law does the state have the rightful power to put him behind bars. Furthermore, if a prisoner can prove that he is innocent and not guilty as previously charged, then the state would be required to release him from prison. Remove the *guilt*, and you remove the just basis for *bondage*.

Similarly, Satan's power over sinners is tied directly to their guilt through sin. His hold on them is because of their sinful rebellion against God. But remove the guilt through Christ's payment for their sin, and you remove the basis for Satan's hold on them. So it is through Christ's death and its payment for sin that the rightful hold that Satan had upon us is necessarily broken. Forgiveness of sin's penalty and freedom from Satan's prison go together. Remove the guilt, and you remove the bondage. As Christ bought the former—forgiveness of the guilt of our sin—he won also the latter—victory over the bondage of our sin. Praise be to our Savior for his gracious and complete forgiveness that accomplishes also this glorious and powerful deliverance from Satan's dominion, bondage, and death (Colossians 1:13–14).

Questions for Thought

1. Why did Jesus have to pay the penalty for sin in order to conquer also the power of sin? How are these two (paying sin's penalty and conquering sin's power) related?

2. Satan and demons are powerful, and they are evil. But Christ has conquered Satan. Since this is true, how should we live to make sure Satan cannot succeed in bringing about his evil plans in our lives?

Memory Verses

> Colossians 2:13–15—"And you, who were dead in your trespasses and the uncircumcision of your flesh, God made alive together with him, having forgiven us all our trespasses, by canceling the record of debt that stood against us with its legal demands. This he set aside, nailing it to the cross. He disarmed the rulers and authorities and put them to open shame, by triumphing over them in him."

Jesus' Resurrection: The Proof That Christ's Death for Sin Worked

The resurrection of Jesus Christ from the dead was the basis of hope for New Testament Christians. In his sermon on the Day of Pentecost, Peter mentioned the resurrection three times and made it the centerpiece of his sermon. "This Jesus God raised up, and of that we all are witnesses," declared Peter (Acts 2:32). Again, in Acts 4, after healing a lame beggar and speaking constantly about the resurrection of Christ before irritated Jewish leaders, Peter, filled with the Spirit, said, "[L]et it be known to all of you and to all the people of Israel that by the name of Jesus Christ of Nazareth, whom you crucified, whom God raised from the dead—by him this man is standing before you well" (v. 10). Again in his sermon to Cornelius, Peter proclaimed that "God raised him on the third day and made him to appear" to witnesses chosen by God to testify that he was alive (Acts 10:40–41). And Paul's sermon in Athens ended suddenly because of the controversy that arose when he said that God had "fixed a day on which he will judge the world in righteousness by a man whom he has appointed; and of this he has given assurance to all by raising him from the dead" (Acts 17:31). Without question, the faith of the early Christians was based on the truth that the Christ who died for sins had been raised. Without the resurrection there would be no Christian faith.

Perhaps the strongest teaching in the New Testament about the importance of the resurrection comes in 1 Corinthians 15 where Paul declares that if the resurrection of Christ has not taken place, the Christian faith is worthless. Paul writes here to correct false teaching that there is no resurrection at all. So Paul says that "if the dead are not raised, not even Christ has been raised. [17] And if Christ has not been raised, your faith is futile and you are still in your sins. [18] Then those also who have fallen asleep in Christ have perished. [19] If in Christ we have hope in this life only, we are of all people most to be pitied" (1 Corinthians 15:16–19). Again we see that these early Christians were convinced that the resurrection was not only important but necessary to the Christian faith. If the resurrection was the basis of their hope, the opposite was also true. If Christ has not been raised, the Christian faith is a complete fake.

A very important question to think about at this point is this: why were the apostles and early Christians so convinced that if Jesus had not been raised from the dead, the Christian faith would be a lie? After all, don't we believe that it was through the *death* of Christ that our sins were paid for? As Paul even says earlier in 1 Corinthians 15, don't we believe that "Christ died for our sins in accordance with the Scriptures" (v. 3)? If so, what would be the problem with a Savior who died for our sins, making a full payment and satisfying God's just demands, and then simply remained dead? What's wrong with that? Or another way to put the question is this: could our Savior have really done on the cross what we Christians believe without also being raised from the dead? That is, is there some connection between 1) Christ's death that actually did *pay for* and *conquer* our sin and 2) Christ's resurrection from the dead?

Well, the short answer is, yes, there is a connection—a very important connection—between the atoning death of Christ that really worked to deal with our sin and his resurrection from the dead that followed. The best way to see this, oddly, is to think together again about the nature and results of sin.

Sin brings to us (sinners) two problems in one. Sin comes to us, first, as a *penalty* we cannot pay and, second, as a *power* we cannot overcome. And if we think further about how sin's penalty and power affect us, we see something interesting. Regarding the *penalty* of sin, Romans 6:23 makes clear that "the wages of sin is death." Of course, this echoes God's warning to Adam in the Garden of Eden in Genesis 2 that the day he ate of the tree of the knowledge of good and evil, he would surely die (v. 17). Regarding the *power* of sin, this is a bit more complicated. Sin, after all, has many different powers, we might say. It has the power to lead someone to steal or murder or lie or covet or hold a grudge or complain or seek revenge and so on. Sin has almost endless ways in which its power is shown in our lives. But in all of those examples, we have at least some possibility to fight against the urges of sin within us. It may want us to be angry, but we can endeavor to resist. It may urge us to engage in jealousy, but we can try to turn our minds to other things. But there is one power that sin has over us that we simply cannot fight against: sin has the power to kill us. So while sin has many different kinds of power, without question sin's greatest power is death (1 Corinthians 15:53–56).

We've come to an interesting place. We see that while sin comes to us both as a penalty and as a power, both of these have the same effect on us in the end. For the penalty of sin is death, and the greatest power of sin is death. So how does this help with our question of whether the resurrection of Christ is connected to the death he died for our sins?

Here's the connection, taking sin as penalty and sin as power separately. First, if Christ by his death on the cross has actually and fully paid the *penalty* for sin, and if the penalty for sin is death, then what is the only way it could be shown that Christ's payment for sin has truly worked? Answer: he has to be raised from the dead. For if Christ supposedly paid sin's penalty, the penalty of death, but then remained in his tomb dead and buried . . . well, he would still be paying the penalty (death). If he really and truly paid sin's penalty fully, since sin's penalty is death, then the only way this could be shown is as he is raised alive again from the dead. The resurrection of Christ, then, is necessary to prove and show that his payment for sin was full and final. He finished paying sin's penalty! He rose from the dead!

Second, if Christ by his death on the cross has actually and completely conquered the *power* of sin, and if sin's greatest power is death, then what is the only way it could be shown that Christ's victory over sin's power has truly worked? Answer: he has to be raised from the dead. For if Christ supposedly conquered sin's power, and its greatest power was death itself, but then he remained in his tomb dead and buried, well, he would still be under the power of sin (death). So, if Christ really and truly conquered sin's power completely, since sin's greatest power is death, then the only way this could be shown is as he is raised alive again from the dead. The resurrection of Christ, then, is necessary to prove and show that his victory over sin's power was full and final. He conquered sin's greatest power! He rose from the dead!

Indeed, if Christ has not been raised from the dead, our faith is worthless, and we are still in our sins. But the greatest news ever to be proclaimed by men or angels is this: Christ is risen! Sin's penalty is fully paid! Sin's power is fully defeated! Christ is risen indeed! May God be praised!

Questions for Thought

1. How does the resurrection of Christ show that his death really did pay for the *full penalty* of sin? And how does the resurrection of Christ show that his death really did conquer the *greatest power* of sin?

2. How does Christ's death and resurrection for sin show that the only hope that sinners have is in Christ and what he has done?

Memory Verses

1 Corinthians 15:3–5—"For I delivered to you as of first importance what I also received: that Christ died for our sins in accordance with the Scriptures, that he was buried, that he was raised on the third day in accordance with the Scriptures, and that he appeared to Cephas, then to the twelve."

Jesus Is King over All

One of the greatest and most glorious teachings of the Bible is that God has appointed a King, his own Son, who will reign over the whole of creation forever and ever. One of the first and strongest pointers in this direction comes in God's covenant promise to David in 2 Samuel 7. David wanted to build God a house, but God instead tells David that he, God, is going to establish his house—David's house—forever. God promises David that he will have a son who will build a house for God and that God "will establish the throne of his kingdom forever" (2 Samuel 7:13). Since God's promises cannot fail, we realize that Solomon, David's son and heir to his throne, cannot be the fulfillment of that promise. As great as Solomon was, he did not sit on the throne forever. In fact, right after Solomon's reign, the nation of Israel divided into the Northern Kingdom (Israel) and the Southern Kingdom (Judah) with no one king over all of Israel.

But the promise of a king was never forgotten. Through the prophets, reference would often be made of days to come when God would put "David" or the son of David as king over his people. One of the most glorious of these passages is worth reading here: "My servant David shall be king over them, and they shall all have one shepherd. They shall walk in my rules and be careful to obey my statutes. ²⁵ They shall dwell in the land that I gave to my servant Jacob, where your fathers lived. They and their children and their children's children shall dwell there forever, and David my servant shall be their prince forever. ²⁶ I will make a covenant of peace with them. It shall be an everlasting covenant with them. And I will set them in their land and multiply them, and will set my sanctuary in their midst forevermore. ²⁷ My dwelling place shall be with them, and I will be their God, and they shall be my people. ²⁸ Then the nations will know that I am the LORD who sanctifies Israel, when my sanctuary is in their midst forevermore" (Ezekiel 37:24–28). Wow! What an amazing picture of a future day of glory when the new and greater King David—one from the line of David who will reign perfectly and forever—will come.

Psalm 2 adds another piece to the teaching about the coming king. Here we are told that the King will be not merely David's son but God's own Son. God will install him as King over all the nations, and this Son-King will reign over them with fury. Speaking through the psalmist, God says, "'As for me, I have set my King on Zion, my holy hill.' ⁷I will tell of the decree: The LORD said to me, 'You are my Son; today I have begotten you. ⁸ Ask of me, and I will make the nations your heritage, and the ends of the earth your possession. ⁹ You shall break them with a rod of iron and dash them in pieces like a potter's vessel'" (Psalm 2:6–9). The anticipation builds as we see the promise of a King who will come in the line of David, reigning forever (2 Samuel 7), but also a King who will bring righteousness to the earth (Ezekiel 37) and victory over the godless nations of the world (Psalm 2).

Old Testament history ends, shall we say, not with a bang but with a whimper. If you wish, you may read the books of Nehemiah and Malachi to see the end of the Old Testament story of Israel. Promised a king, a temple, a land, with righteousness throughout the world—well, let's just say that's not quite how the Old Testament story ends. A small portion of Israel is back in her land, true enough, but only because a pagan king (Cyrus) made it possible for them to return. They do have a leader over them, a godly man named Nehemiah, but he's not from the tribe of Judah (David's tribe), and he's governor, not king. The Temple has been rebuilt, but it's a rather sorry one in comparison to the grandeur of Solomon's. And righteousness on earth? Well, the very last chapter of Nehemiah records this godly man literally tearing out some ungodly men's hair because of blatant sin in Jerusalem. Where is this long-awaited King? When will God's promises be fulfilled?

Then we hear Jesus of Nazareth proclaim words almost too good to believe. Right after his baptism, he announced, "The time is fulfilled, and the kingdom of God is at hand; repent and believe in the gospel" (Mark 1:15). Indeed, here is God's own Son who comes as King. And his reign as King begins with his first coming to bring salvation to a sinful world. How glorious to know that Jesus reigns as King even now—God's Son, the King, has come (Colossians 1:13).

But Jesus did not carry out everything that the Old Testament said this King would do. Because of this, many were puzzled and confused. Among the confused was none other than John the Baptist. You would think that if anyone would know that Jesus was the Messiah, the King of Israel who came to bring righteousness on the earth, it would be John.

John, after all, baptized Jesus and heard the voice from heaven declaring Jesus to be God's Son. John was so sure who Jesus was that when people told him that some of his (John's) disciples were now following Jesus, he replied, "He must increase, but I must decrease" (John 3:30). How amazing, then, to see John now in prison, instructing his disciples to ask Jesus, "Are you the one who is to come [i.e., the Messiah], or shall we look for another?" (Matthew 11:3). What happened to John's confidence that Jesus was the Messiah?

Well, it is very simple. John knew his Old Testament very well. He knew the promises associated with the coming Messiah and King, and what he knew was promised wasn't happening. For example, besides passages we've seen, imagine what John would think as he considered Isaiah 9:6–7: "For to us a child is born, to us a son is given; and the government shall be upon his shoulder, and his name shall be called Wonderful Counselor, Mighty God, Everlasting Father, Prince of Peace. [7] Of the increase of his government and of peace there will be no end, on the throne of David and over his kingdom, to establish it and to uphold it with justice and with righteousness from this time forth and forevermore. The zeal of the LORD of hosts will do this." As John sat in prison, wicked King Herod reigned on the throne in Jerusalem, the adulterer who had John thrown in jail and later beheaded him. No wonder John was puzzled and confused. Jesus looked less like the promised Messiah every day, from where John sat.

What's the answer to this? Well, what was not apparent to John the Baptist or really to any of God's faithful people at that time was this: in Jesus' *first coming*, he came as the Suffering Servant to take away the sin of the world. Some of the promises connected with the Messiah were fulfilled (e.g., see Jesus' response to John the Baptist in Matthew 11:4–5), but many were left unfulfilled. But now he has been raised from the dead and ascended to be with his Father, and he will come again someday. And in his *second coming* he will fulfill all the rest of what has been prophesied, from judgment on the nations (Revelation 19:11–21) to righteousness on the earth and the restoration of the people of God (Revelation 20–22). Yes, the risen and exalted King Jesus will come again and will reign in the fullness of the kingdom! With the apostle John, we cry out, "Come, Lord Jesus!" (Revelation 22:20).

Questions for Thought

1. Jesus will come again as King of kings and Lord of lords (Revelation 19:11–16). But does this mean that Jesus did not come as King in his first coming?

2. How is Jesus' kingdom being built now? (See Colossians 1:13–14 for a clue.)

Memory Verses

Isaiah 9:6–7—"For to us a child is born, to us a son is given; and the government shall be upon his shoulder, and his name shall be called Wonderful Counselor, Mighty God, Everlasting Father, Prince of Peace. Of the increase of his government and of peace there will be no end, on the throne of David and over his kingdom, to establish it and to uphold it with justice and with righteousness from this time forth and forevermore. The zeal of the LORD of hosts will do this."

But Is Jesus Really the Only Savior?

Have you ever heard any of your friends or maybe someone on TV say something like, "There are different ways that people can get to God, like different paths up the same mountain. It's wrong for people to say that there is only one way. Those folks should realize that most people have their own relationships with some Higher Power, and we should accept different religions and different ways of being in touch with God."

You may or may not have heard something like this, but these ideas are growing both here where we live and through much of the world. Christian people who believe that Jesus is the only way to God are sometimes made to feel that they are wrong to think this and even more wrong to share with others the good news of salvation through faith in Christ alone. So, we need to see whether the Bible really makes clear that Jesus is the only way. If it does make this clear, and if Jesus really is the only Savior and the only way anyone can be made right with God, then it is not wrong to believe this or to share it. In fact, if Jesus is the only way, the most loving and kind thing we could ever do is to share this good news with others, even if they don't agree.

Well, then, can we be sure that Jesus is the only Savior? Is the Bible clear about this? Do we have good reasons for believing that Jesus' work—his life, death, and resurrection—is the only way that our sins can be forgiven so that we can be brought back into a right relationship with God?

Let's consider some of the most important reasons for believing that Jesus really is the only Savior. And we'll do this by seeing that of all the people who have lived and ever will live, *Jesus alone qualifies*, in his person and work, as the *only one capable* of actually bringing about forgiveness of sin for anyone and everyone in all of the world. Consider the following ways in which Jesus alone qualifies as the one and only Savior.

1. Jesus alone was conceived by the Holy Spirit and born of a virgin (Isaiah 7:14; Matthew 1:18–25; Luke 1:26–38). Because of this, he alone qualifies to be Savior. Why does the virgin conception and birth of Jesus matter? Well, in every other conception and birth, there is both a man and a woman involved in order for a baby to be conceived. But in the case of Jesus, only as the Holy Spirit took the place of the human father in Jesus' conception could it be true that the one conceived is both fully God and fully man. In order for Jesus truly to be a Savior, to bring about forgiveness of sin, he must be both God and man (see below for more on this). But in order for Jesus to be both fully God and fully man, he must be conceived by the Holy Spirit and born of a human virgin. Now here's an important question: was anyone else in the history of the world conceived by the Spirit and born of a virgin mother? Answer: no. Therefore, *Jesus alone meets this qualification* to be Savior.

2. Jesus alone is God incarnate (John 1:1–18; Hebrews 1:1–3; 2:14–18; Philippians 2:5–11; 1 Timothy 2:5–6), and as such, he alone qualifies to be Savior. As Anselm argued in the eleventh century, our Savior must be *fully man* in order to substitute himself for men and die in their place, and he must be *fully God* in order for the value of his life's payment to satisfy the demands of our infinitely holy God. He must be a man, but a mere man simply could not make this infinite payment for sin. He must be God, but as God alone he could not take our place and die for our sin. One who is Savior, then, must be both fully God and fully man. So here's our question: was anyone else in the history of the world both fully God

and fully man? Answer: no. Therefore, *Jesus alone meets this qualification* to be Savior.

3. Jesus alone lived a sinless life (2 Corinthians 5:21; Hebrews 4:15; 7:23–28; 9:13–14; 1 Peter 2:21–24), and as such, he alone qualifies to be Savior. As the book of Leviticus makes clear, animals offered as sacrifices for sin had to be without blemish. This looked forward to the sacrifice of Christ who, sinless, was able to die for the sins of others because he did not have to die for any sin of his own. Here's our question: has anyone else in the history of the world lived a totally sinless life? Answer: no. Therefore, *Jesus alone meets this qualification* to be Savior.

4. Jesus alone died a substitutionary death as payment for the sins of others (Isaiah 53:4–6; Romans 3:21–26; 2 Corinthians 5:21; Galatians 3:10–14), and as such, he alone qualifies to be Savior. The wages of sin is everlasting death (Romans 6:23; Matthew 25:46). And if we pay the penalty for our own sin, we will pay forever and ever. We never could pay off the offense before God; so someone greater than us has to pay for our sin if we are to be saved. Jesus, as the God-man, is greater than us. And Jesus lived a sinless life; so he did not deserve to die. The cause of his death, then, was entirely because the Father placed *our sin* upon him as he hung on the cross (2 Corinthians 5:21). The death that he died was in *our place* paying the full penalty for *our sin*. So, our question is this: has anyone else in the history of the world died because he bore the sin of others and not as the judgment for his own sin? Answer: no. Therefore, *Jesus alone meets this qualification* to be Savior.

5. Jesus alone rose from the dead triumphant over sin (Acts 2:22–24; Romans 4:25; 1 Corinthians 15:3–8, 16–23), and as such, he alone qualifies to be Savior. The Bible indicates that a few people, other than Christ, have been raised from the dead (e.g., 1 Kings 17:17–24; John 11:38–44), but only Christ has been raised from the dead never to die again, having defeated all sin. The wages of sin is death, and the greatest power of sin is death. So, Christ's resurrection from the dead shows that his atoning death for sin brought about both the *full payment of sin's penalty* and *full victory over sin's greatest power*. Question: has anyone else in the history of the world been raised from the dead because he has triumphed over sin? Answer: no. Therefore, *Jesus alone meets this qualification* to be Savior.

Conclusion: Jesus alone qualifies as Savior, and Jesus alone is Savior. Jesus' own words could not be clearer: "I am the way, and the truth, and the life. No one comes to the Father except through me" (John 14:6).

And the apostle Peter confirms, "And there is salvation in no one else, for there is no other name under heaven given among men by which we must be saved" (Acts 4:12). These claims are true of no one else in the history of the world. Indeed, *Jesus alone is Savior*! May God grant us wisdom, boldness, and joy to believe and proclaim the good news—the *only* good news there is—that Christ has died for sinners, who may be forgiven as they place their full trust and hope in him. Praise be to our Savior, Jesus!

Questions for Thought

1. What are some reasons for believing as both true and very important that Jesus is the only person who qualifies to be the Savior of sinners from their sin?

2. If Jesus really is the only way that people can be brought back into right relationship with God, why is it not wrong or intolerant or mean to share this good news with others?

Memory Verse

John 14:6—"I am the way, and the truth, and the life. No one comes to the Father except through me."

7

The Holy Spirit

The Work of the Holy Spirit in Old Testament Times

One of the most exciting and helpful areas of theology for Christian people is the Bible's teaching on the Holy Spirit. Of course, Christians today do not agree on everything about the Holy Spirit's work. The main area where good Christian people differ is this: some believe that spiritual gifts (supernatural abilities) like speaking in tongues, miracles, and prophecies from God are present today, and others believe these kinds of gifts did not continue after the apostles had died and the New Testament books were all written. Much discussion and writing has taken place on this issue without bringing about complete agreement. However, many people on both sides have come to see that other areas of our beliefs as Christians are far more important than this one. We can remain in close fellowship, then, even if we differ on this question of spiritual gifts.

Thankfully, the areas of the work of the Spirit that we will be thinking about in these sections are ones where Bible-loving Christians have wide agreement. We will focus on the Bible's teaching on the Spirit's work from Old Testament times to what happens in the New Testament. We'll see the amazing and wonderful enlargement or increase of the Spirit's work as we move forward. This should lead us to rejoice in the amazing gift that the Holy Spirit is for Christian people now, for all who have trusted in Christ are promised that they will receive the Spirit into their lives. What a great gift the Spirit is to us as Christians, as will become clearer as we tell this story.

Our story begins, then, with the work of the Spirit during Old Testament times. If you were to look through all thirty-nine books of the Old Testament and notice every time that the Spirit of God (by one name or another) was mentioned, you would count about one hundred references to the Spirit. But as you did this, you might notice that some of these references to the Spirit talk about his actual work during Old Testament times themselves, and other references are in passages that speak of a future work that the Spirit will do. If you count these up, you'll find that about sixty references are to the Spirit's actual work during the Old Testament, and about forty refer to the future work that the Spirit will do in an age to come. In this section, let's take a look at the actual work of the Spirit during Old Testament times.

In all of the Old Testament, the Holy Spirit is said to "come upon" or "fill" people in four main groupings. You read about the Holy Spirit coming upon different *prophets* (e.g., Numbers 24:2; 2 Kings 2:15; 2 Chronicles 15:1–7; 20:14–17), upon some of the *leaders* of the people of Israel (e.g., Numbers 11:17, 25; 27:18; 1 Samuel 11:6; 16:13), upon some of the *judges* (e.g., Judges 3:10; 6:34; 11:29; 14:6), and upon a few of the *craftsmen* responsible for building either the Tabernacle or the Temple (e.g., Exodus 31:3; 35:31). Let's take a look at a few examples.

An interesting account is that of the Spirit coming upon Bezalel, giving him supernatural power for building the Tabernacle. We read that he was filled with the Spirit "to devise artistic designs, to work in gold, silver, and bronze, ⁵ in cutting stones for setting, and in carving wood, to work in every craft" (Exodus 31:4–5). The Lord wanted the Tabernacle built exactly the way he instructed it to be, and so he gave Bezalel (and possibly some others, see Exodus 31:6) Spirit empowerment to build it just as God wanted him to. What we see here, then, is something we'll see again in other examples we'll consider: the Spirit's coming upon people in Old Testament times was primarily to give them supernatural power to carry out what God was calling them to do. And it seems also to be the case that when the work was finished, the Spirit's filling would also end. At least we have no reason to think that Bezalel was Spirit-filled in all of his craftsmanship for the rest of his life. If so, I bet he was a very popular handyman throughout Israel! It is more likely that when the reason for the Spirit's coming was completed, the Spirit would leave. We'll come back to this idea soon.

Another very important passage concerns the Spirit who was upon Moses as Israel's leader during their forty years of wilderness wanderings before they entered the Promised Land. For quite a long time, Moses was the only leader for this whole company of people—perhaps around one million or more!—and the time came when he was very frustrated. The people kept grumbling, and Moses grew tired of trying to satisfy them. In Numbers 11 God decided the time had come for others to join Moses in leadership. But the way this happened is fascinating. As the only leader, Moses alone had the Spirit upon him. But when seventy others were selected to become leaders along with Moses, God took the Spirit who was on Moses and gave the Spirit also to the seventy. As proof that they now had the Spirit, all seventy prophesied (see Numbers 11:16–17, 24–25). Two of the seventy, however, were not with the rest when this happened, and many of the people of Israel heard these two men prophesy. This angered Joshua, since he thought that the people might start following these two men instead of Moses. But Moses replied to Joshua, saying, "Are you jealous for my sake? Would that all the LORD's people were prophets, that the LORD would put his Spirit on them!" (Numbers 11:29). What we see here is a tiny glimpse of Pentecost—a hint of what would happen when God put his Spirit upon all of the people of God (Acts 2). Moses understood how good this would be, but the time had not yet come for the Spirit to be poured out on all God's people. Moses and the seventy had the Spirit, not the rest.

Most of us know the story of Saul, the first king of Israel. Saul was the people's choice, not God's choice, but God used him anyway. In fact, God even put the Spirit on Saul to give him power to lead the people (1 Samuel 11:6). But Saul sinned in some ways that were dishonoring to God. Instead of waiting as he should have for Samuel to come, he offered burnt offerings himself (1 Samuel 13). He also disobeyed God's command to kill all of the Amalekites and their livestock (1 Samuel 15). Because of Saul's disobedience, God took the kingship from Saul. This involved taking the Spirit from Saul (1 Samuel 16:14) at the same time that God gave the Spirit to David, God's newly appointed king of Israel (1 Samuel 16:13). To lead the people of God requires the Spirit; so the Spirit was given first to Saul and then to David. But when Saul no longer was to be king, the Spirit was taken from him. Again we see that the connection between granting the Spirit to people and the tasks they were called to do requires Spirit empowerment.

The story will continue in the next section, but let's close with three things we should pick up from what we've seen here of the Spirit's work in Old Testament times. First, the Spirit came upon just a few people—Moses, the seventy, Bezalel, some prophets, Saul, David, etc. But very few are said to have the Spirit on them in the Old Testament. Although the Spirit was in the "midst" of the people of Israel all along (Haggai 2:5; Isaiah 63:11), he came upon only some of God's people. Second, the Spirit's coming was for the purpose of granting supernatural power to fulfill some specific calling or task that God had given someone to do. Third, the length or duration of the Spirit's coming seems to be tied to the length or duration of the task. When the task was done, the Spirit would leave (the Spirit's leaving Saul is the clearest example). So, the Spirit's coming was 1) selective, 2) task-oriented, and 3) of limited duration, tied to the duration of the task. As we move into the teaching in the Old Testament about a day when the Spirit would come with might and power, we'll see how much greater his work will become. The story continues . . .

Questions for Thought

1. What did the Holy Spirit do in the lives of people in the Old Testament when he came upon them? How was this work of the Holy Spirit important for doing the work that God wanted done?

2. In what ways was the work of the Holy Spirit limited during Old Testament times? Why do you think this was so?

Memory Verse

> Numbers 11:29—"Are you jealous for my sake? Would that all the LORD's people were prophets, that the LORD would put his Spirit on them!"

Old Testament Promises of Future Spirit Transformation

The story of the Spirit in the Bible continues as we turn next to Old Testament teaching of a coming day when the Spirit will be poured out in far greater measure than before. This new outpouring of the Spirit will bring about wonderful and widespread changes, especially for the people of God. You'll recall we ended the last section by noting that the Spirit's work in Old Testament times tended to be upon a select number of people, primarily to empower them to carry out specific callings or tasks, and when the task or calling ended, most likely the Spirit-empowerment also ended. Now, when we look at Old Testament teaching about the future coming of the Spirit in an age to come, we will notice that all three of these features are overturned. The Spirit's coming will no longer be on a select few of God's people but on them all! And his coming will not merely empower tasks to be done or callings to be carried out, but now the Spirit will transform God's people to become holy and obedient. And his coming will not be limited in duration but forever and ever! Let's look at a few of the passages that speak of this wonderful day of Spirit transformation.

Isaiah 32:1–14 describes a very sad scene. Israel is far from the Lord, yet they're not even aware that God's heavy hand of judgment is about to come upon them. They are at ease, enjoying their sinful ways. God assures them, however, that they will soon be brought to ruin, their cities plundered, and their vineyards abandoned to dry up and perish. In his mercy, though, God does not end the story here. God's final word to his own chosen people is not a word of judgment (though they deserve this) but rather a word of restoration, healing, salvation, transformation. So Isaiah writes that God's judgment will come upon them "until the Spirit is poured upon us from on high, and the wilderness becomes a fruitful field, and the fruitful field is deemed a forest. [16] Then justice will dwell in the wilderness, and righteousness abide in the fruitful field. [17] And the effect of righteousness will be peace, and the result of righteousness, quietness and trust forever. [18] My people will abide in a peaceful habitation, in secure dwellings, and in quiet resting places" (Isaiah 32:15–18). What an amazing word this is. Israel has sinned, and God has judged this nation. But then God will turn again toward his people, this time to save and restore her, to transform her and make her new. How will God do this? Answer: when he pours out his Spirit upon her from on high. And when God sends his Spirit, huge changes will occur. The barren wilderness will flourish, so people will think they're in a forest! Idolatry and immorality will be replaced throughout the land with righteousness and peace! No longer will there be fear of invading armies, for God's people will dwell in secure habitations and quiet places of rest. What a transformation indeed! And when will this occur? Answer: when the Spirit comes.

Isaiah 44:1–5 likewise provides an amazing picture of the transformation of God's people in the latter days: "But now hear, O Jacob my servant, Israel whom I have chosen! [2] Thus says the Lord who made you, who formed you from the womb and will help you: Fear not, O Jacob my servant, Jeshurun whom I have chosen. [3] For I will pour water on the thirsty land, and streams on the dry ground; I will pour my Spirit upon your offspring, and my blessing on your descendants. ⁴ They shall spring up among the grass like willows by flowing streams. ⁵ This one will say, 'I am the Lord's,' another will call on the name of Jacob, and another will write on his hand, 'The Lord's,' and name himself by the name of Israel." God speaks of Israel here as his chosen ones, whom he formed and made to be his own people. This is not a reference to God's creation of all things in Genesis 1, but rather to God's special and particular formation of this people to be his own, chosen by God to be his. Because of God's commitment to this people of his own making and choosing, God promises one day to make of them the holy and faithful people he has called them to be. Although they now live in outright rebellion, the day will come when God will remake them, transform them, entirely. When will this occur? When the Spirit comes. And notice what happens. They will grow and flourish like trees planted alongside rivers of water (see also Psalm 1). They will say to each other, with joy and righteous pride, "I belong to the Lord!" Others will write this on their hand, filled with joy to be God's chosen people (see also Deuteronomy 6:4–7). Consider this question: how often in Israel's history did God's people feel and think and act like this? How often were they proud to be the people of God and eager to walk in his ways? Answer: far, far too seldom. What an amazing transformation will occur to all of God's people! And when will this transformation take place? When the Spirit comes.

Ezekiel 36:22–28 reads: "Therefore say to the house of Israel, Thus says the Lord God: It is not for your sake, O house of Israel, that I am about to act, but for the sake of my holy name, which you have profaned among the nations to which you came. ²³ And I will vindicate the holiness of my great name, which has been profaned among the nations, and which you have profaned among them. And the nations will know that I am the Lord, declares the Lord God, when through you I vindicate my holiness before their eyes. ²⁴ I will take you from the nations and gather you from all the countries and bring you into your own land. ²⁵ I will sprinkle clean water on you, and you shall be clean from all your uncleannesses, and from all your idols I will cleanse you. ²⁶ And I will give you a new heart, and a new spirit I will put within you. And I will remove the heart of stone from your flesh and give you a heart of flesh. ²⁷ And I will put my Spirit within you, and cause you to walk in my statutes and be careful to obey my rules. ²⁸ You shall dwell in the land that I gave to your fathers, and you shall be my people, and I will be your God." When God says, "It is not for your sake . . . that I'm about to act," he means, "I'm not bringing these amazing blessings on you because you deserve them." So why will he so bless them? Because of his holy name. God has pledged himself to this people, and he cannot go back on his word. He has promised that they will be his people and that he will be their God. He has promised that they will be blessed. So in faithfulness to his oath, God will do it! He will make them his obedient people and bless them richly. How will God transform these rebellious people to walk in God's statutes and to be careful to obey his rules? Answer: he will put his Spirit within them. With his Spirit in them, they will have new hearts and new spirits, created by God for obedience and faithfulness. As his Spirit comes to dwell within the people of God, they will be changed—radically and comprehensively changed!

Joel 2:28–29 also speaks of the Spirit as one day coming "on all flesh" (v. 28). Sons, daughters, old men, young men, male servants, female servants—these all will be recipients of the coming transforming Spirit of God. Clearly the promises of the future coming of the Spirit surpass by far his actual work in the Old Testament. His coming will not be selective but on all, not task-oriented only but transformational, and not limited in duration but forever.

Well, the story isn't over yet. The movement from the Old Testament's promised Holy Spirit to its New Testament fulfillment has some surprises of its own. Just how and when will the Spirit come and do this transforming work? The story continues . . .

Questions for Thought

1. What are some ways that the actual work of the Spirit during Old Testament times differs from the later work of the Spirit that the Old Testament promised and foretold?

2. What is the main and most important work the Spirit will do when he comes upon all of God's people, according to these Old Testament promises?

Memory Verses

Ezekiel 36:26–27—"And I will give you a new heart, and a new spirit I will put within you. And I will remove the heart of stone from your flesh and give you a heart of flesh. And I will put my Spirit within you, and cause you to walk in my statutes and be careful to obey my rules."

The Spirit on Jesus and on Jesus' Followers

Our story of the Spirit's work through the Bible now moves into the New Testament. In a minute we'll look at the outpouring of the Spirit on all of the people of God, as many Old Testament passages had said would happen. But first we must notice that the New Testament begins with the Spirit being poured out again on one individual, one man called by God to carry out a very specific and important mission. The Spirit is poured out on Jesus.

In the third section of Chapter 5 of this book, we looked briefly at Jesus' life and ministry carried out in the power of the Spirit. As Isaiah 11, 42, and 61 had all indicated, the coming Messiah would be Spirit-anointed. As his ministry began, at his first opportunity, Jesus read the opening verses of Isaiah 61. In doing this, Jesus surprised fellow Jews in the synagogue in Nazareth with his announcement that he was the fulfillment of this promise. He, Jesus of Nazareth, was the long-awaited, Spirit-anointed Messiah. Jesus could have read from Isaiah 53 to announce that he was the Suffering Servant, but instead he chose Isaiah 61. Being seen as the Spirit-anointed Messiah was so important to a correct understanding of who Jesus is that he chose Isaiah 61 as his opening passage.

As we saw earlier, the obedient life he lived and the miracles he performed should be seen in large part as being done in the power of the Spirit. Peter's summary captures the idea perfectly: "God anointed Jesus of Nazareth with the Holy Spirit and with power. He went about doing good and healing all who were oppressed by the devil, for God was with him" (Acts 10:38). In a real sense, Jesus lived out perfectly the Spirit-filled and Spirit-empowered life that the Old Testament prophets foretold would happen for all of God's people. So Jesus might be seen, then, as the perfect example of what our human lives should look like when we also receive the Spirit as he did. Jesus gladly carried out everything that the Father sent him to do, and he did all of this in the power of the Spirit.

But there is much more to the story of the Spirit in the New Testament. Just before Jesus died for our sins and rose from the dead, he prepared his disciples for the next step in God's plan. Jesus would go back to be with his Father, sitting at his Father's right hand and ruling over the world and over his church. But when Jesus told his disciples that he would be going to be with his Father, they were puzzled. Jesus even said it was good news that he was leaving! They were very sad and confused (John 16:5–6). After all, Jewish believers had been waiting a very long time for the promised Messiah to come, and they didn't want him now to leave! But then he explained more to them. He said, "I tell you the truth: it is to your advantage that I go away, for if I do not go away, the Helper [the Holy Spirit] will not come to you. But if I go, I will send him to you" (John 16:7). Why do you think Jesus said, "It is to your advantage that I go away"? How could it be good for Jesus to leave? Well, consider also this question: what could possibly be better than having Jesus living *with* you, walking *alongside* you day by day? Answer: having Jesus, by his Spirit, living his own life *within* you.

Jesus promised his followers that the Spirit who now "dwells with you" would soon "be in you" (John 14:17). Yes, Jesus knew the day would come when all of his followers would receive the Spirit into their own lives, the same Spirit who lived in Jesus' life. They did not have the Spirit yet though. Earlier Jesus said that "those who believed in him were to receive" the Spirit, but that "as yet the Spirit had not been given, because Jesus was not yet glorified" (John 7:39). Jesus knew that when he went to be with his Father—that is, when he was raised and glorified, sitting at the Father's right hand—then it would be time for Jesus to send to his followers the same Spirit who lived within him. As believers in Jesus, they would receive Jesus' own Spirit and would have Jesus' own life and power at work in them. This was good news after all!

The day of the pouring out of the Spirit on all of Jesus' followers finally happened. Forty days after Jesus had died and been raised, on the Day of Pentecost, Jesus poured out the Spirit upon all those who believed in him (Acts 2:33). They were all gathered together waiting for "the promise of the Father" (Acts 1:4–5) to come through the giving of Jesus' Spirit to them. When the Spirit came upon them, they all did something quite amazing. These Spirit-filled believers began telling other people about God's wonderful saving work in Jesus, and they were able to say all of this in languages they had never learned! Those who heard were amazed and also puzzled. So Peter took the opportunity to explain that what was happening was exactly what the Old Testament said would happen. Peter read from Joel 2, where God promised that a day would come when "I will pour out my Spirit on all flesh, and your sons and your daughters shall prophesy, and your young men shall see visions, and your old men shall dream dreams; even on my male servants and female servants in those days I will pour out my Spirit, and they shall prophesy" (Acts 2:17–18; quoting Joel 2:28–29). Finally, the day had come when all of those who truly believed in God would receive his Spirit. The time when God's Spirit—the very Spirit of Jesus—would work powerfully in the lives of God's people was now here!

There is one more important part of this story that we need to notice. Jesus said that when the Spirit comes upon his followers, they would be given power for one job that was very special. Before the Spirit came, Jesus had said to his disciples, "you will receive power when the Holy Spirit has come upon you, and you will be my witnesses in Jerusalem and in all Judea and Samaria, and to the end of the earth" (Acts 1:8). One of the main reasons that the Spirit has come upon Jesus' followers, then, is clear: the Spirit gives us power to tell others about Jesus' death and resurrection for their sin. The Spirit gives us power to share the good news of the gospel with those who need to hear it. The Spirit wants to bring praise to Jesus as his followers speak about the salvation that Jesus has won for sinners. This makes sense because Jesus said that when the Spirit comes, "[h]e [the Spirit] will glorify me" (John 16:14). One of the most important ways the Spirit wants to bring honor and glory to Jesus is as he gives Jesus' followers power to share about Jesus and his saving work on the cross. Sharing the gospel of Jesus, then, is not something we can rightly do in our own power. But when we believe in Jesus and so receive his Spirit into our lives, we too are given this power to share the good news about Jesus with others. How far should we share this good news? Well, as Jesus said, "to the end of the earth." Maybe God will use you one day to take the good news of Jesus to people in a faraway land. What a privilege and what a joy because Jesus really is the one and only Savior of all who put their trust in him.

Questions for Thought

1. What was "the promise of the Father" (Acts 1:4–5) that Jesus told his disciples to wait in Jerusalem to receive? What is so important about this promise?

2. When the Spirit comes upon persons, he comes to transform their character to be more and more like Christ and also to empower them to tell others about

Christ. Are there people you know who show these marks of the Spirit at work in their lives?

Memory Verses

John 14:16–17—"And I will ask the Father, and he will give you another Helper, to be with you forever, even the Spirit of truth, whom the world cannot receive, because it neither sees him nor knows him. You know him, for he dwells with you and will be in you."

The Holy Spirit Gives New Life in Christ

The Bible talks about us sinners as people who are both living and dead at the same time. I know it sounds funny, but it's true! All of us are born into this world both alive and dead. We are alive in our bodies, but there are really two ways in which we are born dead. You may remember that in Chapter 4 we talked about how sin has brought the punishment of death to all of us. As Paul put it, "the wages of sin is death" (Romans 6:23). So, the first way we are dead is that in our sin we face the punishment of everlasting death. That is, we will receive the penalty of being separated from God forever if we remain in our sin and do not trust Christ as our Savior. (So thank God that he sent his Son to die for our sins! If we place our trust in Christ and his payment for our sin on the cross, we will not die eternally but instead will live forever with God—more about this in the next section of our book.)

But there is another way that we are born dead and can be dead even now. You might ask, "But how can this be, since I know that I am very much alive right now?" Paul helps us again, for he tells the Ephesian believers something amazing about who they were before they trusted in Christ. He wrote, "And you were dead in the trespasses and sins in which you once walked, following the course of this world, following the prince of the power of the air, the spirit that is now at work in the sons of disobedience" (Ephesians 2:1–2). Did you notice that Paul described these people as "dead" in the sin in which they once "walked"? So, they were the "walking dead," people who were both alive and dead at the same time. But what could this mean?

What it means is this: even though we are alive in our bodies, so we can think and eat and play and do all kinds of things, yet we are dead spiritually. To be dead spiritually means this: in our sin we do not have real love for God and his ways, and we do not truly desire to obey his word. Our spirits or our inner lives instead are selfish. We want to do the things we enjoy, and we don't like being told what to do. So, because we are sinners, we are separated from God. And because of this, we will not come to God or love God on our own. As sinners we're dead, and we're as unable to do what pleases God as a dead person is unable to ride a bike or swim or throw a Frisbee (see Romans 8:6–8).

So, what does all of this have to do with the Holy Spirit? Answer: everything! If we are ever to be changed so that we no longer are dead spiritually but instead are alive toward God, we must be given this new life that we don't have. Because we are dead in our sins, we cannot make ourselves alive. God has to make us come to life. And the way God does this is through the work of the Holy Spirit.

You may remember a very famous, true story in the Bible about a Jewish leader who came to Jesus at night. He knew that Jesus was from God, but even so, he wasn't ready for the first words that Jesus spoke to him. Jesus said to Nicodemus, "unless one is born again he cannot see the kingdom of God" (John 3:3). This puzzled Nicodemus greatly. *How can one be born again?* he wondered. *Can you go back into your mother's womb and be born a second time?* To this, Jesus answered, "Truly, truly, I say to you, unless one is born of water and the Spirit, he cannot enter the kingdom of God" (John 3:5). In talking about "water" and "the Spirit" together, Jesus was thinking of many verses in the Old Testament that speak of the life that comes when the Spirit is given, like plants that grow when water is brought to them. For example Isaiah 44:3–4 had predicted, "For I will pour water on the thirsty land, and streams on the dry ground; I will pour my Spirit upon your offspring, and my blessing on your descendants. They shall spring up among the grass like willows by flowing streams." By speaking of "water and the Spirit," then, Jesus meant that spiritually dead people have to be brought to life as the Spirit makes them alive. Just as water brings life to plants and trees that are made to drink of that water, so the Spirit brings spiritual life to those who are made to drink of that Spirit. The Spirit gives life to sinners who are dead in their sin. Only God can make us alive, and God does this through his Spirit.

The next words that Jesus said to Nicodemus are also very important. Jesus continued, "That which is born of the flesh is flesh, and that which is born of the Spirit is spirit. . . . The wind blows where it wishes, and you hear its sound, but you do not know where it comes from or where it goes. So it is with everyone who is born of the Spirit" (John 3:6–8). The main thing Jesus wanted to get across is this: when we are born into this world as babies, we are alive physically, but our physical life does not and cannot make us alive spiritually. In fact, as we've seen, when we are born into this world as babies physically, we are actually born spiritually dead. Because we are born sinners, we are not alive toward God, and so we are the living dead, as we said earlier—alive in this world but dead toward God in our sin. We must be born again. We must be born not only physically but also spiritually. But as Jesus said, only if we are born of the Spirit can we be alive spiritually. There is nothing we can do to make ourselves become spiritually alive. The Spirit must cause us to be born again. The Spirit must cause us to become spiritually alive. And can we control the Spirit and make him do what we want? Jesus said that just as the wind blows where it wishes and we cannot control where it goes, so the Spirit gives life to those whom he wishes, and we cannot control what the Spirit chooses to do.

If we are thinking carefully about what Jesus said to Nicodemus, we should be very humbled. We should realize there is nothing we can do to make ourselves be born again. There are no actions or works we can perform to bring to ourselves spiritual life. So, what should we do then? If the Spirit must work for us to be born again, and if we cannot control what the Spirit does, what should we do? The only thing we can rightly do, and the one thing we should do, is this: we should bow our heads and admit before God that we are helpless to save ourselves. We are unable to make ourselves come alive. We know that we are spiritually dead because of our sin, and we know that we don't deserve to be made alive.

But that's not all! We also know that God is kind and that he comes to those who are humble before him (see Isaiah 57:15). Paul once said that because of the loving-kindness of God, he saved people through a washing that made them to be born again, through the Holy Spirit who made them new (Titus 3:5—notice "washing" and "Spirit" together also here). We should put our hope in the kindness of God, his mercy toward sinners, and his power to save those who admit they cannot save themselves. Our trust must be in God, not in ourselves. We must admit, if we are to be born again, that God must do this. His Spirit must give us life. He alone is our hope!

Questions for Thought

1. What are some ways the Bible describes all sinners who do not have the Spirit of God living within them?

2. Because we are dead in our sins, we cannot make ourselves alive. God has to make us come to life. How does God work to make someone come to life spiritually?

Memory Verse

John 3:5—"Truly, truly, I say to you, unless one is born of water and the Spirit, he cannot enter the kingdom of God."

The Holy Spirit Unites Believers Together in Christ

The Holy Spirit works in a personal and individual way when he brings new life to someone who has been dead in his own sin. But something else happens at the same time. As the Spirit gives new life to an individual sinner so that he or she trusts in Christ, the Spirit also does something else that is wonderful and amazing, involving many others and not just one individual person. The Spirit also brings that one born-again person together with all other born-again people so that they become a "family" of new brothers and sisters in Christ. They also are joined together in one new "body" in Christ. The Spirit, then, works in an individual, personal, and loving way to bring new life to each person who is saved. But the Spirit also works to unite all saved people together within a beautiful and joy-filled family, a body of Christ's own people.

The Bible uses both *family* and *body* as illustrations of how the Holy Spirit unites believers together in Christ. Let's think about each. First, the Holy Spirit works to help those who have trusted Christ come to understand that God is now their very own Father. Amazing! But that's not all. The Spirit also works to help them understand that *all* believers are their brothers and sisters, adopted into one big family in Christ. Amazing again! Yes, for all who have trusted Christ, God is their Father, and they are adopted with all other believers into God's family.

Do you know some children who were adopted into their families? One wonderful thing about adoption is this: often adopted children are taken from places that might have been difficult or unsafe and brought into homes where they are cared for and loved dearly. Also, adopted children have a special place in their new families. They know they don't belong there by birth. But they belong there because they have been chosen, loved, and wanted by others. Although adopted children don't deserve this love and kindness, they are shown great love by their new parents and families.

John speaks exactly this way about God and his love for his children. He writes, "See what kind of love the Father has given to us, that we should be called children of God; and so we are. The reason why the world does not know us is that it did not know him. ² Beloved, we are God's children now, and what we will be has not yet appeared; but we know that when he appears we shall be like him, because we shall see him as he is" (1 John 3:1–2). How precious and beautiful to know that if you are a believer in Jesus Christ, you are a child of God. And how precious to know that God is your Father and that all true believers are your brothers and sisters. What love God shows to sinners who don't deserve his kindness by loving them and adopting them into his family, to become his own children!

The Holy Spirit plays a very important role in this adoption process. Paul writes about this wonderful work of the Spirit when he says, "For all who are led by the Spirit of God are sons of God. ¹⁵ For you did not receive the spirit of slavery to fall back into fear, but you have received the Spirit of adoption as sons, by whom we cry, 'Abba! Father!' ¹⁶ The Spirit himself bears witness with our spirit that we are children of God, ¹⁷ and if children, then heirs—heirs of God and fellow heirs with Christ, provided we suffer with him in order that we may also be glorified with him" (Romans 8:14–17). The reason we are adopted into God's family, then, is that God has used his Spirit, "the Spirit of adoption," to bring us into his family. The Spirit unites us together as brothers and sisters in Christ, with God the Father as our own Father.

In his letter to the Galatians, Paul speaks of these wonderful new relationships with God and with others that all believers should enjoy. Paul reminds believers that when they trusted in Christ, God worked to make them his own sons. He writes, "in Christ Jesus you are all sons of God, through faith" (Galatians 3:26). A few verses later he explains more, saying, "But when the fullness of time had come, God sent forth his Son, born of woman, born under the law, ⁵ to redeem those who were under the law, so that we might receive adoption as sons. ⁶ And because you are sons, God has sent the Spirit of his Son into our hearts, crying, 'Abba! Father!'" (4:4–6). So, sinners become sons of God when they trust in Christ. And because they now are sons, the Holy Spirit works in their lives to help them understand that God is their very own Father and that they are part of a new family filled with many, many adopted children. As hard as it might be to imagine, each person who has truly believed in Christ is united with every other Christian believer in one glorious family. All believers have one heavenly Father—"Abba! Father!" God is the Father of all these believers, and they are brothers and sisters together forever.

The second way that the Spirit works to unite believers together in Christ is by putting them together into one new "body" in Christ. Paul writes, "For in one Spirit we were all baptized into one body—Jews or Greeks, slaves or free—and all were made to drink of one Spirit" (1 Corinthians 12:13). Paul uses the idea of believers being different parts of one body to help us understand a couple of things.

First, each part of the body needs all of the other parts. So, when the Spirit unites believers together with other believers, he does this so they can help each other. When one hurts, another believer can comfort. When one worries, another believer can encourage. When one suffers, another believer can give hope. We need each other, and so the Spirit puts us together, even giving each of us special gifts so we can help each other grow in our relationship with Christ (1 Corinthians 12:4–26).

Second, when Paul speaks of "Jews or Greeks, slaves or free" all joined together in one body in Christ, he is making a very important point. Paul is teaching that those who come together in Christ are often very different from each other. When they were sinners in this world, these people may not have liked each other or gotten along. Certainly this was true of unsaved Jews and Greeks who often hated each other. But now because believers are united as brothers and sisters in Christ, they are to accept and love all believers, even if they are from a different culture or their skin is a different color or they speak a different language. All believers are brought together into new and greater relationships than ever were true for them before.

Since believers are brothers and sisters of one heavenly Father, and since they are parts of the same body, doesn't it make sense that they should seek God's grace to truly love one another? Believers will show that the power of the Spirit is really alive in them when now, by the Spirit, they love as their own brothers and sisters people who used to be very hard to love. The Spirit is at work in believers' lives. Although he has come to unite us to God—praise God for this!—he has also come to unite us to one another in Christ. May God's Spirit do this work, for the glory of Christ and for the good of his body, God's own family.

Questions for Thought

1. The Spirit unites believers in the family of God and into the body of Christ. What do both of these images illustrate about how Christians ought to relate to each other?

2. When you consider that you can become a child of God by faith in Jesus Christ, what does this do within your own heart? Do you see the beauty and great joy this involves?

Memory Verses

> Romans 8:14–15—"For all who are led by the Spirit of God are sons of God. For you did not receive the spirit of slavery to fall back into fear, but you have received the Spirit of adoption as sons, by whom we cry, 'Abba! Father!'"

The Holy Spirit Fills Believers to Live for Christ

The Holy Spirit gives new life to people who were dead in their sins. How amazing that he is able to make the dead live, causing them to be born again! The Holy Spirit also brings these born-again people together into a wonderful new family, as parts of one new body. How amazing that he unites believers as adopted children of God and members of the body of Christ!

But the Holy Spirit works in even more ways than this. After giving people new life and uniting them together and with Christ, the Spirit continues his work in each believer's life. The Bible speaks about this part of the ongoing work of the Spirit as the filling of the Spirit. Listen to how Paul talks about this wonderful truth: "And do not get drunk with wine, for that is debauchery, but be filled with the Spirit, [19] addressing one another in psalms and hymns and spiritual songs, singing and making melody to the Lord with all your heart, [20] giving thanks always and for everything to God the Father in the name of our Lord Jesus Christ, [21] submitting to one another out of reverence for Christ" (Ephesians 5:18–21). So what does it mean to be filled with the Spirit? How can believers live so that they obey this command in Scripture to be filled with the Spirit?

The best help here comes from Paul himself with the illustration he chooses to use when he teaches about the filling of the Spirit. His command, "do not get drunk with wine" is important in itself, of course. Believers should never take something into their lives that would cause them to lose control of how they think and behave. While wine is often used in the Bible to illustrate joy and God's blessing (e.g., Isaiah 55:1; Joel 3:18), drinking too much wine so that one becomes drunk is wrong and sinful. But why is this so? Because when one is under the influence of too much wine, one cannot control one's own thoughts and actions. He might say things he should never say or do things he should never do, and yet he might not even be aware of it. The wine has become a controlling influence in his life, leading him to speak and act as the wine would direct.

So, when Paul says, do not get drunk with wine, *but* "be filled with the Spirit," we have a pretty good idea what he means. Instead of taking in too much wine that ends up influencing you to speak and act in ways that are wrong and sinful, let the Spirit be such a strong influence in your life that you end up speaking and acting in ways that are holy and honoring to Christ. After all, the Spirit is called "the Holy Spirit" ninety-four times in the New Testament. If the Holy Spirit controls a believer's life, this Spirit will lead the person to think and talk and behave and live in ways that are good and right. Just as Paul says, when the Spirit controls one's life—that is, when he is "filled" with the Spirit (Ephesians 5:18)—that person will talk to others with speech that honors God (5:19), give thanks to God for all that he brings into their lives (5:20), and serve others out of love and respect for Christ (5:21). So, to be filled with the Spirit means having the Spirit influence strongly or control one's thoughts, attitudes, words, and actions.

Paul uses another illustration for the Spirit's control over a believer's life. In Galatians 5, rather than talking about the filling of the Spirit, he rather speaks of the "fruit" of the Spirit in the lives of those who "walk" by the Spirit or are "led" by the Spirit. He writes, "But I say, walk by the Spirit, and you will not gratify the desires of the flesh. [17] For the desires of the flesh are against the Spirit, and the desires of the Spirit are against the flesh, for these are opposed to each other, to keep you from doing the things you want to do. [18] But if you are led by the Spirit, you are not under the law. . . . [22] But the fruit of the Spirit is love, joy, peace, patience, kindness, goodness, faithfulness, [23] gentleness, self-control; against such things there is no law. [24] And those who belong to Christ Jesus have crucified the flesh with its passions and desires. [25] If we live by the Spirit, let us also walk by the Spirit" (Galatians 5:16–25).

The main point of this beautiful passage is seen in the last verse of that passage: "If we live by the Spirit, let us also walk by the Spirit." Paul means this: since the Spirit is the One who has used his great power to give sinners new life in Christ, so the Spirit is the One who also gives believers that same power to live lives that are pleasing to Christ. The Holy Spirit leads those in Christ to holy living through the power he gives them as he dwells within them. And when his power is at work, the Spirit's control is shown through love, joy, peace, and all of the other good qualities that the Spirit causes and brings about. The "fruit" of the Spirit, then, are those good ways of thinking, feeling, speaking, and acting that express what the Spirit is like lived out through his people. So we might think of what we have seen this way: good and godly thoughts, attitudes, words, and actions are shown in the lives of those who are influenced and controlled by the Spirit. Or more simply, the "fruit" of the Spirit (Galatians 5:22–23) are shown in the lives of those who are "filled" with the Spirit (Ephesians 5:18).

One more question needs to be answered: if the "fruit" of the Spirit is shown in the lives of those who are "filled" with the Spirit, how can a believer be filled or controlled more and more by the Spirit? What can Christians do in order to have the Spirit influence and direct more of their lives? While the Bible gives a number of answers here, one main teaching from Scripture seems to stand on top. You'll remember that in Ephesians 5:18, Paul taught that believers should be "filled with the Spirit," so that their thoughts, attitudes, words, and actions would be directed by the Spirit. But in the book of Colossians, Paul wrote something similar to this but also different. Colossians 3:16–17 says, "Let the word of Christ dwell in you richly, teaching and admonishing one another in all wisdom, singing psalms and hymns and spiritual songs, with thankfulness in your hearts to God. ¹⁷ And whatever you do, in word or deed, do everything in the name of the Lord Jesus, giving thanks to God the Father through him." Do you notice how similar these passages are? In both, the results are about the same—words and deeds that are honoring to Christ—but what brings about the results is stated differently in the two passages. In Ephesians 5:18 Paul says to be "filled with the Spirit" in order for these results to happen. But in Colossians 3:16 he says to "let the word of Christ dwell in you richly" in order for the same kinds of results to come about. What can we learn from this? The Spirit will have a greater influence and will provide more direction in our lives as God's Word "dwells" more and more within us. Our reading of his Word, our time spent memorizing and meditating on Scripture, is one of the main tools that the Spirit uses to help us think, feel, speak, and act in ways that are more and more pleasing to Christ. Since this is so, it's pretty clear what we should do. Believers should long to be more "filled" with God's Word so they will be more "filled" with his Spirit. Word and Spirit go together, and the better we learn this, the more we will live to the honor of Christ.

Questions for Thought

1. How are the "filling" of the Spirit and the "fruit" of the Spirit related to each other?

2. How does comparing Ephesians 5:18 and Colossians 3:16 help us understand better what it means to be filled with the Spirit? Can you think of other places in the Bible where "Spirit" and "word" are related?

Memory Verses

Ephesians 5:18–20—"And do not get drunk with wine, for that is debauchery, but be filled with the Spirit, addressing one another in psalms and hymns and spiritual songs, singing and making melody to the Lord with your heart, giving thanks always and for everything to God the Father in the name of our Lord Jesus Christ."

8

Our Great Salvation

God's Kindness and Wisdom in Choosing Some to Save

Have you ever been in a church service, or maybe at family devotions, when those present were asked to mention some reasons why God should be praised? Most often Christian people will give a number of good answers. Often they will talk about Christ dying on the cross for sinners, or the comfort God gives during difficult times, or the ways in which God has answered prayer in their lives. These are all good reasons for praising God.

But there is something amazing and different about how the apostle Paul talks about why God should be praised. Beginning in Ephesians 1:3, he gives a list of reasons for praising God, and the very first reason is one that few Christian people would likely bring to mind. He writes this: "Blessed be the God and Father of our Lord Jesus Christ, who has blessed us in Christ with every spiritual blessing in the heavenly places, ⁴ even as he chose us in him before the foundation of the world, that we should be holy and blameless before him. In love ⁵ he predestined us for adoption as sons through Jesus Christ, according to the purpose of his will, ⁶ to the praise of his glorious grace, with which he has blessed us in the Beloved" (Ephesians 1:3–6). So, what is the first thing that comes to Paul's mind when he thinks about why God should be praised? Answer: God has chosen some sinners to be in Christ (v. 4), and God has predestined them for adoption into his family through Christ (v. 5). This is very important to see. If the apostle Paul thinks that one of the greatest reasons why God should be praised is that he chose people to be saved, then we should think the same way. After all, what Paul writes here is the teaching of the Bible, that is, God's own Word. So, if Paul thinks that God's choosing some to be saved is wonderful and good, then we should seek to understand just why. So, here's our question: why is it good and wise of God to choose some sinners to save? Why is his choosing to save some people a very important reason for why he should be praised?

Our answer to these questions starts with remembering some things we've learned about who we are as sinners. Because of Adam's sin in the garden, we are born into this world with inner lives that are sinful. Those sinful inner lives do not love God and do not want to follow God's ways. Rather, as sinners we love things in this world and want to go our own way instead of loving God and gladly doing what he has told us. Our sin has resulted in our death, our separation from God both in this life and forever in the life to come. We are guilty before God, and we deserve the punishment that is ours. "The wages of sin is death" (Romans 6:23a), and so as sinners, we are getting what we have earned, what we deserve. It is very important, then, to understand that all human beings who have come from Adam are in this condition. We all, with Adam, are sinners in our inner lives and sinners who deserve God's full and final punishment. If God gives us what we deserve, we will receive one and only one thing—separation from God that will last forever (2 Thessalonians 1:9).

In understanding God's choosing of some to be saved, why is it important to be reminded of our sin and guilt before God? There are two reasons for this. First, because of our sin we are rebels against God, running away from him and hating his ways. A rebel is someone who doesn't like to be told what to do and tries every way he can to do the opposite of what he's told. And as sinners, though we may not be aware of it, this is how we are toward God and his ways. We love many things in this world that we shouldn't love, yet we don't love God as we should (John 3:19). We gladly choose to do many things that we shouldn't do, yet we don't do the very things God commands that we should do (John 3:19–20). Our inner lives as sinners are hardwired, you might say, against God and his ways. Well, if we love the world instead of loving God, and if we do what is wrong instead of desiring to do what God says is right, then as sinners we are not running toward God, longing to live with him. Instead, we are running away from God as fast as we can, hoping he never catches up with us. Though we may have no idea what rebels we are, that is exactly what we are!

The second reason we should recall the nature of our own sin is this: as we begin to think about God's plan to save people, we need to understand from the very beginning that no one—absolutely no one!—deserves the kindness and mercy that God decided to shower upon them. It is hard for us to think this way about ourselves because we live at a time when many people think they deserve many good things. But this just is not true. We don't deserve from God any good thing we might think we do. We don't deserve a new bike or a new video game or a new pair of shoes or a new dress. We might want them badly, and we might think in our own hearts that we deserve to have them. But as sinners before God, there is only one thing that we rightly and justly deserve—everlasting separation from God and punishment for our sin. The fact that we are breathing at this moment or have food to eat today or often feel well and enjoy good health is because God, in his kindness, gives us what we *don't* deserve (Acts 17:25). Well, if we don't deserve breath or food or health, we also don't deserve to be saved. None of us does. And until we take this truth deep within our own thoughts and lives, we will not understand the grace and mercy of God in choosing some to be saved.

So, as God looks at all sinful human beings in Adam, this is what he sees. He sees every single person from Adam down to you and me as sinful rebels who are running fast and furiously away from him and as guilty sinners who deserve his just punishment. Now can you begin to see why the truth about God's choosing some to be saved is so important? Some people would lead us to believe that when God looks at the human race, he sees many people reaching out to him, wanting to be with him, and desiring to live in ways that please him. In this view, if God chooses some to be saved, this means that he turns away others who have also wanted to be with him, but he didn't choose them. But this is not true, not true at all. No person born in the line of Adam is ever like this. The Bible says that "no one seeks for God. [12] All have turned aside . . . no one does good, not even one" (Romans 3:11–12). If God were to leave it up to us, not a single person would ever want to be with God, and no one would ever desire to do what pleases God.

But God, in his mercy and undeserved kindness, has decided that he will not leave all of us in our sin to face his judgment. Instead God has done something so good, so gracious, so wise that it is almost unthinkable. God has decided to choose some sinners to be the objects of his most precious love, to receive kindness and grace that they do not deserve, to have their sins forgiven by the death of his Son, and to enter into fellowship with him now and forever. You see, God's choosing is never a matter of his turning away some who wanted to come. His choosing is always a matter of his bringing to him those who never would have come. What kindness and wisdom is shown in God's choosing undeserving rebels to become part of his family. Can you now see how God's choosing some to be saved is a very good reason for praising God?

Questions for Thought

1. Why is it good and wise of God to choose to save some sinners? Why is his choosing to save some people an important reason for why he should be praised?

2. How does Scripture show that it is *not* true to think that as God chooses some to be saved, this means that he turns away others who wanted to be with him? How, instead, should we think of the biblical teaching that God, in his mercy and grace, chooses some sinners to be saved?

Memory Verses

> Ephesians 1:3–6—"Blessed be the God and Father of our Lord Jesus Christ, who has blessed us in Christ with every spiritual blessing in the heavenly places, even as he chose us in him before the foundation of the world, that we should be holy and blameless before him. In love he predestined us for adoption as sons through Jesus Christ, according to the purpose of his will, to the praise of his glorious grace, with which he has blessed us in the Beloved."

"Sirs, What Must I Do to Be Saved?"

Many of you know the story about Paul and Silas who were beaten and thrown into prison for preaching Christ and for casting a demon out of a young girl. After Roman soldiers "had inflicted many blows upon them" (Acts 16:23), Paul and Silas spent much of that night in a prison cell praying and singing hymns to God. After some hours, God showed both his mercy and his mighty power by causing an earthquake that broke apart their shackles and opened the prison doors. When the prison guard saw the doors had flown wide-open, he was terrified. He knew that he would be held responsible for the prisoners' escape, and this would cost him his life. But amazingly, Paul and Silas didn't leave. Instead, when the guard was about to kill himself, they called out loudly and said, "Do not harm yourself, for we are all here" (Acts 16:28). The guard was amazed, for he could tell that the God these prisoners wor-shipped had brought this earthquake to pass. And having overheard the prayers that Paul and Silas had offered and the hymns that they had sung, he then asked them the most important question anyone ever could ask. He brought them out of their prison cell and said to them, "Sirs, what must I do to be saved?" (v. 30).

How would you answer this question? Do you know the Bible's answer? Do you know how Paul and Silas responded? Well, let's start with this last point and see what Paul and Silas said. They replied, "Believe in the Lord Jesus, and you will be saved, you and your household" (v. 31). Here, as in many passages of Scripture, we are told that sinners are saved when they "believe" in Christ or "trust" in Christ or put their "faith" in Christ. Belief, trust, and faith in Christ are different ways to talk about the same idea in the Bible. To believe in Christ (or trust in Christ or put faith in Christ) means to count or rely completely on what Christ has done in his death and resurrection for my sin, so that my hope of being right in God's sight is *all* because of Christ and has *nothing* to do with any good thing I might ever say or do.

This is very much what Paul means when in another place he says, "For by grace you have been saved through faith. And this is not your own doing; it is the gift of God, not a result of works, so that no one may boast" (Ephesians 2:8–9). To be saved "by grace" means that God gives to the sinner who trusts in him what that sinner does not deserve and could never earn. This is why he calls salvation a "gift" from God rather than something they have worked to receive. And because salvation is given to them by God's grace (undeserved favor) and as a gift from God (not as something they worked for), those who receive salvation from God can never boast or brag about the fact that they are saved. They did nothing to deserve it, they did no works that could earn it, and so they have no basis for boasting, except in the God who has given it to them out of his grace (see also 1 Corinthians 1:26–31).

Since salvation is God's gift by his grace, it should now be clear why sal-vation comes by "faith" and not by works. When someone works at a job, he receives payment for what he's done. But because he has earned his pay, we would never call the paycheck he receives a gift, would we? No; if he earned it, the paycheck is not a gift but what he deserves to receive. This is exactly why Paul states that "faith" is the opposite of "works." If by works we get what we deserve, then by faith we get what we do *not* deserve. Faith in Christ, then, trusts completely in what Christ has done to save me since there is nothing I can do—no works that I can carry out—that would make me deserving of the salvation God offers. If we are to be viewed by God as right in his sight, forgiven of our sin, and able to be brought back into fellowship with him, then we must believe that Christ has done everything that is needed for us to be forgiven and saved. We can add nothing to the completed work that Christ has done; so our hope for salvation must be placed fully in Christ, and in Christ alone (see also Romans 4:4–5).

There is something else about believing in Christ that we need to see. John's Gospel speaks much about the need to believe in Christ to be saved, and in one place we read this: "Whoever believes in the Son has eternal life; whoever does not obey the Son shall not see life, but the wrath of God remains on him" (3:36). You'll remember that we have just learned that faith or belief in Christ is the opposite of works. Here in John 3:36 something like this also happens. But here one who "believes" in Christ is not the opposite of one who works for what he receives but of one who "does not obey" Christ and so is lost forever. So, while faith is the opposite of "works" (Ephesians 2:8–9), faith is also the opposite of "not obey[ing]" (John 3:36).

What does this tell us about the faith we need to put in Christ to be saved? If true faith by which we are saved is the opposite of not obeying Christ, it means that the faith we put in Christ involves a hope in Christ and a love for Christ that leads us to obey Christ. After all, why would we really want to trust Christ to remove our sin and guilt if we continued to want to hold on to our sin and disobey Christ day after day? If the Spirit has caused us to see that our sin has hurt us deeply and has made us deserving of God's judgment, then the Spirit has also caused us to see Christ as good and loving in taking that horrible sin from us. So, trusting Christ to remove our sin and make us right with God means also that we want to turn from our sin with new desires now to obey Jesus with our lives.

This is why the Bible sometimes would answer the jailer's question, "Sirs, what must I do to be saved?" (Acts 16:30), by speaking together about turning from our sin (repentance) and believing in Christ. For example, in the very first words of Jesus recorded in Mark's Gospel, Jesus says, "The time is fulfilled, and the kingdom of God is at hand; repent and believe in the gospel" (1:15; see also Acts 20:21). *Repentance* involves seeing sin for the deceitful and deadly thing that it is, so that we turn from it. *Belief* in Christ involves seeing Christ for the gracious and powerful Savior that he is, so that we turn to him. These two acts go together in a person's salvation. Repentance and belief are like two sides of the same coin. You can't have one side of the coin without having the other side also.

Have you ever noticed that whenever you turn, you turn in two ways? Suppose you are walking to go out the front door of your house when you remember you left your house key on the kitchen table. When you turn to go back *to* the kitchen table, you also turn *from* the front door of your house. Every turning to involves a turning from, and every turning from involves a turning to. And this is what saving faith is. It involves turning from the horror of sin because we want to turn solely to Christ in trust and hope. And it involves turning to Christ alone in trust and hope because we now see the ugliness of sin and turn away from it. So, how would you answer the jailer's question? What must you do to be saved?

Questions for Thought

1. To believe in Christ for salvation means to rely completely on what Christ has done in his death and resurrection for my sin, so that my hope of being right in God's sight is *all* because of Christ and has *nothing* to do with any good thing I might ever say or do. Is this really what the Bible teaches? Can you point to some passages to support your answer?

2. How do repentance and faith relate to each other? What role does each of them play in the salvation of a sinner?

Memory Verses

Ephesians 2:8–9—"For by grace you have been saved through faith. And this is not your own doing; it is the gift of God, not a result of works, so that no one may boast."

Declared Right in God's Eyes When We Believe

Have you ever been to a play? If you have, you'll know that a play is quite different from a movie. Plays are performed on stages with live actors and actresses. Most often they tell a story through a series of "acts" that gradually unfold the plot of the story from beginning to end. The plan of salvation in the Bible can also be understood as having a series of acts. Like a play that moves the story forward through its series of Act 1, Act 2, and Act 3, the salvation story of the Bible moves the plan of salvation forward through three acts.

In Act 1, Adam sins in the garden, eating the forbidden fruit, so that his sin is charged not only to him but also to all who have come from Adam (Romans 5:12–19). Just like if you used your dad's credit card to buy something, charging the expense to him, so God charges us with the sin of Adam. In so doing, this brings to Adam and to us both the stain and bondage of sin in our inner lives and the guilt of sin before a holy God.

Act 2 involves God the Father taking all of that sin—both the sin we received from Adam and all of our own sin—and charging that sin to Christ. As we've thought about earlier, when Jesus died on the cross, he bore our sin and took the punishment that we deserved. Even though he was sinless and innocent of any wrongdoing, yet for our salvation, God the Father put our sin on his Son and satisfied his own just wrath against our sin through his Son's death. As Paul states, "For our sake he [God the Father] made him [Christ] to be sin who knew no sin" (2 Corinthians 5:21a).

Act 3 is crucial to the story of salvation, and it involves God the Father now crediting us with the righteousness of his own Son when we put our faith solely in Christ. To credit means to add something positive that increases the value from what was true before. When you deposit money into a savings account, you credit the account by the amount of that deposit, making the account more valuable than it was previously. God does this with sinners who turn to Christ in faith. At the moment that they trust Christ alone for the forgiveness of all of their sins and the only hope they have of receiving eternal life, he credits them with the righteousness of his own Son. The remainder of 2 Corinthians 5:21 makes this point. The whole verse reads, "For our sake he [God the Father] made him [Christ] to be sin who knew no sin, so that in him we might become the righteousness of God."

These three acts in the plan of salvation are sometimes referred to as the three acts of imputation. To impute is either to charge someone with something bad or to credit someone with something good. In Act 1, God imputes (charges) Adam's sin to us. In Act 2, God imputes (charges) our sin to Christ. But in Act 3, God imputes (credits) Christ's righteousness to all those who believe. As you can see, 2 Corinthians 5:21 speaks of the acts of imputation that happen both in Act 2 and in Act 3. God made Christ to be sin—imputing (charging) our sin to his Son—so that we might become the righteousness of God through Christ—imputing (crediting) Christ's righteousness to those who believe. Some have referred to this as "the great exchange." God imputes our sin to Christ, and in exchange God imputes Christ's righteousness to those who believe. That's the greatest exchange that ever could be!

There's something else about Act 3 that we need to understand clearly. When God imputes (credits) the righteousness of Christ to those who believe, those believers are seen by God as righteous. That is, God views them as being in right standing or in good favor before him. But here is something very important: the reason God sees them as righteous is not because their inner lives have been cleaned up and all of their sin removed. No; those who put their faith in Christ continue to have sinful inner lives—they continue to struggle with not always thinking the right thoughts, having the right attitudes, saying the right words, or doing the right things. But if they continue to have sin within them, how can God view them as being in right standing before him? After all, even after they've believed, they are still sinners. The answer is amazing, an answer that is at the heart of what the Christian faith is all about. How can God view sinners as righteous? Answer: because they have been credited with the righteousness of Christ, a righteousness that is not their own, a righteousness that is complete and perfect. Their standing before God is now as sinners who have been forgiven of the guilt of their sin because Christ paid the penalty for their sin on the cross, and they have trusted in Christ's death as their only hope. By faith, then, those who have trusted in Christ are credited with Christ's righteousness. When God looks at them, he sees his Son's perfect righteousness now as theirs, imputed to them by faith.

One of the most surprising statements in all of the Bible is found in Romans 4. Paul writes: "Now to the one who works, his wages are not counted as a gift but as his due. [5] And to the one who does not work but believes in him who justifies the ungodly, his faith is counted as righteousness" (vv. 4–5). Did you notice a surprising, even shocking statement? It's in verse 5, when Paul says that God "justifies the ungodly." To *justify* is to declare that one is righteous or in right standing with God. To *justify* is to make a legal statement, as in a court of law, that someone is innocent of wrongdoing. But notice here that the one whom God justifies—declares to be innocent and righteous—is an ungodly person! How can this be? God himself has made clear that doing such a thing is wrong. Proverbs 17:15 says, "He who justifies the wicked and he who condemns the righteous are both alike an abomination to the LORD." So notice this: in Proverbs 17:15 God says that the one who "justifies the wicked" is an abomination (something God deeply dislikes), and in Romans 4:5 Paul says that God "justifies the ungodly." Why is God not guilty of doing what he considers to be such a bad thing?

The answer hinges on the fact that the ungodly person has been declared righteous *by faith*. Look at Romans 4:5 again: "to the one who does not work but *trusts him* who justifies the ungodly, his *faith* is counted as righteousness." You see, if this ungodly man tried to "work" for his righteousness, he could never receive what he worked to get. No amount of works, even all the good works in the world, could make a sinner righteous before God. But this verse says that the ungodly man "does not work" but instead "believes in" the One who "justifies the ungodly," so that "his faith is counted [credited to him] as righteousness."

In Act 3, then, God credits sinners with the righteousness of Christ when they put their hope and trust in Christ alone. As sinners trust in Christ's work, not their own work, God credits them with Christ's righteousness, not their own righteousness. God declares as righteous those who are still very unrighteous only because they have been given the righteousness of another—the perfect righteousness of Christ. Justified by faith, not by works—this is the heart of what the story of God's salvation plan is all about.

Questions for Thought

1. *Imputation* is a difficult word, but it has a very important meaning in the Bible. What does *imputation* mean, and where in the Bible do you see this idea being used?

2. Why is it true that when God looks at those who have trusted Jesus Christ for the forgiveness of their sin and the hope of eternal life, God sees his Son's perfect righteousness now as theirs?

Memory Verses

Romans 4:4–5—"Now to the one who works, his wages are not counted as a gift but as his due. And to the one who does not work but believes in him who justifies the ungodly, his faith is counted as righteousness."

Made More Like Christ through All of Our Lives

Do you remember talking about different ways that sin has hurt us? The sin that we receive from Adam and the sin we do in our own lives is bad for us in *two ways*. Sin is both a *penalty* that we cannot pay, and sin is a *power* that we cannot overcome. The *penalty* of sin comes in the form of punishment we deserve to pay, a punishment that would never, ever come to an end if we had to pay the penalty for sin ourselves. And the *power* of sin is so strong that we are in slavery to it in this life and are held in its grip of death forever if its power over us is not broken.

But there is good news! God has sent his Son to take care of sin fully for us. The resurrection of Christ from the dead proves that Christ's death on the cross really did do this! The penalty of sin is death, so when Christ rose from the dead, he proved that he had paid sin's penalty fully. And the greatest power of sin is death, so when Christ rose from the dead, he proved that he had conquered sin's power fully. Yes, Jesus truly is the one and only Savior of sinners since he alone has dealt fully with their sin.

But how is this great saving work of Christ applied to the lives of those who have trusted Christ for their salvation? Well, the Bible talks about *two ways* that God works in believers' lives that deal with the *two ways* that sin has hurt them. Through the work of Christ on the cross, God has planned a way to take care of the *penalty* of sin we deserve to pay and a way to take care of the *power* of sin that holds us as its prisoners. Because God wants to save people fully from their sin, he has the perfect answer to both of the problems we face because of our sin—sin as a penalty and sin as a power.

God's way to deal with the *penalty* of sin that we cannot pay is God's plan of justification. Our last section focused on this biblical teaching, showing that God justifies or *declares righteous* those who believe in Christ. Although sin remains in their inner lives, when God looks at them, he sees his Son's perfect righteousness now as theirs, imputed (charged) to them by faith. When we are justified by faith, we no longer stand before

God as guilty, deserving to pay sin's penalty. Christ has paid our penalty fully, and we receive his payment and his righteousness when we believe, even though sin remains in our lives.

But God does not want sin to continue always in our lives. So God's way to deal with the *power* of sin that we cannot overcome is God's plan of sanctification. The term *sanctification* means to be set apart or separate, to be different, to be holy. In sanctification, God goes to work in our lives to overpower sin's power, to bring to an end sin's control, to free us from sin's slavery. God separates us from sin's complete control of our lives as we are separated unto God, in Christ. So, God has planned not only to save us from the penalty of sin through justification by faith, God has also planned to save us from the power of sin as he separates us unto himself, in his Son, making us more and more like Christ. Here God's work is not to declare us as righteous (that is done in justification) but to *make us righteous*. God works to remove our sin and make us like his Son, making us the holy and happy people he planned for us to be.

God's work of sanctification—setting his people apart to himself through their being in Christ—is a work that goes on throughout the whole lifetime of believers. God is determined to make his people a truly holy people, to remove sin from their lives. He will not stop until this is finished. But he doesn't finish it all at once. Instead, his work of sanctifying them—making them more like Christ and less like the sinful world we live in—is a work he continues to do in them every day until they are with him in heaven.

It is helpful to think in two ways of God's work to remove sin from our lives, making us more like Christ. First, at the very moment that a sinner puts faith in Christ to be saved, God separates that person from the control of Satan and frees that person from slavery to sin. God does this as he places that person instead in Christ. You might say, then, that a person's position changes when he trusts in Christ. Paul writes about God separating us from slavery to sin and Satan and bringing us into the wonderful rule of Christ over our lives. He gives thanks to God the Father because "he has delivered us from the domain of darkness and transferred us to the kingdom of his beloved Son, in whom we have redemption, the forgiveness of sins" (Colossians 1:13–14). What a wonderful truth to think deeply about and take in. The very instant that someone puts his or her faith in Christ for salvation, that person moves. No longer is that person in the place where sin and Satan rule but is now in a new place where Christ rules in his glorious kingdom.

The fact that believers have been transferred from the rule of Satan to the rule of Christ cannot be more true tomorrow than it is the day they first believed. It's like moving from California to Illinois, or Texas to Maryland. Once you've moved to your new home state, you can't be more in your new state tomorrow than you are today. You've moved. You don't live where you used to live. You are living in a completely different area. So it is when we trust in Christ. We've moved! God moves us out of the area of Satan's hateful control and into the beautiful realm of Christ's wise and loving control. Our position has changed, and it cannot change back.

We might call this way in which we are separated from Satan and unto Christ our *positional* sanctification. Our position has changed. We are not where we used to be, and we are not what we used to be. Things have changed that are permanent and can't be changed back. Besides the Bible's teaching that we are transferred into the kingdom of Christ when we believe, there are other ways we see that our position has changed. For example, at the moment a sinner trusts in Christ for salvation, that sinner is now a new creation in Christ; old things have passed away, and new things have come from God (2 Corinthians 5:17–18). The believer is now a temple of the Holy Spirit, whom he has received from God (1 Corinthians 6:19). He has died and been raised with Christ, so that sin can no longer have complete control over his life (Romans 6:3–7). And he now knows that he was chosen by God before the foundation of the world, predestined to be adopted into God's own family (Ephesians 1:4–5). For sure, then, a believer's position before God changes in amazing ways the moment he trusts Christ alone for his salvation.

The second way we should think of God's work to remove sin from our lives, making us more like Christ, might be called *progressive* sanctification. This involves God's daily work in us, helping us to turn from sin and become more like Christ day by day. God has given us tools to help us grow. The Bible is the actual Word of God, and its truth can work powerfully to change how we think, how we feel, and how we live. Giving much attention to reading the Bible and hearing it faithfully preached can bring about great growth in our lives. Prayer is a very important tool that God uses to help us understand how much we need God, how dependent we are on God. And the fellowship of other believers can give us comfort, encouragement, correction, and instruction to see better how Christ would have us live. Through these and other tools, God works to make us more like Christ and to defeat completely the power of sin over our lives. So, sin's *penalty* is removed by justification; sin's *power* is removed by sanctification. Praise God for saving sinners so well!

Questions for Thought

1. What is the main difference between justification and sanctification? Is one more important than the other? Which matters more to sinners who need to be saved from their sin?

2. What kinds of activities are needed for growth in progressive sanctification? That is, what kinds of things should a follower of Christ be doing to help him or her grow to become more like Christ?

Memory Verses

> Colossians 1:13–14—"He [God the Father] has delivered us from the domain of darkness and transferred us to the kingdom of his beloved Son, in whom we have redemption, the forgiveness of sins."

Saved *by* Good Works? No— Saved *for* Good Works? Yes

I f anything is clear from the teaching of the New Testament, it is this: sinners are saved by faith, not by works. In the earliest days of the church, just after Jesus went back to his Father, some Jews who had believed in Jesus taught something different. They taught that along with trusting in Jesus, you still had to keep the Law and do certain good works that would bring you into right relationship with God (see Acts 15:1–5). The apostles of Jesus argued strongly against this teaching. No, we are saved not by doing works of the Law, but only and completely by putting our full trust in Jesus and in his death on the cross for our sins. We are saved by faith and not by any good works that we might do, they insisted (see Romans 3:19–22; Galatians 2:15–16).

So now a very important question might be asked: since we are saved by faith and not by doing good works, is there any place in the Christian life for these good works? Maybe Christians should think of good works as a bad thing, as strange as that sounds. For if we are saved by faith, and if we should not bring good works into how we are saved, then maybe good works don't belong at all. Could this be?

A very important passage that can help us answer this question is Ephesians 2:8–10. We've looked already at verses 8–9, verses that make it clear that we are saved by God's grace, through faith in Christ, and not at all by any good things that we do. These verses say, "For by grace you have been saved through faith. And this is not your own doing; it is the gift of God, 9 not a result of works, so that no one may boast." The teaching here could not be any clearer. We cannot do anything to add to what Christ has done for us or else we would be able to "boast" or brag that we've helped save ourselves. No, we cannot help in saving ourselves. All we can do to be saved—in fact, what we *must* do—is to accept by faith the gift of salvation that God gives us by his grace, by his kindness to those who don't deserve any bit of it. So as we've seen before, we are saved by grace through faith and not by any good works we might do.

But many people stop reading at this point and miss what Paul says next in verse 10. Here he writes, "For we are his workmanship, created in Christ Jesus for good works, which God prepared beforehand, that we should walk in them." Isn't it amazing that right after Paul made it so very clear that good works have nothing to do with how we are saved, the very next thing he says is that believers were "created in Christ Jesus *for good works*"? We might think of what Paul is saying this way: while we are not saved at all *by good works* that we do (2:8–9), we are saved *for good works*, works that God has prepared for us to do (2:10). Or this: while good works have nothing to do with *why* we have been saved, good works truly show *that* we have been saved. And this: while good works are not the *reason* or the *basis* for our salvation, good works are the *outworking* or *demonstration* of our salvation.

This idea is found in a number of places in the New Testament. For example, Paul writes to Titus: "For the grace of God has appeared, bringing salvation for all people, 12 training us to renounce ungodliness and worldly passions, and to live self-controlled, upright, and godly lives in the present age, 13 waiting for our blessed hope, the appearing of the glory of our great God and Savior Jesus Christ, 14 who gave himself for us to redeem us from all lawlessness and to purify for himself a people for his own possession who are zealous for good works" (Titus 2:11–14).

According to this passage, those who are truly saved have been given God's grace and power to show that they are saved in two ways. They should live in a way that shows they are turning away from the sinful attitudes and actions with which the world tempts them.

This is what Paul means when he says that God's grace in salvation is training believers "to renounce ungodliness and worldly passions" (v. 11) and turn away from "lawlessness" (v. 14). So, just as we turn from sin when we first come to Christ to be saved, so believers continue to turn from sin in their Christian lives, showing that God's grace and power continue to work within them. Paul's main point, though, is a positive one. The main thing Paul wants Titus and other believers to see is this: Christ's saving work involves changes in believers' lives so that they not only seek to live in ways that please God, but even more, they have a deep desire or a passion to do the good works God has called them to do. Paul expresses both of these truths together in verse 14 where he says that Christ "gave himself for us to redeem us from all lawlessness [turn away from doing what is bad] and to purify for himself a people for his own possession who are zealous for good works [deeply desiring to do what is good]."

So we see that good works, then, are a very important part of the Christian life. While we are not saved *by* good works, we definitely are saved *for* good works. But some might wonder, can we take or leave good works in the Christian life? Isn't it true that once we are saved, it doesn't matter whether we do good works or not, since no matter how we live we'll still be in heaven in the end? This is a very hard question to answer because it says something that is partly true, but also something that is very, very wrong.

What is partly true is this: once we trust Christ alone for the forgiveness of our sins and the hope of eternal life, we can never lose our salvation or have our salvation taken from us. Sometimes this is stated with the phrase, *once saved, always saved*. And this is true. Many passages of Scripture teach this. For example, Jesus says, "For this is the will of my Father, that everyone who looks on the Son and believes in him should have eternal life, and I will raise him up on the last day" (John 6:40). To say that someone may truly believe in Christ and not be raised up to eternal life would be to say that Jesus was wrong. But Jesus is never wrong! So, all who truly believe will have eternal life and will be raised up to be with Christ. And Romans 8:30 says, "those whom he [God] predestined he also called, and those whom he called he also justified, and those whom he justified he also glorified." The key part right now is that last phrase, that all of those whom God justified he also glorified. This means that every person who truly puts faith in Christ alone for salvation and is justified (see Romans 5:1) will also be made fully like Christ ("glorified"). There is no one, then, who is truly saved (justified) who will not be made fully like Christ (glorified). If you wish, look also at these passages: John 10:27–29; Romans 8:31–39; 1 Corinthians 1:8–9; Ephesians 1:13–14; Philippians 1:6; 1 Thessalonians 5:23–24; and 1 Peter 1:3–5. Yes, the Bible is clear. God will save in the end those who truly have trusted in Christ for their salvation.

But does this mean that it doesn't matter how we live? Absolutely not! Why? Because when we are truly saved, God begins a new work in our hearts and inner lives, giving us power to turn more and more from sin and to desire more and more to please him. If we say that we have trusted Christ, but we have no desire to obey Christ or please Christ or do the good works God wants us to do, then it may be that we have not truly trusted Christ. We are saved for good works, and those good works will begin to show more and more in the lives of Christ's real followers. So, do good works have a place in the Christian life? Yes, they do. Good works, done in God's power, please God and show that we really belong to him.

Questions for Thought

1. We are not saved *by* good works, but we are saved *for* good works. Can you explain these important biblical ideas in your own words?

2. Jesus promises that the person who believes in him will have eternal life and that he will raise that person up on the last day (John 6:40). If a person has trusted Christ as Savior, does it matter how he lives? Does it still matter whether he grows in becoming more like Christ? Does it matter if he grows in doing good works?

Memory Verses

Titus 2:11–14—"For the grace of God has appeared, bringing salvation for all people, training us to renounce ungodliness and worldly passions, and to live self-controlled, upright, and godly lives in the present age, waiting for our blessed hope, the appearing of the glory of our great God and Savior Jesus Christ, who gave himself for us to redeem us from all lawlessness and to purify for himself a people for his own possession who are zealous for good works."

But Must People Know about and Believe in Christ to Be Saved?

Anumber of people in our day, some of them Christians, are asking questions like this: "Can God rightly hold people responsible for their sin if they have never heard the gospel? How would it be fair for God to judge them when they never had a chance to hear?" Or, "Is it possible that those who have never heard of Christ or the gospel might be accepted by God some other way? Maybe God knows that their hearts are seeking him, and so he will save them. It just doesn't seem fair that people must hear about Christ in order to be saved since so many never do."

Some who claim to be Christians and who claim to follow the Bible agree with what these kinds of questions and ideas are suggesting. Some, in fact, are writing books defending the idea that people who have never heard of Christ may be saved by faith in God as they believe him to be from creation or from their own religion and culture. All people, they insist, are saved by Christ, but people don't have to actually believe in Christ to be saved. So, even though Christ is the only Savior, they argue, people can be made right with God even if they do not know about Christ or believe in Christ to be saved.

This is a very important question for us to think hard about. Are there good reasons from the Bible for thinking that faith in Christ is necessary to be saved? That is, does the Bible teach that people are really lost and without hope unless they learn the gospel of Christ and trust in Christ for the forgiveness of their sins? Or is God at work saving people around the world who have never heard of Christ by some way other than through knowing and believing in Christ?

We will look at some of the Bible's teaching to support the idea that people must learn about Christ and his death and resurrection and believe in what Christ has done for them in order to be forgiven of their sins and saved. Consider the following biblical teachings, then, that support the conviction that people are saved *only* as they know about and trust in Christ as their Savior.

1. Jesus' own teaching shows that the nations need to hear and repent to be saved (Luke 24:44–49). Look with me at what Jesus says in Luke 24:46–47: "Thus it is written, that the Christ should suffer and on the third day rise from the dead, ⁴⁷ and that repentance and forgiveness of sins should be proclaimed in his name to all nations, beginning from Jerusalem." Here are some very important questions from this short passage (note: look again carefully at the passage to answer each question): 1) What is the present condition of people, as Jesus describes them here? Answer: unforgiven and unrepentant sinners. And since they are still in their sin, they are not saved. 2) What must happen for them to be forgiven (saved)? Answer: they must repent of their sin. 3) What is needed for them to repent of their sin so they can be forgiven and saved? Answer: a proclamation is needed that calls them to repent. 4) What is the content of the proclamation? Answer: they are to hear a proclamation "in his name"; so the content must be about Jesus who suffered and rose on the third day (see verse 46 for a summary of the content of this proclamation). 5) Finally, to whom does all this apply? That is, who are these unrepentant and unforgiven sinners who need to repent to be saved but who can only repent as they hear a proclamation of Christ and the gospel? Answer: "all nations, beginning from Jerusalem." Jesus does not consider the vast numbers of people making up the "nations" as already having saving revelation available to them. Rather, believers must proclaim the message of Christ to all the nations for people in those nations to be saved. So all people in all the nations, even those in Jerusalem who have the Law of Moses and the whole Old Testament, need to hear about Christ in order to repent, to be forgiven, to be saved.

2. Paul teaches that even devout Jews, and everyone else, must hear and believe in Christ to be saved (Romans 10:1–4, 13–15). In Romans 10:1–4, Paul expresses his heart's desire and prayer for the salvation of his fellow Jews. This is amazing because even though they have the Law and a zeal for God, they are not saved. Why? They do not know that God's righteousness comes only through faith in Christ. So these Jews, even though religious and devoted to God, are not saved. But whoever will call upon the name of Christ (see Romans 10:9 along with Romans 10:13) will be saved. The line of reasoning in Romans 10:13–15 should not be missed. Here Paul writes: "For 'everyone who calls on the name of the Lord will be saved.' ¹⁴ How then will they call on him in whom they have not believed? And how are they to believe in him of whom they have never heard? And how are they to hear without someone preaching? ¹⁵

And how are they to preach unless they are sent? As it is written, 'How beautiful are the feet of those who preach the good news!'" It could not be more clear! Moving in the opposite direction from what Paul said, we conclude this: someone must send, for someone to go, for someone to preach, for another to hear, then to believe, and then to call upon the Lord to be saved. If even devout Jews who have the Law and a zeal for God must hear about and believe in Christ to be saved, the other peoples of the world surely also need the same. Missions, then, is necessary, since people must hear the gospel of Christ and trust in Christ to be saved.

3. Cornelius's story demonstrates that even devout Gentiles must hear and believe in Christ to be saved (Acts 10:1–2, 38–43; 11:13–18; 15:7–9). Far from being saved before Peter came to him, as some think, Cornelius was a very "devout" and religious Gentile (10:2) who needed to hear about Christ and believe in Christ to be saved. When Peter finally came to Cornelius's home, the very last part of his sermon, before the Holy Spirit came upon Cornelius, was nothing other than the gospel of Christ. Peter spoke these words: "And he [Christ] commanded us to preach to the people and to testify that he is the one appointed by God to be judge of the living and the dead. [43] To him all the prophets bear witness that everyone who believes in him receives forgiveness of sins through his name" (Acts 10:42–43). Notice that Peter ended by clearly stating that those who believe in Christ receive forgiveness of their sins. Most surely, then, at that very moment Cornelius believed in Christ, as Peter had said, and he was then saved. But we don't have to wonder if this is so since the next chapter in Acts confirms that this is what happened. When Peter later reported about the conversion of the Gentiles, he says that only when he preached did Cornelius hear the message that he needed to hear by which he would "be saved" (Acts 11:14; cf. 15:8–9). Even though Cornelius was religious and pious, he needed to hear the proclamation of the gospel of Christ to be saved. God sent Peter to Cornelius precisely for this reason, and so it is the case with all unsaved people of our day, pious or not. The gospel of Christ is good news. And people need to hear this gospel and trust in Christ alone for their salvation.

Conclusion: Jesus is the only Savior, and people must know and believe in Christ to be saved. May we honor Christ and the gospel and show forth our faithfulness to God's Word by upholding both of these important truths. And may the Spirit grow strong desires within our hearts to see that the gospel of Christ is proclaimed to the peoples of this world. The gospel is true, Christ alone is Savior, and sinners must hear and believe in Christ to be saved; so the task of missions is mandatory. This is so simple but so powerful. By God's grace, let's live as those who believe it.

Questions for Thought

1. How does the story of Cornelius (Acts 10) help us understand that even if a person is religious, that person still needs to hear about Jesus and believe in Jesus to be saved?

2. If the Bible teaches that people must hear about Christ in order to believe in Christ to be saved, what does that tell us about the importance of sharing the gospel and going to other countries as missionaries?

Memory Verses

> Romans 10:13–15—"For 'everyone who calls on the name of the Lord will be saved.' How then will they call on him in whom they have not believed? And how are they to believe in him of whom they have never heard? And how are they to hear without someone preaching? And how are they to preach unless they are sent? As it is written, 'How beautiful are the feet of those who preach the good news!'"

9

The Church of Jesus Christ

Jesus Is the Lord of the Church

Sometimes we talk about churches in funny ways. We might refer to a church as "our family's church" or "Pastor Smith's church" or even "my church." Of course, it isn't wrong to talk this way, as long as we realize this: if a church really is a church, then it doesn't belong to a family or to a pastor or to me as a member. All real churches, and the whole church from the beginning, belong to one Person—the Lord Jesus Christ. He alone is the Lord of the church.

You can hear this in Jesus' teaching to his disciples. After it was revealed to Peter that Jesus was "the Christ [that is, the anointed One, the Messiah], the Son of the living God" (Matthew 16:16), Jesus looked at Peter and said, "you are Peter, and on this rock I will build my church, and the gates of hell shall not prevail against it" (Matthew 16:18). Jesus could not have been clearer. "I will build my church" means that the church belongs to Jesus alone ("I will build *my church*"), and he will not fail to build it as he chooses ("*I will build* my church"). To make sure we understand that nothing can stand in his way in building the church as he chooses, he adds, "and the gates of hell shall not prevail against it." Satan and all of his demons simply cannot keep Christ from building his church exactly as he has planned and decided. Yes, the church belongs to Jesus, for Jesus is the Lord of the church.

All of the examples in the New Testament for the church show that Jesus has the highest place over the church. Since the church is his and he is Lord of the church, he is shown as most important. For example, in John 10 the church is said to be like sheep that need to be fed and watered, sheep that also need protection from dangerous wolves. Are these sheep on their own, to fend for themselves and to protect each other if a wolf enters? No; along with the sheep is "the good shepherd" who leads them to find pasture and protects them from the wolves (vv. 7–15). This good shepherd cares so much for his sheep that he even "lays down his own life for the sheep" (vv. 11, 15). Even though it will cost the life of the shepherd himself, he proves that he is truly the "good" shepherd since he protects and cares for them, even to the point of giving his life for them.

But there is one more truth in John 10 we should not miss. What is the one thing that the sheep are supposed to do? Answer: hear the voice of the shepherd and follow. The shepherd leads, and the sheep follow. The shepherd provides food and water, and the sheep eat and drink as the shepherd directs. The shepherd protects against danger, and the sheep trust and follow the shepherd. As Jesus says of the shepherd, "The sheep hear his voice, and he calls his own sheep by name and leads them out. [4] When he has brought out all his own, he goes before them, and the sheep follow him, for they know his voice" (vv. 3–4).

A number of years ago I traveled with a group to Israel. One day we stopped for lunch on the side of a hill with a deep valley in front of us. Hundreds of sheep grazed below. I noticed that each sheep had a colored spot on the wool of its neck. Some sheep had a green spot and others a red spot, but these sheep were all mixed together as they looked for grass to eat. I had not noticed at first that two shepherds were sitting on a rock, talking, at the base of the valley. All of a sudden the shepherds got up, walked in opposite directions, and each made a sound, calling his sheep. I was amazed at what I saw next! Even though all the "greenish" sheep were mixed in with the "reddish" sheep, when the two shepherds called, the sheep separated. All of the sheep with green spots turned one direction, following one shepherd. And all of the sheep with red spots turned the opposite direction, following the other shepherd. Yes, sheep do hear the voice of their shepherd, and they follow. Pretty simple, isn't it—and what a good lesson for Christians who are part of the church. Since Jesus is our Good Shepherd, we are called to do one thing all the time, under all circumstances, no matter what we may think or how we may feel: we must hear and follow the voice of our Shepherd. Jesus is the Shepherd, and we are the sheep. It would be a really good thing if we remembered which is which.

Another way the church is pictured is as a bride, with Christ as the bridegroom. To a group of believers whom he led to Christ, Paul writes, "I betrothed you to one husband, to present you as a pure virgin to Christ. [3] But I am afraid that as the serpent deceived Eve by his cunning, your thoughts will be led astray from a sincere and pure devotion to Christ" (2 Corinthians 11:2–3). One of the most important parts of this picture of the church is her call to be pure. After all, the very name *church* literally means "called out ones." We are people called out of the sin and rebellion of the world to be devoted completely to Christ. In human relationships, a young woman should keep herself pure for her husband on their wedding day. In the same way, Paul longs for these believers to turn from other attractions and keep themselves "sincere and pure" in their devotion to Christ.

Since Christ is to become the husband to his bride, the church, we who make up the church are to submit to him as a wife submits to her husband (Ephesians 5:24). After all, the day of our marriage is coming. We're told at the end of the book of Revelation about the wonderful and joyous day when the church will be clothed in white for her marriage to Christ. Seeing this day in the future, John writes, "'Let us rejoice and exult and give him the glory, for the marriage of the Lamb has come, and his Bride has made herself ready; 8 it was granted her to clothe herself with fine linen, bright and pure'—for the fine linen is the righteous deeds of the saints. 9 And the angel said to me, 'Write this: Blessed are those who are invited to the marriage supper of the Lamb.' And he said to me, 'These are the true words of God'" (Revelation 19:7–9). What great motivation for devotion to Christ and purity of life now as we await the day when we will be joined to Christ forever.

One final picture of the church will help us see, again, that Christ has the highest position over the church, as Lord of the church. Often the church is spoken of as the body of Christ. Of course, this picture includes the idea that each member of the body needs all the other members, as Paul says in 1 Corinthians 12:12–26. But another very important part of this picture relates to Christ's position in the body. Christ is the head of the church, showing that he is Lord over the church. He directs the church forward, to grow and to become what he wants it to be. Paul refers to Christ's headship when he writes that God the Father has "put all things under his [Christ's] feet and gave him as head over all things to the church, 23 which is his body, the fullness of him who fills all in all" (Ephesians 1:22–23). His authority over all things in creation is for the purpose of reigning over the church. What an amazing thought. As he sits at the right hand of the Father (see Ephesians 1:20) with everything subjected to him, Christ has complete control of all things for the sake of his body, the church. What confidence we can have that Christ will build his church, just as he said. Hell or Satan or demons or human kings or presidents cannot keep the Lord of the church from doing as he has purposed and planned. So remember, the church where you worship may in one sense be your church, but more accurately, it is Christ's church.

Questions for Thought

1. What is involved in Jesus' statement in Matthew 16:18, "I will build my church"? What does this tell us about the importance of the church, as God views things?

2. What are some pictures of the church in the New Testament that help us understand how Christ is the Lord of his church? How do these pictures of the church talk about Christ? How do they talk about Christ's people?

Memory Verse

Matthew 16:18—"And I tell you, you are Peter, and on this rock I will build my church, and the gates of hell shall not prevail against it."

A People of the New Covenant

Have you ever had to sign a piece of paper saying that you agreed to do certain things? Maybe it was a form for school saying that if you got injured playing sports, you wouldn't blame the school for what happened. Or maybe you've been with your mom or dad when they signed an agreement for buying a car or your house. An agreement like this is between two people or two groups of people, and it tries to say very clearly what each person or group has agreed to do, as well as what will happen if one party or the other doesn't do what he or she or they said.

In the Bible, there are a number of agreements that take place between God and his people that are sort of like this. These agreements are often called covenants. They say what God's people are responsible to do before God, and they also state what God promises he will do. Sometimes they also make clear what will happen if God's people do not do what the covenant says they must do. There is one big difference, though, between most human agreements and the covenants in the Bible. The covenants are drawn up or stated by God without asking for his people's ideas about how they think things should be. In other words, God does not negotiate with his people.

The requirements and promises of the covenants in the Bible do not come about as God and his people discuss what we all think would be best. No, God decides *period*. After all, he is God! And whatever God has decided, his people must do. This is how God's covenants with his people work.

There's one covenant in the Old Testament that was especially important to the everyday lives of the people of Israel. After God delivered his people from their slavery in Egypt, he took them into the wilderness where God spoke to Moses on a mountain. God gave Moses the Law, including the Ten Commandments (Exodus 20), which Israel was commanded to carry out. God made it clear that if they obeyed this Law, they would receive great blessing from God. But if they disobeyed the Law, God would bring horrible punishment upon them (see Leviticus 26; Deuteronomy 28–30). This law, sometimes called the Law of Moses or the Mosaic Covenant, gave very clear and detailed instructions for the people's lives. It taught them how God was to be worshipped, what they should do when they sinned, and how to treat each other and their neighbors.

But throughout the history of the people of Israel, sadly they often turned away from the Law and disobeyed what God had told them. And just as God had warned, when they disobeyed day after day, year after year, God brought punishment to them. The greatest forms of God's punishment came when he raised up two different nations to come and almost wipe out his own people, Israel. The Assyrians fought against the northern tribes of Israel and took them captive in 722 B.C. Later God raised up the Babylonians who came against the tribes of the southern kingdom of Judah and took them captive, destroying the wall and the Temple of Jerusalem itself in 586 B.C. How very sad. God had said that if his people would obey his Law, he would keep all these nations away from them and grant them unspeakable blessing. But they refused to obey. So God did as he warned and punished this people whom he had chosen.

God's plans for his people were not ruined, though. You see, even though Israel disobeyed, God knew that they would. He planned all along to replace this Old Covenant, the Mosaic Covenant, with "a new covenant." In Jeremiah 31:31–34, God promises a day when he will no longer write the demands of his Law on tablets of stone but will write it on the hearts of his people. When the Law becomes a part of their very inner lives, then they will choose to keep the Law. They will delight in doing God's will and will find joy in obeying his Word. This new covenant that takes the place of the Law of Moses is a covenant that God's people will keep. And because they will keep this covenant, all of the blessings that God had promised for his people will finally be theirs.

So as it turns out, the Law of the Old Covenant, the Law of Moses, was intended by God to show his people the sin of their own hearts. God knew that they could not keep the Law since their own sin would urge them to break the Law. Paul makes this point in Romans 7 when he talks about what happened when the Law was given. He comments that "if it had not been for the law, I would not have known sin. For I would not have known what it is to covet if the law had not said, 'You shall not covet.' [8] But sin, seizing an opportunity through the commandment, produced in me all kinds of covetousness. For apart from the law, sin lies dead" (Romans 7:7–8). Why did God give the Law then? Paul answers this in another place, saying it was given to expose the sin and transgressions of our lives, to teach us how much we need Christ and his work on the cross to free us from our sin (Galatians 3:19–25). The Law could not bring God's people righteousness and newness of life, Paul says. Nor did God ever think that it would. Paul writes, "[I]f a law had been given that could give life, then righteousness would indeed be by the law. [22] But the Scripture imprisoned everything under sin, so that the promise by faith in Jesus Christ might be given to those who believe" (Galatians 3:21–22).

The church of Jesus Christ, then, is not under the Law of Moses, a law that sinners cannot keep on their own. Rather, the church is under the New Covenant in which God writes his laws and commands on our hearts. His Spirit works within the hearts of believers to remake their inner lives so that they learn to love the things of God. Over time the Spirit gives God's people new tastes, new longings, new desires, so that what they want to do is what God wants them to do. The New Covenant, then, is kept only because the Spirit works within believers' lives to make them, day by day, grow more in wanting to follow God's ways.

In a helpful passage, Paul explains this so well. He writes, "For God has done what the law, weakened by the flesh, could not do. By sending his own Son in the likeness of sinful flesh and for sin, he condemned sin in the flesh, [4] in order that the righteous requirement of the law might be fulfilled in us, who walk not according to the flesh but according to the Spirit" (Romans 8:3–4). Because of the sin of our inner lives (our "flesh"), we did not want to keep God's Law. So God sent his Son to forgive our sin (sin's penalty is paid) and to break its hold on us (sin's power is conquered), so that by faith we would receive Christ's work in our lives. Jesus sends us his Spirit for this very purpose, to give us power we did not have before. By breaking the control of sin and by giving us the Spirit's new power, we grow in becoming able to live in obedience to what God commands us. By the Spirit, not by our own efforts, we grow to become more like Christ and live more pleasing to the Lord.

Aren't you glad that the church is under the New Covenant and not the Old? Under the Law of Moses, God's people were told the right way to live (Romans 7:12), but they could not do what they were told. By the works of the Law, they could not please God. But now in the New Covenant, God has given his Son to die for their sin and has given his Spirit to bring power to their lives. By God's gracious work, God's people can grow in obedience and holiness. What hope there is for Christ's church! What joy to be a people of the New Covenant!

Questions for Thought

1. What is a covenant? How do covenants work to help explain how God relates to his people at different times throughout history?

2. What is the heart of the "new covenant" that God has made with his own people? How is it different from the "old covenant" (the Law of Moses)? Why is it such wonderful news that those who are part of the church are under this new covenant?

Memory Verses

> Romans 8:3–4—"For God has done what the law, weakened by the flesh, could not do. By sending his own Son in the likeness of sinful flesh and for sin, he condemned sin in the flesh, in order that the righteous requirement of the law might be fulfilled in us, who walk not according to the flesh but according to the Spirit."

Communities of Christians Who Worship and Serve Together

The books of the New Testament were written in the Greek language. The word *church* in our English Bibles is a translation of the Greek word *ekklesia*. This word comes from two Greek words joined together—

kaleo meaning "to call" and *ek* meaning "out"—so that the word *church* really refers to those who are "called out" by God to join together as his people, the followers of his Son. Sometimes *church* is used of all of the followers of Jesus from the very first disciples down to today. For example, when Jesus said, "I will build my church" (Matthew 16:18), he did not have in mind some specific local church on the corner of First and Main Streets in Jerusalem. No, he meant that he would build together all of those, in all of the years to come, who would be his followers, the members of his body. Or when Paul said that he was unworthy to be called an apostle because he "persecuted the church of God" (1 Corinthians 15:9; Galatians 1:13), he did not mean that he went after Christians from one local church only. Rather, Paul (Saul) sought to bring an end to all Christians everywhere. Sometimes the term *universal church* is used for this wider meaning, the church seen as all true Christians from the time of Christ to today, from all places in the world (see also 1 Corinthians 10:32; 12:28; Ephesians 3:10; Colossians 1:24).

But *church* is more often used in a narrower way, referring to specific gatherings or communities of Christians who meet together regularly for worship and for service. Sometimes the term *local church* is used for these individual gatherings of Christians in specific places. Paul writes, for example, "to the church of God that is in Corinth" (1 Corinthians 1:2) and to "to the churches of Galatia" (Galatians 1:2) and "to the church of the Thessalonians" (1 Thessalonians 1:1). As he closes his letter to the Colossians, Paul sends a greeting to "Nympha and the church in her house" (Colossians 4:15).

Why does it matter that we think of the church in both its wider and narrower ways? A couple of reasons come to mind. First, we should understand that there are many more Christians, many more true followers of Christ, than those who meet in any of our own local churches. Whether you go to a large or small church, still there are millions more Christians who have been true and faithful followers of Jesus throughout history and across the world. It is important to know that we are part of this larger church even though we don't know most of those people. But as we know from Revelation 5:9 and 7:9–10, when all Christians are gathered together in the end before the throne of Christ, there will be people there from every tribe, language, people group, and nation. What strength and joy it will be to know the large gathering of the full church when Christ has completed the building of his church.

But, second, it also matters that we think of the church as specific local communities of Christians who gather together on a regular basis to worship God and to serve both God and one another. You see, Christians cannot sing songs of praise and gather to worship God in the universal church—where would they meet? And Christians cannot hear the Bible taught and proclaimed in the universal church—who would teach and preach? And Christians cannot gather to baptize new followers of Christ or take the Lord's Supper in the universal church—how could this happen? Rather, Christians must meet in smaller local gatherings to sing, pray, worship, hear preaching, be baptized, take the Lord's Supper, serve one another, hold each other accountable, and urge one another to love and do good deeds.

Meeting in local churches is important to the life and well-being of all Christians. The writer to the Hebrews was concerned throughout his letter to encourage Christian people to remain faithful to Christ to the end. Many of these followers of Christ were being persecuted, and some were leaving the Christian faith to avoid suffering. Others left Christ simply because they wanted to fit in with those around them. So, this writer is deeply concerned that Christian people are helped to grow in their faith and to stand against the many temptations to leave Christ for the world. In light of this deep concern for faithfulness to Christ, these words are so very important: "Let us hold fast the confession of our hope without wavering, for he who promised is faithful. 24 And let us consider how to stir up one another to love and good works, 25 not neglecting to meet together, as is the habit of some, but encouraging one another, and all the more as you see the Day drawing near" (Hebrews 10:23–25). Sometimes you hear Christian people say that they have "church" by themselves out in the woods or walking along a beach. But this simply is not "church." Such times alone with the Lord, enjoying the beauty of creation and praying quietly to him, can be encouraging and calming and beneficial in many ways. But this is no substitute for gathering together on a regular basis with other Christians. Why? Much could be said, but let me suggest two main answers.

First, Christians gather together to *worship* God in communities of faith. While worship is sometimes private and silent, worship in the Bible also requires the regular gathering of God's people to do what can only happen when they come together (Acts 2:42). Christians can grow much and can encourage others to grow in Christ as they participate in different parts of the worship of God. Meeting together, Christians grow as they participate in singing hymns and songs of praise, as they pray for one another and for needs in many places, as they listen to the reading of God's Word week by week, and as they hear the Scriptures faithfully taught and preached. God has chosen to use these gatherings of local churches as one of his main ways to encourage his people to be faithful and to teach them more about himself and his ways. No wonder the writer to the Hebrews is grieved that some have made a habit of "neglecting to meet together." We need what God has planned to bring to his people only as they gather in local churches. The prayer, preaching, teaching, singing, fellowship, encouragement, accountability, and other parts of church worship provide us much that we need for resisting temptation and following Christ. Yes, much is at stake in our regular participation in a strong and faithful local church.

Second, Christians gather together to *serve* God especially as they serve one another in local communities of Christian people. Each Christian is given some spiritual gift or other, and every one of these gifts of the Spirit (there are no exceptions) is given "for the common good" (1 Corinthians 12:7). While God could have chosen to do all of his work in each of us by himself, as it were, he didn't. Instead God chose to do a large part of his work in you and me through the gifts he has given to others. Likewise, God has gifted you and me as believers so that we will use our gifts in serving other people. We rob ourselves of being served by others, and we rob others of how we could serve them, when we neglect to meet together regularly in our local churches. And, of course, all of this shows the importance not only of regular gatherings, but even more, of committing ourselves to one another as members of local churches. Membership in a local church matters because only then can we know those who have made commitments to love each other, pray for one another, encourage and even confront each other, and in everything help each other grow more in Christ. The church is Christ's body, his bride, his flock. And local churches are God's means of seeing the universal church grow to be all that Christ has planned that it should be.

Questions for Thought

1. Why is it important for Christians to meet together regularly in local churches? What can be accomplished in local churches that cannot be done by Christians on their own who don't meet regularly in churches?

2. How are the activities of worshipping God and serving God greatly affected by the kind of local churches in which Christians gather together? What are some characteristics that should mark local churches that are being true to what the Bible wants them to be?

Memory Verses

> Acts 2:41–42—"So those who received his word were baptized, and there were added that day about three thousand souls. And they devoted themselves to the apostles' teaching and the fellowship, to the breaking of bread and the prayers."

Baptism: Picturing Jesus' Death and Resurrection

Jesus gave his followers two practices, two lived-out pictures, that show what it means to believe in the Son of God who died and rose again to save them from their sin. Both of these practices were commanded by Christ for his people to carry out; so they are often referred to as *ordinances* of the church. This simply means that Jesus ordained or charged his followers to continue to do both of these throughout the life of the church. Baptism is the ordinance Christ gave to be carried out when a person first puts his or her trust in Christ for salvation, at the beginning of new life in Christ. The Lord's Supper was ordained by Christ to be carried out throughout a believer's life along with other believers within local churches. What they have in common is that both of them picture in quite different ways something of the meaning of Christ's death and resurrection for sinners. It is clear that Christ wants his people to have constant reminders of the greatest event that has ever happened in human history. And he wants them to remember that by faith they now are joined together with Christ in his death and resurrection for sin so that they now live new lives in Christ. Yes, the gospel of Jesus' death and resurrection should always be in the front of our minds as believers as we recall what Christ did for us and who we now are in Christ.

Baptism was ordained by Christ after he had died and been raised from the dead. In Matthew 28:18–20, we read that Jesus said to his disciples, "All authority in heaven and on earth has been given to me.

[19] Go therefore and make disciples of all nations, baptizing them in the name of the Father and of the Son and of the Holy Spirit, [20] teaching them to observe all that I have commanded you. And behold, I am with you always, to the end of the age." The term *baptize* means "to dip under water," "to submerge," or "to immerse." Baptism is a beautiful picture of what it means for a believer in Jesus Christ to be joined together with Christ in his death for sin and in his resurrection to newness of life. Of course, it is a picture that is shown through drama. Baptism isn't a still picture, like a photograph. It's more like a movie (which used to be called a motion picture). Action takes place in baptism, and what occurs is very important and wonderful. One who has trusted Christ for his salvation is dipped completely under water, only a moment later to be brought back up again. His being dipped under the water (often called immersion) is meant to picture that this believer is now so closely connected to Jesus Christ by faith that Christ's own death has become this believer's death. As he goes under the water, then, the Christian sees his own sin being paid for and his own death taking place as he is joined to Christ who died and paid for his sin in his place.

But just as Jesus did not remain in the grave, so the believer does not stay under the water. An instant after this believer's immersion into the water, he is brought up out of the water, showing that he is joined as well to Jesus' resurrection life. As he now stands up with water streaming down him, he pictures the cleansing of his sin and the newness of life that he has been granted. United with Christ in his death and united with Christ in his resurrection from the dead—this is what the drama of baptism is meant to picture.

Paul talks about this when he writes, "Do you not know that all of us who have been baptized into Christ Jesus were baptized into his death? [4] We were buried therefore with him by baptism into death, in order that, just as Christ was raised from the dead by the glory of the Father, we too might walk in newness of life. [5] For if we have been united with him in a death like his, we shall certainly be united with him in a resurrection like his. [6] We know that our old self was crucified with him in order that the body of sin might be brought to nothing, so that we would no longer be enslaved to sin. [7] For one who has died has been set free from sin" (Romans 6:3–7).

Let's be sure we are clear about something. Believers' baptism does not save believers, but it does provide a vivid, living picture of what happened when they were saved. Their salvation happens when they trust in

Christ alone and in his death for their sin. They believe in their hearts that when Christ died on the cross, Christ bore their sin and paid the punishment of death that they deserved to pay. And because Christ's death was a full payment for their sin, Christ then rose from the dead, showing he had completely dealt with their sin. By faith, they are saved by trusting Christ who died for them, taking their punishment and defeating their sin, then rising from the dead triumphant. Their baptism, though, gives an outward picture of what is true of their own inner life. By faith these believers are joined with Christ in his death and resurrection, and by baptism believers present a living picture of just what has happened. So, while baptism doesn't save them, it does show beautifully what their salvation is all about. They are saved only because by faith they are joined to Christ who died and rose for their sin.

Baptism, then, is sometimes called a sign that the baptized person has been forgiven of his sin. Baptism *signifies* or points to the fact that because the believer is joined to Christ in his death, the death that Christ died is the believer's own death to sin. And because the believer is joined to Christ in his resurrection, the resurrected life of Jesus is now the believer's own new life in Christ. Baptism, then, is like a sign along the road that points at a person who has trusted Christ and says, "Sins forgiven in Christ! Raised to new life in Christ!"

For most of the church's history, Christian people who love Jesus and have trusted in Christ alone for their salvation have not been able to agree on some parts of the Bible's teaching on baptism. The understanding that we've looked at here is one that is held by Christians who are also known as Baptists. Baptists believe two things about the Bible's teaching on baptism that not all agree with. First, Baptists believe that only those who have already believed in Christ for their salvation should be baptized—this is called *believer's baptism*. Second, they believe that the best and proper way of baptizing someone is through dipping them under the water and bringing them back out of the water—this is called *baptism by immersion*. Those who hold this Baptist view see this as the only clear practice that is recorded for us in the book of Acts and the rest of the New Testament.

But many fine Christian people, both past and present, do not hold this same view of baptism. Many believe that the infants of believers should be baptized by sprinkling them with water—this is called *infant baptism* or *paedobaptism*. This is meant to show that they are part of the community of those who believe in Christ, even though they still must personally trust Christ later in life to be saved. Where we all agree, though, is this: Christ commanded baptism, and this practice is meant to picture the precious truth that only those who are joined to Christ by faith can know that they have died to sin and been raised to newness of life in Christ. The gospel is true and is believed by many whose understanding and practice of baptism may differ. So, let's be gracious with those of a different practice, and yet let's work to understand and follow as best we can what the Bible teaches. Baptism matters, to be sure. But the truth that baptism points to matters even more. Our hope is in Christ, who died and rose for our salvation. Praise be to Jesus, the only true Savior of sinners.

Questions for Thought

1. Have you seen someone baptized by immersion? In baptism, a believer is placed under water and then raised out of the water. What does this picture?

2. Baptism doesn't save the person who is baptized. So, what is the role of baptism in someone's life? How does it relate to that person's belief in Christ?

Memory Verses

Matthew 28:18–20—"All authority in heaven and on earth has been given to me. Go therefore and make disciples of all nations, baptizing them in the name of the Father and of the Son and of the Holy Spirit, teaching them to observe all that I have commanded you. And behold, I am with you always, to the end of the age."

The Lord's Supper: Remembering Jesus' Death and Resurrection

Have you noticed how important the idea of remembering is through the story line of the Bible? The first time we come across it is in the story of the Flood. Noah, his family, and many pairs of animals were on the ark that Noah built, safe from the rains that flooded the whole earth.

Long days passed before the waters began to lower, and then in the opening verse of Genesis 8 we read this: "But God remembered Noah and all the beasts and all the livestock that were with him in the ark. And God made a wind blow over the earth, and the waters subsided." We learn something very important here about the biblical idea of remembering. Since God is the one doing the remembering here, it is not a matter of bringing to mind some facts or information that one might have forgotten. God hadn't forgotten Noah, I dare say! So the main idea must be something different. For God to "remember" Noah is to bring directly to mind something important and to choose to act upon it. It's sort of the way a wedding ring reminds a husband or wife that he or she is married. When a married man looks at his wedding ring, he hasn't forgotten that he's married, but the ring focuses his mind to remember the importance of the vows he made, and it instructs him to be faithful to his wife. This is how God remembered Noah. He brought to mind his promise to Noah and began at that very moment to act on his promise, causing the floodwaters to lower.

Of course, there are many examples through the Bible of either God or humans remembering (or not remembering) different things. One of the most important is this: while the Israelites were slaves in Egypt, God instructed them to eat a particular meal just before he sent the angel to strike the homes of the Egyptians, killing the firstborn in every Egyptian home and stable. This was called the Passover meal because when the angel of death came to the camp of Israel in the land of Egypt, he saw the blood on the doorposts of their houses and "passed over" their homes, sparing them from death (Exodus 12:1–20; 13:3). From that time on, Israel was to celebrate the Passover meal each year, so that they would "remember the day" when God brought them out of the land of Egypt (Deuteronomy 16:3). Clearly this meal served to remind Israel of the facts of what happened. It would give opportunity for fathers to tell their children the story of God's marvelous deliverance from slavery under Pharaoh. But it was more than this, wasn't it? By remembering that God brought them out of Egypt by a mighty hand, they were honoring God for saving them and thanking him for his mercy. And even more, they were calling to mind again that they were God's chosen people. By God's great power and love, he had delivered them to show the world that Israel was his people, and he was their God. As a result, Israel was responsible to live in obedience to God and to his Law. By remembering the exodus from Egypt, Israel was called to live as the people of God, the chosen and saved people God had made them to be.

It is no surprise, then, that one of the ordinances that Christ put in place for his church to practice is one in which they would regularly remember his death for their sin. At his last supper with the disciples, Jesus used some of the items of their meal as symbols for his own upcoming death. Paul records that what Jesus had taught him took place at this last supper. He writes, "For I received from the Lord what I also delivered to you, that the Lord Jesus on the night when he was betrayed took bread, 24 and when he had given thanks, he broke it, and said, 'This is my body which is for you. Do this in remembrance of me.' 25 In the same way also he took the cup, after supper, saying, 'This cup is the new covenant in my blood. Do this, as often as you drink it, in remembrance of me.' 26 For as often as you eat this bread and drink the cup, you proclaim the Lord's death until he comes" (1 Corinthians 11:23–26). Bread and wine, two very common items at a meal in Jesus' day, and items that he commanded his followers to eat and drink regularly as they meet together, are symbols of his own broken body and his shed blood for their sins.

Notice with me a few things from these verses and the larger context of this passage. First, the disciples of Jesus are to carry out Jesus' instructions when they come together in a group, as a community of believers. Paul's whole teaching about the Lord's Supper actually runs from 1 Corinthians 11:17–34. Throughout these verses Paul mentions "when you come together" or a similar phrase no fewer than five times. Clearly, Paul understood this ceremony is to be carried out when Christians gather for worship and teaching. Acts 2:42 confirms this idea. The early Christians gathered to learn from the apostles' teaching, for fellowship, for the breaking of bread (the Lord's Supper), and for prayer. So it seems that the Lord's Supper is not best viewed as a personal or family activity. The practice of the early Christians was to celebrate Christ's death and resurrection at the Lord's Table when they came together for worship.

Second, notice that the main focus is on the death of Christ. The broken bread is meant to picture Christ's body broken as he hung on the cross. The wine or juice pictures Christ's blood shed for sinners. Both elements are meant to focus our attention on the suffering and death of Christ, but not for some crude or gory purpose. Rather the suffering of Christ itself focuses our attention on the purpose of his suffering, to suffer and die in our place, taking the penalty for our sin. But there is another focus as well. Paul says that as often as we eat this meal, we proclaim Christ's death "until he comes." The certainty of both the resurrection and the return of Christ are also part of the joy of this ceremony of worship.

Third, with the cup Jesus says something that is especially important. He refers to the cup as "the new covenant in my blood," and we might wonder just what he means by this. While the main focus of the New Covenant in Jeremiah 31:31–34 is on the new hearts that God's people will have as God writes his Law upon them, the statement of this New Covenant ends with some very important words: "For I will forgive their iniquity, and I will remember their sin no more" (v. 34). What this means is that the only way God can bring about the changes in our lives that he wants to do is if he first forgives our sin. How could God make us new if the sin that ruined us remains? So, Jesus brings about forgiveness of sin by his death on the cross. Only because of this may we be sure that the promise of the New Covenant will come true.

Finally, notice that while the New Covenant says that God will remember our sins no more, in the Lord's Supper we are to remember Christ's death for us. For God not to remember our sins cannot mean he literally forgets them. At the final judgment, all of our words and deeds, both good and bad, will be brought to light. God always knows all we ever think, say, and do. So, when it says that he doesn't remember our sins it must mean this: God chooses not to bring our sins directly to mind as a basis of his judgment against us. He chooses not to hold sins against us that he justly could. But in contrast, we are called to remember Christ's sacrifice. There's no doubt that part of what this means is recalling the story of Jesus' suffering that all four Gospels tell us. But there's more. As we recall God's great act of salvation in his Son, we honor and worship God, and we thank him with all our heart for his mercy. In addition, we remember now that we are not our own, but we have been bought with a very costly price, the broken body and shed blood of Christ (1 Corinthians 6:19–20). We are his people, bought by him to live for him. Our purpose now is to follow him, love him, and obey him. This, too, is part of what it means to remember Christ's death and resurrection for our sin.

Questions for Thought

1. Like baptism, the Lord's Supper is another picture of Christ's death for sinners. What is pictured by the elements used in the Lord's Supper, the bread and the wine or juice?

2. When Jesus tells his disciples to take each of the elements in "remembrance" of him, what does he mean by this? What should happen to us as we remember Jesus' broken body and shed blood for our sins?

Memory Verses

1 Corinthians 11:23–26—"For I received from the Lord what I also delivered to you, that the Lord Jesus on the night when he was betrayed took bread, and when he had given thanks, he broke it, and said, 'This is my body which is for you. Do this in remembrance of me.' In the same way also he took the cup, after supper, saying, 'This cup is the new covenant in my blood. Do this, as often as you drink it, in remembrance of me.' For as often as you eat this bread and drink the cup, you proclaim the Lord's death until he comes."

Growing the Church through Making Disciples

Among Jesus' most important words in explaining what the church should be doing are these instructions to his disciples as recorded in Matthew 28:18–20: "And Jesus came and said to them, 'All authority in heaven and on earth has been given to me. [19] Go therefore and make disciples of all nations, baptizing them in the name of the Father and of the Son and of the Holy Spirit, [20] teaching them to observe all that I have commanded you. And behold, I am with you always, to the end of the age.'" Because he speaks these words from the position of having "all authority in heaven and on earth," we must listen carefully to what Jesus says. He alone has complete authority over everything in all of creation because of his obedient death and triumphant resurrection. The Father has given to him this highest of all positions (Ephesians 1:20–23), and so whatever Jesus says, we must hear and do. There is no bargaining, no compromise, and no negotiation. As Lord of all, and as Lord of the Church, he speaks and we listen, he commands and we obey, he leads and we follow.

And what exactly does he command his people in the church to be doing? Some have thought that Jesus has given two commands: 1) to go, and 2) to make disciples. After all, our English translations lead us to think along these lines. But looking at the Greek language of these verses shows something different. There really is only *one* command. There really is just *one* thing that Jesus says we must do. But this one thing involves three activities. So, what is the one command, and what are these three supporting activities?

The command Christ gives here is to "make disciples of all nations" (Matthew 28:19). Disciples are those who have come to believe that a certain teacher speaks what is both wise and true. Because of this, what he teaches should be learned well, and his instructions should be followed with care. Disciples, then, listen attentively to their teachers and seek to follow in their ways. Disciples want to think like their teachers, feel like their teachers, and live like their teachers. So when Jesus says to "make disciples of all nations," he means that our job is to lead people from anywhere and everywhere in the world to see Jesus as the great teacher whom they should want to listen carefully to, learn from, and model their lives after. Let's be sure we are clear about something: we are not being called here to seek to make disciples of ourselves. The idea is not that we want others to look to us, admire us, learn from us, and live like us. While there is something correct in thinking this way (see Philippians 3:17, for example), the main thing Jesus commands here is to make disciples of himself. We only obey Christ when we direct people's attention to the teaching of Christ, the wisdom of Christ, the grace and compassion and truth of Christ. We must have the attitude that John the Baptist had. When people noticed that some of those who had been following John were now following Jesus, John's response was amazing. He said, "He [Jesus] must increase, but I must decrease" (John 3:30). Our main job as believers in Christ and as those who make up his church is this: we are commanded to make disciples of Jesus from people throughout the world.

Now, three words are used in these verses to describe how making disciples of Jesus will take place. The first word describes an activity that must happen if disciples are to be made from around the world. That word is "go." Though this word sounds like a command, Jesus should be understood as saying, "while going into the world" or "since you are going into the world . . . make disciples [command] of the nations." In some of his last teaching to his disciples, Jesus made it clear to them that the Sprit would come and give them power to bear witness about Christ (John 15:26–27; Acts 1:8). So he assumed that they understood that they must go. He knew that the Spirit who was coming would give them power to speak of Christ wherever they went. But this much is clear: they have to go to where the people are throughout the world if disciples are to be made from all the nations. Although the command in this verse relates to making disciples, going is a very important and needed part. We must go wherever Christ leads us. Our task is to make disciples, and going is part of what has to happen for this command to be fulfilled.

Second, Jesus says to make disciples (command) by baptizing them in the name of the Father, the Son, and the Holy Spirit. As we've seen in our reflections on baptism, it is not the outward form of baptism that saves people. What saves them is their joining with Christ by faith, trusting his death and resurrection alone for the forgiveness of their sin. Their baptism is an outward sign that points to what is true of their new relationship with Christ. So, when Jesus says to make disciples by baptizing them into the name of the Christian God, he means to declare to them the gospel of Christ so they can believe in Christ and be saved. Their baptism is only real and it is only truly a sign of their union with Christ if they have in fact trusted Christ alone for the forgiveness of their sins and their only hope for eternal life. So, the activity of baptizing them means you have first shared the gospel with them. It focuses on the quantitative growth of the church—more people being saved and becoming part of the church. We want larger numbers of people to hear of Christ and come to Christ, to be sure. And Christ's command urges this to happen. Bringing people to the waters of baptism assumes that we have told them about Christ and his death and resurrection for their sins, and they have responded in faith and hope in Christ.

Third, Jesus says to make disciples (command) by "teaching them to observe all that I have commanded you." Sometimes we may think that once we have shared the gospel with people, and they've believed and been baptized, we have fulfilled what Christ commands in these verses. But this certainly is not the case. This teaching of Christ, the "Great Commission" as it is often called, involves teaching those who have put their faith in Christ as much as it involves leading them to their initial faith in Christ. Remember what disciples are. Disciples don't come to a teacher only once, hearing his words and believing what he says only to leave him and learn no more from him. No, a disciple wants to learn everything he can from his teacher, to master the truth he knows and to live out the wisdom of his life. This must be true also of disciples of Jesus. The instruction Jesus gives here is almost shocking: "teaching them to observe *all that I have commanded you.*" As those called to make disciples of all the nations, we have our hands full. As important as sharing the gospel is to obeying the Great Commission, the rich and full role of teaching all that Christ himself taught is also needed. And notice also that Christ wants us to make disciples who not only know his teaching but who "observe" what he has taught. Knowing the truth of Christ, loving that truth, and living it out are all parts of what Christ has commanded his followers to do in making disciples. If baptizing them had more to do with quantitative growth—seeing that more people are saved—"teaching them to observe" has more to do with qualitative growth—seeing that those saved also grow to be like Christ.

Going, baptizing, and teaching—these are the three activities of the one command Christ gives to make disciples of all the nations. Since Jesus' last words to us commanded us to do one thing, we'd better be sure we do it.

Questions for Thought

1. What is involved in making disciples of all the nations (Matthew 28:19)? How are you involved in this? How is your church involved in fulfilling this command of Christ?

2. Disciples need to be baptized and taught all that Jesus commanded them. What do these two activities (baptizing and teaching) focus on, and how can they be carried out?

Memory Verse

Acts 1:8—"You will receive power when the Holy Spirit has come upon you, and you will be my witnesses in Jerusalem and in all Judea and Samaria, and to the end of the earth."

10

What Will Take Place in the End

Knowing the Future Helps in the Present

Have you ever listened to a friend tell you a story when the end of the story suddenly gets cut off? You know, just as the bridge he's walking over starts to collapse, or just as she quietly rounds the corner and sees someone's shadow, or just as the phone rings and it's "him" calling—just when you come to the most exciting part, something happens and you don't hear the end of the story. It can make you go a little bit crazy. How hard it is to know the buildup of the story but not know how it ends!

Just imagine how sad it would be if this were how the Bible had been written. Suppose we knew about God creating the world, and the mess we made by our sin, and what God planned to do to save lost people, and his sending his Son to conquer sin—but then suddenly the end of the story is cut off. We don't know for sure whether God wins in the end or not. We don't know what happens to Satan. We don't know where we will go when we die. And we don't know anything about either heaven or hell that awaits each and every person who has ever lived. How troubling this would be! We could easily be filled with worry and fear, not knowing how things are going to be in the end.

But thank God, he has told us the end of the story. True enough, he hasn't told us everything about what is coming, and some things he has told us are not given in exact detail. But he has told us a lot. And he's told us enough so that if we are trusting in Christ, we can put away our fears and worries. We *know* what happens when we and others die. We *know* that Christ is coming again. We *know* that the Kingdom of God will be established upon the whole earth. We *know* that all evil will be judged. And we *know* that those who have trusted in Christ for their salvation will live forever with Christ, in the presence of God. What great hope and confidence we can have as followers of Christ who *know* these things are true. How kind and gracious and good of God to let us *know*!

There are many good reasons why knowing the Bible's teaching about the future helps us in the present. One of these may surprise you, though. When we understand the Bible's teaching about what happens in the end, we realize something we probably never would have imagined: we are in what the Bible calls "the last days" right now! This idea can be a little confusing, so let's think about it as clearly as we can. When the prophets in the Old Testament speak about what God will do in the last days, they often speak about some things that took place at the first coming of Christ right along with some other things that won't take place until the second coming of Christ. In other words, the last days include some things that have *already* happened and other things that have *not yet* happened.

Let's look at one example. Isaiah speaks about the day when the Messiah from the line of David will come. What he describes includes some things that Christ did in his first coming, for sure. But other things won't happen until he comes again and brings righteousness to all the earth. Isaiah 11 describes the Messiah in both ways in the same passage. On the one hand, "the Spirit of the LORD shall rest upon" the Messiah (v. 2), and "his delight shall be in the fear of the LORD" (v. 3). "He shall not judge by what his eyes see, or decide disputes by what his ears hear, but with righteousness he shall judge the poor, and decide with equity for the meek of the earth" (vv. 3–4). These are things that are true of Jesus in his first coming. But on the other hand, Isaiah also says that the Messiah "shall strike the earth with the rod of his mouth, and with the breath of his lips he shall kill the wicked" (v. 4). And the result of Messiah's coming will be that "the wolf shall dwell with the lamb," "the cow and the bear shall graze," and "the nursing child shall play over the hole of the cobra" (vv. 6–8). Clearly, these are things that will only happen when Christ comes again. In his second coming he will bring judgment on the wicked and peace on the earth.

Consider briefly one other example. When Jesus went into the synagogue in his hometown, Nazareth, to worship on the Sabbath (Luke 4:16–21), he was asked to read from the book of Isaiah. He read from Isaiah 61 and then said that this passage was about him. As he read this passage, he included the statement from Isaiah 61:2 saying that he would "proclaim the year of the Lord's favor." But he stopped his reading and did not include the very next phrase, "and the day of vengeance of our God." So Isaiah 61:2 says the Messiah will bring about the year of God's favor—which happens in Christ's first coming—and he will bring about the day of God's vengeance—which happens in Christ's second coming.

So, it is clear that both Isaiah 11 and Isaiah 61 put the two comings of Christ together. How, then, do we answer this question: has the coming of the Messiah promised in Isaiah 11 and Isaiah 61 happened? In answer, we have to say, yes, part has already happened in his first coming, but no, other parts have not yet happened and await his second coming. This *already* and *not yet* idea helps us explain how many Old Testament promises are fulfilled. For example, we already are in the kingdom of Christ, but that kingdom has not yet come in its fullness. Already we are new creatures in Christ, but our being remade in the likeness of Christ is not yet completed. Already the New Covenant has replaced the Old Covenant, but many parts of the promised New Covenant have not yet happened fully.

This means that we really are living in a time when promises of our future life are here in the present. In one way followers of Christ live in this old world, and in another way his followers live in Christ's new kingdom. In one way we are citizens of this earth, and in another way we are citizens of heaven. I love to put together two sayings from two different passages, both of which describe our lives as believers right now. Galatians 1:4 describes us as living in "the present evil age," but Hebrews 6:5 says that "the powers of the age to come" are here now. So, which is it? Do we live in this present evil age? Or do we live when the powers of the age to come are already here? Answer: both are true. On the one hand, the powers of the age to come are here so that we already have some portion of the promised power of the future available for our lives in the present. On the other hand, the evil of this age continues to be strong, and God's promised age of peace and righteousness is not yet fully here. We live in two worlds at the same time. But as followers of Christ, we need to realize that the power of the new world is greater than the power of this present evil world. We have great hope as we see what God has promised will take place in the age to come and as we realize how much of that is here for us now.

Questions for Thought

1. God has not told us everything about the future. But he has told us some wonderful things. What has God revealed about the future that should fill his followers' hearts with hope and joy?

2. Is it true that the future the Bible speaks of has come into the present? What are some ways that we see the promises of future blessing *already* here in the present? What are some other parts of the promised future blessing that have *not yet* come fully to pass?

Memory Verse

2 Corinthians 5:17—"Therefore, if anyone is in Christ, he is a new creation. The old has passed away; behold, the new has come."

What Happens to Grandma When She Dies?

Funerals are difficult for most people. Even in the best of circumstances, questions often come to people's minds about what has happened to family members or friends who have now left us. There's no question: death is final. All of us who have lost loved ones or close friends know this reality all too well. My dear wife, Jodi, had a precious relationship with her dad and loved him so much. Over the years that he's been gone she has often commented, "I just wish I could talk to him about this." You probably will experience (or maybe you have) the sadness that comes when someone you love dies. Unless the Lord returns in our lifetimes, we know that the reality of death faces us as it does everyone. So, what happens to Grandma when she dies? Or more generally, what follows physical death?

In answer to this last question, the first thing we should be clear on is this: life follows physical death. As the Bible teaches, death is not an ending of our existence as human beings. Rather, it is a point of transition to our lives for the rest of eternity. Hebrews 9:27 teaches that "it is appointed for man to die once, and after that comes judgment." So death should not be seen as bringing life to an end, but as taking our lives to the next phase of life—the final place where we will live forever.

Physical death, then, involves the separation of who we are on the inside from the bodies that make up part of our lives. Now granted, our full and normal human life includes living in our bodies, but the Bible teaches that at physical death we continue living even though our bodies go into the grave. Most Bible teachers believe Scripture says that we have both physical and non-physical parts to our lives as humans. Many fine

Christian people have differed over whether we are made up of body, soul, and spirit—three parts, as it were—or just body and soul (or spirit)—two parts to our human lives. For our discussion here, we won't try to settle this difference, since both sides agree that we are part physical and part non-physical, part material and part immaterial. Death, then, results in the separation of the material part of our lives from the immaterial. Our inner lives (immaterial) separate from our bodies (material) at death, but we continue living in our inner lives. So, while the physical part of us does cease to live, we—our inner lives, our immaterial part(s)—continue living even though our bodies are now gone.

What is the experience of those who have died? What may we expect will happen to us when we die? The Bible makes clear that the experiences of the believer and unbeliever at death are very different. As we might expect, the believer enters into real joy and blessing at his physical death, even though he still awaits the resurrection of the body when the fullness of his transformed life will come. The unbeliever may expect to enter into real misery and torment at his physical death, even though he also awaits the resurrection of his body and his final judgment before a holy God.

One passage that helps much in seeing the reality of life after physical death and the different experiences of the believer and unbeliever is Luke 16:19–31. You may wish to read the entire passage. Some of the most important verses are these: "The poor man died and was carried by the angels to Abraham's side. The rich man also died and was buried, [23] and in Hades, being in torment, he lifted up his eyes and saw Abraham far off and Lazarus at his side. [24] And he called out, 'Father Abraham, have mercy on me, and send Lazarus to dip the end of his finger in water and cool my tongue, for I am in anguish in this flame.' [25] But Abraham said, 'Child, remember that you in your lifetime received your good things, and Lazarus in like manner bad things; but now he is comforted here, and you are in anguish. [26] And besides all this, between us and you a great chasm has been fixed, in order that those who would pass from here to you may not be able, and none may cross from there to us'" (Luke 16:22–26). From this passage we see that both the rich man (the unbeliever) and the poor man (the believer) continued living after they died. The experiences of the two men were very different, however. Lazarus enjoyed the comfort of being with the people of God, while the rich man suffered torment and anguish. He longed for someone to come and bring him relief, but no one could come. A chasm separated them, so that no one could travel from one place to the other. This shows us, then, that where we will live forever is fixed at the point of physical death. As much as the rich man would have loved to be with Lazarus, he could never change the torment he experienced. As 2 Peter 2:9 says, God keeps "the unrighteous under punishment until the day of judgment."

The greatest hope for Christians is the return of Christ and our resurrection to be with Christ forever. But the joy of life for the believer at the point of physical death is also taught in Scripture, something that brings much comfort when a believer dies. Paul was very aware of the shortness of life. In addition, the regular affliction and persecution he experienced made him realize that his life could come to an end at any time. In a couple of places in Scripture he spoke about what he expected when he died. In one passage he wrote, "So we are always of good courage. We know that while we are at home in the body we are away from the Lord, ⁷ for we walk by faith, not by sight. ⁸ Yes, we are of good courage, and we would rather be away from the body and at home with the Lord. ⁹ So whether we are at home or away, we make it our aim to please him" (2 Corinthians 5:6–9). His use of the phrases "at home" and "at home with the Lord" were his way of speaking about being with Christ after physical death. But notice how clear he was in expecting to continue living after he died (when he's "away from the body"). Even more, he commented in verse 8 that he would rather die physically ("away from the body") so that he would be with Christ ("at home with the Lord"). Paul looked forward to his death as something he wanted more than he wanted to keep living on earth. This shows that Paul was truly living by faith in God's promise and was not living by sight (v. 7).

Finally, Paul's most moving passage is this one: "For to me to live is Christ, and to die is gain. ²² If I am to live in the flesh, that means fruitful labor for me. Yet which I shall choose I cannot tell. ²³ I am hard pressed between the two. My desire is to depart and be with Christ, for that is far better. ²⁴ But to remain in the flesh is more necessary on your account. ²⁵ Convinced of this, I know that I will remain and continue with you all, for your progress and joy in the faith" (Philippians 1:21–25). Paul understood the time of his physical death as one of "gain" (v. 21), one that would be "far better" (v. 23). How can this be? There is one and only one reason for this: Paul knew that when he died, he would "depart and be with Christ," and it is this that was "far better" (v. 23). As we learn from chapter 3 of Philippians, Paul gave up everything he considered important to him and viewed all of it as garbage. Paul came to see Christ as the greatest treasure, the only real joy. If death would be the time that he would flee into the arms of Christ, then death would be "gain." Leaving this world to be with Jesus is "far better."

What happens to Grandma when she dies? Answer: she lives. But the most important question for her and for all of us is this: has she—and have we—trusted in Christ alone as Savior and Lord? That we all will die is certain. That we will live after we die is also certain. Where we will live depends, though, on where we place our hope.

Questions for Thought

1. The Bible teaches that physical death is not the end of our lives. What happens to people when they die? Does it matter whether they have trusted in Christ or not at the point of their physical death?

2. What do you think Paul means when he says, "For to me to live is Christ, and to die is gain" (Philippians 1:21)? Can you say this about your own life? What might keep someone from truly believing that his or her dying would bring about a gain, an increase to his or her joy and happiness?

Memory Verses

2 Corinthians 5:6–9—"So we are always of good courage. We know that while we are at home in the body we are away from the Lord, for we walk by faith, not by sight. Yes, we are of good courage, and we would rather be away from the body and at home with the Lord. So whether we are at home or away, we make it our aim to please him."

The Promise-Keeping God and the Salvation of Israel

The God of the Bible loves to make promises, and he also loves to show that he always keeps the promises that he's made. God is faithful to his word. He always does exactly what he said he would do. God is a promise-maker and a promise-keeper. His very name and honor and glory are linked to the truthfulness of his word and the faithfulness of his pledge. When God says something, you can count on him doing it.

Through the Old Testament, God made some amazing promises to the people of Israel that have not yet come to pass, at least not completely. From the very beginning of his calling Abraham to become the father of the nation of Israel, God has promised to bless Israel. His promise to Abraham did not have any strings attached either. Listen to the covenant promise God made with Abram (who became Abraham): "Now the LORD said to Abram, 'Go from your country and your kindred and your father's house to the land that I will show you. ²And I will make of you a great nation, and I will bless you and make your name great, so that you will be a blessing. ³I will bless those who bless you, and him who dishonors you I will curse, and in you all the families of the earth shall be blessed'" (Genesis 12:1–3). God didn't say here that he would bless Israel only if they did certain things. Although the Law that was later given to Moses required obedience for blessing, this promise to Abraham simply stated what God would do *period*. God will make of him a great nation. God will make his name great. And God will bless the nations of the world through Abraham. God's covenant with Abraham is what is called an *unconditional covenant*. God simply promised what he would do, and because God promised these things, he will keep his word. The people of Israel coming from Abraham are promised God's blessing. They will be his people, and God will be their God.

Moses reminded the people of Israel of their very special place in God's heart and in God's plans. After God delivered them from Egypt but before they entered into the Promised Land under Joshua, Moses said to them, "For you are a people holy to the LORD your God. The LORD your God has chosen you to be a people for his treasured possession, out of all the peoples who are on the face of the earth. ⁷It was not because you were more in number than any other people that the LORD set his love on you and chose you, for you were the fewest of all peoples, ⁸but it is because the LORD loves you and is keeping the oath that he swore to your fathers, that the LORD has brought you out with a mighty hand and redeemed you from the house of slavery, from the hand of Pharaoh king of Egypt" (Deuteronomy 7:6–8). Because God chose Israel to be his people, he also gave them his Law (the Law of Moses, in the Old Covenant), which told them how to live before him. God made very clear that if they obeyed his Law, he would bless them greatly (see Leviticus 26:3–13; Deuteronomy 28:1–14). If they disobeyed his Law, he would punish them (see Leviticus

26:14–43; Deuteronomy 28:15–68). God's covenant with Israel through Moses, then, had strings attached. It stated what Israel must do in order to receive God's blessing. So, unlike God's covenant with Abraham, which was unconditional, God's covenant through Moses was conditional—it stated conditions that had to be met or certain things that had to be done in order to receive God's blessing.

As you know, Israel disobeyed God's Law over and over, and God punished them just as he said he would. But now we wonder something as we think about these two covenants. In God's covenant with Abraham, God promised that he would bless Israel, with no strings attached (unconditional covenant). But in God's covenant through Moses, God promised that he would bless Israel only if they did certain things (conditional covenant). How can we understand both together since they seem to be opposite? Will God bless Israel *period* as in God's covenant promise to Abraham? Or will he only bless Israel if they obey him as stated in God's covenant made through Moses?

The answer is that God will be true to both of these covenants. He did punish Israel when they broke his Law and turned from him in their sin. He even raised up other nations (Assyria and Babylon) to destroy Israel and Judah. But through the Law of Moses that God gave to Israel, he wanted them to learn something important. God wanted them to learn that they were not able to keep God's Law. Sin within them controlled them so that they did not want to keep the Law. Instead they wanted to be like the other nations around them, doing things that went against God's Law. Even though God promised to bless Israel if they would obey the Law, Israel wanted instead to live the way other people lived and so go against how the Law said they must live. So, if Israel had to be obedient to the Law in order to receive God's blessing, God could not bless Israel. If they obeyed, they would be blessed. But that's just it—they would not obey! And so under the Law, God could not bring them blessing.

But God never forgot about his earlier promise that, no matter what, he would bless Israel, that Israel would be his people and that he would be their God. He had promised that he would bless Israel *period*, and God would not go back on his word. But this is also clear—he could not bless Israel if the only way he could do this was as they obeyed him. But they wouldn't obey him! So, what was God to do? How could he bless his people if they wouldn't obey him by keeping his Law?

The solution God planned is amazing. What he did was to make another covenant with Israel, a new covenant that would be uncondi-tional like God's covenant with Abraham. In this new covenant made with "the house of Israel and the house of Judah" (Jeremiah 31:31), God promised that he would take the Law that they did not want to obey and he would "write it on their hearts" (Jeremiah 31:33). What God means is that he would remake their hearts so that instead of them wanting to disobey God's Law, they would now want to be obedient to God, from their hearts. He also would give them the Spirit to change them into his obedient people. God said to Israel, "I will put my Spirit within you, and cause you to walk in my statutes and be careful to obey my rules" (Ezekiel 36:27). No strings attached! God will simply make his people the obedi-ent people they should be, and they will receive all the blessing that God long ago promised they would have.

No wonder, then, that Paul devotes three chapters in the book of Romans (9–11) to explaining that God has not forgotten his promise to Israel. God has not cast them away from him. Yes, God is working now to save many people from all the nations of the world (Gentiles). So right now few Jewish people will be saved. Because of their disobedience, God has hardened their hearts for a time (see Romans 11:25). But the day will come when God will finish what he started. God will keep his promise to Israel. God will save the people of Israel and bring blessing upon them, making them his obedient people. As Paul states, when God has saved people from all of the nations, he will turn again to Israel, so that "all Israel will be saved" (Romans 11:26).

God is a promise-keeping God. God's salvation of Israel in the days to come will show in one of the most amazing ways that God is faithful to his promises. God will keep his word. The people of Israel will one day be saved!

Questions for Thought

1. God is the original promise-maker and promise-keeper. He never goes back on his word. How should this truth fill you with hope and confidence? What are some promises of God that he's made concerning you? What does it mean to you to know that God will never break these promises?

2. What was the kind of promise (or covenant) that God made with Israel? And what did God promise Israel? If God never breaks his promises, what does this mean for the people of Israel?

Memory Verses

Genesis 12:1–3—"Now the LORD said to Abram, 'Go from your country and your kindred and your father's house to the land that I will show you. And I will make of you a great nation, and I will bless you and make your name great, so that you will be a blessing. I will bless those who bless you, and him who dishonors you I will curse, and in you all the families of the earth shall be blessed.'"

Jesus Will Come Again

One of the greatest promises Jesus gave his followers was that, after leaving them for a time, he would come back again. Jesus had told them that the Father would be sending them the Spirit to give them Jesus' power to live new lives and to witness about Christ. But still, they longed to have not only Jesus' Spirit within them, but they loved Jesus and wanted him to be with them forever. Jesus was the Messiah, the Christ, and they wanted to serve him, under his reign as King. But Jesus was leaving, and so the disciples were sad. Listen to Jesus' own words given to comfort and encourage them: "Let not your hearts be troubled. Believe in God; believe also in me. ² In my Father's house are many rooms. If it were not so, would I have told you that I go to prepare a place for you? ³ And if I go and prepare a place for you, I will come again and will take you to myself, that where I am you may be also" (John 14:1–3). What hope and joy this gives the followers of Jesus. Even though he has gone now to be with his Father, he promised that he would return. Since Jesus always keeps his word, we know that this great day is coming. Jesus is coming back!

After Jesus' death and resurrection, Jesus' disciples watched him go up into the clouds to be with his Father. Jesus' last words to his disciples had reminded them again of the good news that the Spirit was coming to live within them and to give them his power. They would have the very

Spirit of Jesus living within them, and they would be witnesses throughout the world for this Christ who had died and now had been raised. And as they were thinking about what Jesus had just said, all of a sudden they could hardly believe their eyes. They watched as Jesus went up into the sky where a cloud took him out of their sight. Two angels appeared and said to them, "Men of Galilee, why do you stand looking into heaven? This Jesus, who was taken up from you into heaven, will come in the same way as you saw him go into heaven" (Acts 1:11). What wonderful news that confirmed what Jesus had already told them. Yes, Jesus would be with his Father for a time, but then he will return from the sky just as the disciples watched him go. Jesus will come again!

When Jesus returns, his second coming will be very different from his first coming. You may know some familiar words from John's Gospel about Jesus' first coming, when he came to die to save us from our sins. John writes, "For God so loved the world, that he gave his only Son, that whoever believes in him should not perish but have eternal life. 17 For God did not send his Son into the world to condemn the world, but in order that the world might be saved through him" (John 3:16–17). In his first coming, then, Jesus did not come as a judge. He did not come to condemn sinners in the world. Instead, he came to save the world. He came to carry out what the Father sent him to do, to die on the cross and to be raised from the dead so sinners could be saved from their sin.

But Jesus' second coming will not be like this. When Jesus comes again, as he promised his disciples he would, his purpose will no longer be to save sinners. Rather, he will show God's anger at the sin of our world. He will bring God's judgment against all of those who continue to rebel against God. Of course, the followers of Jesus will rejoice at his second coming. We who have trusted Christ for our salvation will be raised and united forever with Christ. We will begin our new resurrected lives now freed entirely from sin and enjoying the presence of God forever. But those outside of Christ—those who have not trusted Christ alone for the forgiveness of their sin and their only hope for eternal life—will be judged by Christ when he returns to earth.

Jesus told his disciples about this when he was with them in his first coming. Jesus said to them, "The Father judges no one, but has given all judgment to the Son" (John 5:22) and told them that the Father "has given him authority to execute judgment, because he is the Son of Man" (John 5:27). At the resurrection of all people, then, followers of Jesus will be raised to life, but those who continue doing evil against God will be part of "the resurrection of judgment" (John 5:29). And in one of Jesus' longest teachings about the judgment that will come on the whole earth (Matthew 24–25), Jesus also states that he will stand as judge over all people. He calls his own followers "the sheep" and those outside of Christ "the goats." He says, "When the Son of Man [Christ] comes in his glory, and all the angels with him, then he will sit on his glorious throne. [32] Before him will be gathered all the nations, and he will separate people one from another as a shepherd separates the sheep from the goats" (25:31–32). He goes on to say that the sheep (his followers) will enter into the new place that he has prepared for them. But to the goats (unbelievers who have not trusted and followed Christ) he will say, "Depart from me, you cursed, into the eternal fire prepared for the devil and his angels" (25:41).

Other passages in the New Testament also teach us about Christ's judgment at his second coming. To encourage believers who are suffering for their faith, Paul tells them that when Christ comes again they will suffer no more. Instead God will bring suffering on those who have been mean and have done what is wrong to his own followers. He writes, "God considers it just to repay with affliction those who afflict you, [7] and to grant relief to you who are afflicted as well as to us, when the Lord Jesus is revealed from heaven with his mighty angels [8] in flaming fire, inflicting vengeance on those who do not know God and on those who do not obey the gospel of our Lord Jesus. [9] They will suffer the punishment of eternal destruction, away from the presence of the Lord and from the glory of his might, [10] when he comes on that day to be glorified in his saints, and to be marveled at among all who have believed, because our testimony to you was believed" (2 Thessalonians 1:6–10).

When Christ comes again to bring judgment on the earth, he also comes as the King of kings and the Lord of lords. No one can stand against him. He comes with all authority and power. And he comes to express the righteous anger and just judgment of God. One of the last chapters in the Bible speaks of Christ's coming as Judge and King. We read, "Then I saw heaven opened, and behold, a white horse! The one sitting on it is called Faithful and True, and in righteousness he judges and makes war. . . . [15] From his mouth comes a sharp sword with which to strike down the nations, and he will rule them with a rod of iron. He will tread the winepress of the fury of the wrath of God the Almighty. [16] On his robe and on his thigh he has a name written, King of kings and Lord of lords" (Revelation 19:11–16).

Jesus will come again! That day will be one of great joy for Christ's followers, for they will be raised and brought into Christ's kingdom to live in God's presence forever. But for those who continue in their sin, not trusting in Christ for their salvation, this day will be one of great sadness. They will know that Jesus really was the only hope for sinners, but now they can no longer trust in him to be saved. He comes in his second coming as their Judge, not as their Savior. How important it is, then, to trust in Christ now for the forgiveness of our sin and the hope of eternal life. We also should share with others now that Jesus is Savior, for he will come again one day as Judge and King.

Questions for Thought

1. The second coming of Jesus is both a source of great hope and encouragement for believers, but a reason for fear for unbelievers. Why is this so?

2. Do you think much about the fact that Jesus could come at any moment? How should the ways we think and live be affected by the truth that Jesus is coming again?

Memory Verses

John 14:1–3—"Let not your hearts be troubled. Believe in God; believe also in me. In my Father's house are many rooms. If it were not so, would I have told you that I go to prepare a place for you? And if I go and prepare a place for you, I will come again and will take you to myself, that where I am you may be also."

The Suffering of Hell and the Joys of Heaven

One of the most serious teachings of the Bible is that all people will live forever either in a place of great suffering or a place of great joy. Jesus spoke much about both of these places. He warned people about the pain they would experience in hell if they did not turn from their sin and follow him, and he told his disciples about the joys they would know in heaven. It seems, then, that if we are faithful to the Bible and faithful to Christ we will desire to understand what they have taught us. We also will desire to tell others about these matters that are very important to their lives now and forever without end.

I've often wondered what people would think about someone who knew about a planned disaster but didn't do anything to warn people that it was going to happen. Suppose you had a friend who knew for sure about a plan to set off a bomb at a local school. And suppose your friend thought, "Yes, I know that the school is going to be bombed tomorrow. But I don't want to tell this to the school principal or teachers or students. After all, this is not very happy news, and I want people to be happy. I want the things I tell them to lift them up. I don't want to say things that will make them feel afraid." What would you think about your friend? Or suppose a doctor found cancer in one of his patients, but this doctor thought, "I don't want to talk about cancer. After all, cancer is a horrible disease, and no one wants to hear that they have it. I want my patient to be encouraged by her visits to my doctor's office; so I'm not going to say anything about her cancer." What would you think about this doctor? Unlike the foolishness of this friend and this doctor, the Bible does talk about things that are difficult for us to hear. God knows that heaven and hell are real, and he is right to warn us about the suffering of hell and to let us know about the joy of heaven. God is both good and wise to tell us about these things. Jesus was good and wise when he talked about them. We need to know what the Bible teaches, and others need to know also.

Earlier we talked some about Jesus' teaching on hell (Chapter 24) and saw there that Jesus spoke about hell often and with strong words. He spoke of hell in these ways: "hell of fire" (Matthew 5:22), "eternal fire" (Matthew 18:8), "unquenchable fire" (Mark 9:43), "eternal punishment" (Matthew 25:46), "fiery furnace" or "outer darkness," "weeping and gnashing of teeth" (Matthew 13:42; 25:30). And if you read the larger teachings where these words and phrases are used, it is clear that Jesus taught strongly about the reality and the horror of hell. Hell is a place where people who did evil and refused to trust in him will be sent in the end. The day will come when all those outside of Christ will stand before him in judgment and will receive the punishment they deserve. Some will be punished more strongly than others (see Matthew 11:21–24 for an example), but all will feel the pain and suffering of hell forever.

Two passages in the book of Revelation make it clear that hell is horrible and lasts forever. Revelation 14:10–11 speaks of hell as the place where the unbeliever will "drink the wine of God's wrath, poured full strength into the cup of his anger," and they will be "tormented with fire and sulfur in the presence of the holy angels and in the presence of the Lamb . . . forever and ever . . . [with] no rest day or night." And Revelation 20:11–15 presents the final judgment of all unbelievers. All whose names are not found in the Book of Life will be judged according to what they have done and then "thrown into the lake of fire" (v. 15), which was described a few verses earlier, saying that those in the lake of fire are "tormented day and night forever and ever" (20:10).

I think we would all agree that these are not happy things to think about. Neither is a bomb set to go off at a school. And neither is cancer. But sometimes we have to talk about things that are very hard and unpleasant. Because hell is real, we need to know what the Bible teaches. And we should be very grateful that God, in his infinite wisdom, chose to tell us about this place. To know that hell is so horrible and that its punishment never ends gives us greater thankfulness for the gospel. Jesus paid the full penalty of our sin. He suffered all of the pain of hell that we deserve in our lives. What a joy to know that through faith in Christ and his completed work on the cross we can be spared the punishment of hell and enter instead into the joy of heaven.

Yes, heaven too is real! The Bible speaks about the final home for believers as a place of never-ending joy and happiness, a place always in the presence of God and his beauty, and a place of great satisfaction and fulfillment. The early verses of Revelation 21–22 help us see some of the wonder of heaven. John writes, "Then I saw a new heaven and a new earth, for the first heaven and the first earth had passed away, and the sea was no more. ² And I saw the holy city, new Jerusalem, coming down out of heaven from God, prepared as a bride adorned for her husband. ³ And I heard a loud voice from the throne saying, 'Behold, the dwelling place of God is with man. He will dwell with them, and they will be his people, and God himself will be with them as their God. ⁴ He will wipe away every tear from their eyes, and death shall be no more, neither shall there by mourning, nor crying, nor pain anymore, for the former things have passed away'" (21:1–4). And again, "Then the angel showed me the river of the water of life, bright as crystal, flowing from the throne of God and of the Lamb ² through the middle of the street of the city; also, on either side of the river, the tree of life with its twelve kinds of fruit, yielding its fruit each month. The leaves of the tree were for the healing of the nations.

³ No longer will there be anything accursed, but the throne of God and of the Lamb will be in it, and his servants will worship him. ⁴ They will see his face, and his name will be on their foreheads. ⁵ And night will be no more. They will need no light of lamp or sun, for the Lord God will be their light, and they will reign forever and ever" (22:1–5).

Notice a few things here: First, heaven is on earth—the new earth that God will make. John pictures the new Jerusalem coming down from heaven, showing that our final home will be on the new earth. Believers are in their resurrected bodies (1 Corinthians 15:35–58), and they are made fully like Christ (1 John 3:2). As people fully remade, in both body and soul, we will live and love and work on the new earth that God has made, with great joy and great fulfillment. Second, we will reign with Christ forever. Even though we know very little about all that heaven will be, we know that it will be a place of deep satisfaction in the work God gives us, reigning and working with Christ. In our fallen world, work often does not sound like a good thing. But most of us learn over time that the deepest pleasures in life come through great labor and toil. Work with Christ and work for God will be our great joy in heaven. Third, Revelation 22 pictures us as back in the Garden of Eden with its tree of life. But the picture here shows a Garden of Eden better than before with its twelve kinds of fruit and leaves that heal the nations. So, we are not merely brought back to the place Adam was before he sinned. No, we are taken to a place far beyond what he had. Heaven is not merely restoring the world God made in Genesis 1–2. Heaven far surpasses the first creation.

Finally, heaven is a place of endless joy, happiness, freedom, fulfillment, beauty, and love. Imagine Jesus himself wiping away every tear, so that we never again experience pain, suffering, or sadness. What God has in store for his people is far beyond what we could know fully. But aren't you glad he's told us something about heaven?

Questions for Thought

1. The Bible teaches that both heaven and hell are real. What aspects of heaven should give believers hope for life now, even when facing difficulties and sufferings?

2. If hell is real (and it is), and those who are outside of Christ will go there, how should this affect our relationships with those who do not know Christ? And what about your own life—are you ready to face Christ at his coming, knowing that your sins are forgiven and you'll go to heaven, not hell?

Memory Verses

Revelation 21:3–4—"And I heard a loud voice from the throne saying, 'Behold, the dwelling place of God is with man. He will dwell with them, and they will be his people, and God himself will be with them as their God. He will wipe away every tear from their eyes, and death shall be no more, neither shall there by mourning, nor crying, nor pain anymore, for the former things have passed away.'"

God's Greatness and Glory Shown Forever and Ever

How might you answer this question: What is the greatest thing about God making all things new? Or, what is the best and most important thing about God completing his work to remove all evil and to make his people and all creation good once again? Some of us might give these answers: the greatest thing about the new world that God will make is that the beauty of creation will be restored. Or, the greatest thing is that evil will be judged and ended forever. Or, the greatest thing is that wars will cease and the nations will live in peace forever and ever. Or, the greatest thing is that believers will live with God in endless joy and constant love, never again experiencing pain or sorrow.

All of these answers refer to good things that will take place when God makes all things new. Yes, remaking creation to be pure and beautiful, ending all evil and warfare, and living with God forever in joy and love—all of these are good and wonderful parts of the new world that God will one day bring to pass. But as good as all of these things are, none of them says what the greatest thing really is. What answer does the Bible give, then, to our question? What really is the greatest thing about the new world that God will make?

Our answer is given in many places in Scripture. One of the best can be found in Isaiah 11. After describing the new world that God will make through the work of his Messiah, Isaiah then gives this summary statement of what the world will be like in that day: "the earth shall be full of the knowledge of the LORD as the waters cover the sea" (v. 9; see also Habakkuk 2:14). When all things are completed as God has planned, when the world is remade in righteousness and peace, then all people everywhere will know that God is God, that God is great, and that God is worthy of all glory. The knowledge of the greatness and glory of God will be as wide on the earth as the width of the waters that cover the sea. People will see God for who he is. They will know that his wisdom is perfect, his goodness never-failing, his righteousness flawless, his power limitless, and that every other quality of his life is worthy of nothing but pure awe and wonder. Yes, people—all people—will know God for who he is in that day. And God will be known for being the great and glorious God that he is. Right now, of course, far too few people know God for who he is, and far too few people honor him as he deserves. But in that day, when God makes all things new, then all people everywhere will honor God as he should be honored, for all people everywhere will know God for who he is.

So, what is the greatest thing about God making all things new? Answer: in making all things new, God will grant all people everywhere a true and deep knowledge of him that will lead them to give him the glory, honor, thanksgiving, and praise that he alone deserves as God. When the knowledge of the Lord covers the earth as the waters cover the sea, for the first time since sin entered the world, all of creation will live fully to the glory of God. This will be the greatest thing that will happen when all things are made new.

Another passage from Isaiah gives us this same answer. Through Isaiah the prophet, God says, "'I am the LORD; that is my name; my glory I give to no other, nor my praise to carved idols. 9 Behold, the former things have come to pass, and new things I now declare; before they spring forth I tell you of them.' 10 Sing to the LORD a new song, his praise from the end of the earth. . . . 11 Let the desert and its cities lift up their voice. . . . 12 Let them give glory to the LORD, and declare his praise in the coastlands" (Isaiah 42:8–12). Throughout chapters 41–48 of Isaiah, God (the *true* God) has made fun of the false gods, the idols, who cannot talk or hear or plan or act. Foolish people make their idols and worship them. But these "gods" have no power at all; worship of them is worship robbed from God. So God declares that he will stand for this no longer. He will not allow worship belonging to him to be given to idols. He will not allow his glory and praise to go to carved images. The day will come, declares the Lord, when he will make all things new. He declares them now, and he surely will bring them to pass.

And when this happens, when God completes his work to make creation the perfect and righteous place he has planned, then all of creation will sing to the Lord a new song. All things everywhere will give him glory. From coastland to coastland, all the earth will offer to him the praise that he alone deserves. So, what is the greatest thing about God making all things new? Answer: in making all things new, God will expose the sin and folly of giving glory to anything other than God. He will expose the false gods for the pretenders that they are as he shows forth the greatness of his own character as God. When the glory of the Lord is known for what it truly is, for the first time since sin entered the world, all of creation will sing a new song to the praise of God that is truly worthy of his name. This will be the greatest thing that will happen when all things are made new.

A few last thoughts are needed. First, why is the glory of God the greatest thing about the new creation that God will make? Our answer goes back to some of the earliest sections of our book. The greatest thing about the new creation is the glory of God because God himself possesses everything that is worthy of being honored, thanked, praised, adored, and worshipped. As glorious as creation is—in part or in whole—all of its glory is reflected. All its beauty, goodness, wisdom, and power comes from the one source who alone possesses these and every good quality within his own life, without measure and without end. Just as you don't praise the mirror for the beautiful face shown on it, you don't praise creation for the splendor of God shown through it. God alone deserves glory, since God alone possesses all that is worthy of glory. The greatest thing about the perfection of creation, then, is the perfection of praise that will rightly and fully be given to God, and to God alone.

And, second, how does this relate to the joy and fulfillment that God promises his children will have forever? Well, consider here what may seem an odd prayer request from Jesus. John 17:24 records Jesus saying, "Father, I desire that they also, whom you have given me, may be with me where I am, to see my glory that you have given me. . . ." Why would Jesus pray that his followers would be able to see his glory? The answer is this: Jesus wants this for his followers because in seeing who he really is, they will desire to be more like the character of this One whom they admire and adore. You see, God has made us so that we long to be like what we adore. We want to become like what we love. We wish to take on the qualities of what it is we consider beautiful and good. So, as we see Jesus for who he is, we are drawn to be more like Jesus in who we are. To see Jesus is to love Jesus, and to love Jesus is to become more like Jesus. This is why Jesus prays that his followers will be with him to behold his glory. He wants them to have the joy of being like him in their own lives.

To glorify God, then, is to enter into the joy of being like God in our character. Here is true happiness. Here is true fulfillment. Here is how the glory of God and the good of his people unite forever and ever. Praise be to God for the greatness of his glorious name!

Questions for Thought

1. When all things are made new, and the whole creation is perfected, God's glory will shine forth in new and wonderful ways. What are some reasons that the perfected creation and the greater display of God's glory go together?

2. If God's goal for the renewed earth is that "the earth shall be full of the knowledge of the LORD as the waters cover the sea," what should be our main goal in this life? How is our growing in the knowledge of God here fitting in light of God's goal for his people in the end?

Memory Verse

Isaiah 11:9—"They shall not hurt or destroy in all my holy mountain; for the earth shall be full of the knowledge of the LORD as the waters cover the sea."